SOCIAL AND TECHNICAL ISSUES IN TESTING
Implications for Test Construction and Usage

Buros-Nebraska Symposium
on
Measurement & Testing

Volume 1

Series Editors

STEPHEN N. ELLIOTT
Assistant Director

JAMES V. MITCHELL, JR.
Director

**Buros Institute of Mental Measurements
and
Department of Educational Psychology and
Social Foundations
University of Nebraska–Lincoln**

SOCIAL AND TECHNICAL ISSUES IN TESTING
Implications for Test Construction and Usage

EDITED BY
BARBARA S. PLAKE
University of Nebraska–Lincoln

LAWRENCE ERLBAUM ASSOCIATES, PUBLISHERS
1984   Hillsdale, New Jersey   London

Lawrence Erlbaum Associates, Inc., Publishers
365 Broadway
Hillsdale, New Jersey 07642

Library of Congress Cataloging in Publication Data
Main entry under title:

Social and technical issues in testing.

(Buros-Nebraska symposium on measurement & testing)
Includes bibliographies and indexes.
1. Psychological tests.   2. Ability—Testing.
3. Psychology, Applied.   I. Plake, Barbara S.
II. Series.
BF176.S63   1984   153.9′4   83-20692
ISBN 0-89859-299-2

Printed in the United States of America
10   9   8   7   6   5   4   3   2   1

Contents

**PART II INFLUENCES ON APTITUDE AND ACHIEVEMENT
TEST DEVELOPMENT AND USAGE**

Contributors

BARBARA S. PLAKE   Associate Professor of Educational Psychology
                            University of Nebraska–Lincoln

ELLIS BATTEN PAGE   Professor of Educational Psychology and Research
                            Duke University

ROBERT J. STERNBERG   Associate Professor of Psychology
                            Yale University

LYLE F. SCHOENFELDT   Professor of Management
                            Texas A & M University

DONALD N. BERSOFF   Professor of Joint J.D.–Ph.D. Program
                               in Law and Psychology
                            University of Maryland School of Law
                            and The John Hopkins University

JAMES V. MITCHELL, JR. Director, Buros Institute of Mental Measurements
                               and Professor of Educational Psychology
                            University of Nebraska–Lincoln

ANNE ANASTASI   Professor Emeritus of Psychology
                            Fordham University

ROBERT L. EBEL   Professor Emeritus of Educational Psychology
                            Michigan State University

SAMUEL MESSICK   Vice President and Distinguished Research Scientist
                            Educational Testing Service

Preface

Tests are constructed and used to facilitate assessment and understanding of human beings in all their multifaceted complexity. Hence, testing by its very nature is both a scientific and a social endeavor.

The interplay between testing and society has resulted in both praise and criticism from concerned citizens, psychologists, educators, and numerous other professional and consumer groups. For over 40 years, Oscar K. Buros, as Director of The Institute of Mental Measurements and Editor of the *Mental Measurements Yearbooks,* contributed immensely to this interplay between testing practices and societal issues. On March 19, 1978, Oscar Buros died. Luella Buros, his wife and lifelong helpmate, completed the work on *The Eighth Mental Measurements Yearbook* with the support of the Institute's devoted staff. She also took steps to relocate the Institute to ensure the continuation of the Institute's scholarly work and services for test consumers. The new Buros Institute of Mental Measurements is now at the University of Nebraska–Lincoln and is under grant from The University of Nebraska Foundation.

An important objective of the new Buros Institute is to conduct an extended outreach effort that will help communicate more effectively with test users about contemporary issues in testing. Thus, it was the combination of recent social issues focusing on testing and our desire to fulfill more vigorously the mission of the Buros Institute that motivated the development of an annual scholarly symposium and this series on measurement and testing.

We intend each symposium and volume in this series to present state-of-the-art knowledge that will contribute to the *improvement of test construction and test usage.* Such a schema will incorporate topics across a broad spectrum such as theoretical models of human behavior, test standardization procedures, social and legal factors in testing, administration of testing programs, and test-based decision making. Thus, the series will be focused thematically and yet be flexible enough to integrate current and future measurement and testing issues into its schema.

The success of our first Buros–Nebraska symposium and this volume is the result of the efforts of many individuals. We thank Luella Buros for having faith in us to carry on and extend a tradition that has become so important to the measurement field and to test users. Barbara Plake, as editor of the first volume in the series, made conceptual and editorial contributions that were of critical importance to its success. Finally, we want to thank Larry Erlbaum for his support, encouragement, and commitment to the project and to its timely completion.

Series Editors
Stephen N. Elliott
James V. Mitchell, Jr.
Lincoln, Nebraska

Volume Acknowledgments

The quality of this volume was dramatically influenced by the contribution and efforts of several people. Foremost in dedication and assistance were the members of the staff of the Buros Institute of Mental Measurements. The series editors, Stephen N. Elliott and James V. Mitchell, Jr., were prime movers in maintaining product effort and activity.

The presenters at the Buros–Nebraska Symposium on Measurement and Testing provided what might be considered the official kickoff for the volume. Drs. Ellis B. Page, Donald N. Bersoff, Lyle F. Schoenfeldt, Robert J. Sternberg, and James V. Mitchell, Jr., helped to create an intellectually stimulating atmosphere through their presentations that carried momentum into their chapters of the volume. Those chapters are joined by other chapters by Drs. Anne Anastasi, Robert L. Ebel, and Samuel Messick. All the volume authors are sincerely thanked for their cooperation, persistence, and patience during the editing and revision process. I am especially thankful to have a chapter in the volume by Dr. Robert L. Ebel. Dr. Ebel, who served the measurement community with his dedication, creativity, and intellectual integrity, passed away in November, 1982.

A number of dedicated professionals gave their time and talents to review and to provide comment on the chapters of the book. Drs. Gary Melton, Royce R. Ronning, Harry W. Hennessey, Thomas Mehle, Leonard S. Feldt, and Gerald J. Melican are gratefully acknowledged for their comments on the chapters. In addition, Claire S. Parker, Steven S. Benton, and Elizabeth P. Smith provided essential editorial assistance.

Lawrence Erlbaum and the staff of Lawrence Erlbaum Associates are sincerely thanked for their support, assistance, and guidance. Linda Weber of the Buros Institute of Mental Measurements was extremely helpful by providing a variety of essential secretarial support.

Finally, I would like to thank my husband, Donald H. Plake, and my two daughters, Hilary and Emily, for their support and patience over the long months of intense work that was necessary to produce this volume.

Barbara S. Plake
Volume Editor
Lincoln, Nebraska

Dedication

At the combined annual meeting of the American Educational Research Association and the National Council on Measurement in Education in April of 1980, Luella Buros, widow of Oscar Buros, was presented with a plaque honoring the achievements of her husband. The inscription read as follows:

"TRIBUTE"

"Whereas Oscar K. Buros established the series of Mental Measurements Yearbooks, and continued publishing these brilliantly over the last 40 years of his life; and

"Whereas these yearbooks have achieved recognition as classic contributions to the theory and practice of educational and psychological measurement, and of great benefit to our various professions—

"Therefore, we the undersigned officers of the American Educational Research Association and the National Council on Measurement in Education do hereby pay public tribute to the memory of Professor Buros, and to the high principles of quality and integrity which he represented in his work and in his life."

It was most fitting that Luella Buros received this tribute on behalf of her husband, because she had helped him in many ways from the very beginning of the series, particularly with matters pertaining to business and design. Oscar Buros had dedicated the *Third* and *Seventh Mental Measurements Yearbooks* to his wife, and when she completed *The Eighth Mental Measurements Yearbook* after his death, she dedicated it "To the memory of my beloved husband: Oscar Krisen Buros." The new Buros Institute of Mental Measurements will be dedicating both *Tests in Print III* and *The Ninth Mental Measurements Yearbook* to Oscar Buros. For the first book in this symposium series, however, we decided to take a different path and dedicate the volume to a remarkable couple who had a loving, happy, and productive relationship over so many years. We therefore dedicate this volume to:

Oscar and Luella Buros

1 Filling the Gaps Between Test Outcomes and Usage: An Introduction

Barbara S. Plake
University of Nebraska–Lincoln

Why do we have tests? What useful purposes do they serve? How can test results be used to make decisions? How can a test be proved to provide accurate and usable information? Questions such as these have been posed recently by a concerned public who have become more aware of and concerned about testing, test quality, and appropriate test usage. Their questions are challenging, legitimate queries that can and should be addressed by members of the measurement community.

Some of the questions being asked by the public are value laden, providing topics for many thoughtful but heated debates. For example: Would we be better off as a society if we did not have tests? Should testing be banned? Other questions are technical in nature and require accurate answers from the measurement community, which communicates to the public the present state of the art in measurement, assessment, and interpretation. Finally, questions such as "How can tests be used to eliminate the errors made in the selection process?" can provide an impetus within the measurement field for both theoretical and empirical development and yet are not ones that can, at least so far, be definitely answered.

The measurement field should take serious stock of itself and assess, as well as possible, the boundaries of its capabilities. From this assessment, it would be possible to communicate with the public about what testing *can* do, *may* be able to do, and is *incapable* of ever doing. At the present time, however, there appears to be an informational and expectational gap concerning what can be possible with the use of test results. Unless measurement experts and test users obtain a direct line to the angels, for example, error-free measurement will never be a reality!

Part of the communication and expectation gap can be assigned to a lack of measurement sophistication on the part of the public. Measurement course work and classes are not readily accessible to the public as a whole and may not be truly meaningful and usable to the public even if they were. A well-meaning but confused public provides fertile ground for test misunderstanding and misrepresentation by both knowledgeable and unknowledgeable test representatives. Tests enter into the lives of the public in so many ways; questionnaires, market surveys, school achievement batteries, classroom exams, and admission screenings are only a few possibilities. Yet the knowledge level of the public is minimal at best with regard to test information and interpretation.

Another part of the blame for the communication and expectation gap belongs to the measurement and testing professionals. Careful theoreticians are the first to caution on too rapid application of test advances into test usage and decisions. The state of the art is not as advanced in criterion-referenced testing or latent-trait modeling as some practitioners would want the public to believe. In addition, we are only now beginning to come to grips with decision-making models for test usage. Thus, a clear and purposeful statement (for public consumption) of what tests can and cannot do needs to be addressed by measurement and testing professionals. This would be an important *first* step in narrowing the gap.

Until such a statement is made, societal confusion and concern will abound. Confusion is fostered by the fact that decisions about test quality, application, and utility are made regularly by persons who are not trained as psychometricians. Legislative and legal decisions by politicians and judges who mandate and dictate test usage and disclosure only serve to widen the communication and expectation gap further.

PURPOSE OF THE VOLUME

The purpose of this volume is to investigate social and technical influences on test development and usage. As such, the volume can be viewed as making initial progress toward identifying what testing can and cannot do. This is accomplished first by establishing what some of the social influences are that impact tests and second by documenting some current technical aspects of testing. The volume provides essential preliminary information on how tests can be used and may be interpreted.

The intent of the volume is to present state-of-the-art content on: (1) characteristics that tests should have to be valid for use in decision making; (2) public awareness and social–legal issues that influence the credibility of tests that are used in decision making; (3) applications of tests in the decision-making process; (4) cognitive psychology's impact on test development and vice versa; (5) quality issues of test development, packaging, sales, and usage; and (6) technical advances in test validation. These components are found in the five chapters of

Section I: *Social and Technical Influences*. Section II: *Influences on Aptitude and Achievement Test Development and Usage* is composed of three chapters that provide an integrated example of how social and technical issues have affected the development and usage of aptitude and achievement tests.

OVERVIEW OF THE CHAPTERS

Section I

Section I begins with the keynote presentation, "Struggles and Possibilities: The Use of Tests in Decision Making" from the first Buros–Nebraska Symposium on Measurement and Testing, and is authored by Dr. Ellis B. Page. Breaking from the style found in the other chapters in the volume, Dr. Page's chapter is essentially a transcription of his symposium presentation because it was the keynote presentation for the symposium and therefore set the stage for the subsequent chapters within the section.

Dr. Page brings to focus a series of concerns that are relevant to the topic of uses of tests in a decision-making process. He chooses this forum to emphasize the social as well as technical issues in using tests for decision making. Dr. Page reviews factors that often influence perceptions of test quality, such as attacks on testing by the media, decisions with regard to test usage made by the courts, and concerns for test fairness and bias. Perception of test quality is identified as a fundamental factor in the use of tests for decision making. Unless tests are considered to provide valid, reliable, and reasonable pieces of information, he surmises, their role in making decisions will be subject to controversy and question. The chapter proceeds from a discussion of ways of establishing test quality and the reasons attitudes about the quality of tests may be threatened to a presentation of theoretical foundations for applying test results in the decision-making process. Page's chapter therefore approaches the use of tests in decision making on two levels: initially, it must be demonstrated that the tests in question are in fact appropriate for use in a decision; second, a decision-making process should be employed to determine how the information provided by the test can be applied rationally to aid in making decisions.

Dr. Robert Sternberg presents an account of contributions of cognitive psychology to test development and usage in the following chapter titled "What Cognitive Psychology Can (and Cannot) Do for Test Development." He contends that cognitive psychology stands to make substantial contributions to test development, although most of the contributions will be in the future. Sternberg discusses four topics: (1) what cognitive psychology is; (2) how cognitive psychologists study intelligence; (3) implications of cognitive psychological research for test validation; and (4) score interpretation and modification. Testing is presented in a reciprocal fashion whereby tests are used as assessment tools in cognitive psychological research, the results of which can suggest modifications to test development and usage.

The next chapter presents fundamental and valuable information on the role and status of test validation research. In this chapter, Dr. Lyle Schoenfeldt reviews the history of test validation strategies, identifying methods of establishing test content, criterion-related, and construct validity. New advances in criterion-related validity, such as multivariate validation approaches, are presented and evaluated. In addition, validity generalization and Bayesian statistical approaches are discussed. The chapter presents recent advances and applications of test validation theory and research to the field of business (e.g., applicant selection and job satisfaction). Test validation is presented as an essential and legally necessary step in test usage. Some important and timely ramifications of not using tests with demonstrated validity are also discussed. Because the use of test results is only reasonable if the test is valid, this chapter presents the foundations upon which test usage relies.

"Social and Legal Influences on Test Development and Usage" is the title of the following chapter. After Schoenfeldt's presentation of legal ramifications of inadequate test validation, Dr. Donald N. Bersoff posits three social influences that he regards as underlying all legal decisions pertaining to tests. These social influences are: (1) attempts to undo past injustices due to discrimination; (2) recognition of the public of their rights to privacy; and (3) negligence and lack of care by persons in positions to make decisions. Application of these social influences are illustrated in the fields of education, employment, and forensics. Bersoff continues his chapter with some examples of how social science research has and could be used to aid in court decisions on testing. He relates the impact of social influences and social science research to decisions in the cases of *Larry P v. Riles, PASE v. Hannon, Griggs v. Duke Power Co.,* and *Merriken v. Cressman*. The chapter concludes with a section on psychologists and public policy. Bersoff places the ultimate decision of test usage in the court's hands, recognizing that the court's decision will be influenced by the social and legal climate, which should be influenced further by test quality (validation) and expert psychometric testimony. He points out the final decision, however, is made by the judges, who are not generally psychometrically oriented.

Section I is concluded with a chapter from the Director of the Buros Institute of Mental Measurements, James V. Mitchell, Jr., which is titled, "Testing and the Oscar Buros Lament: From Knowledge to Implementation to Use." Dr. Mitchell reviews the progress made in test development, using information accumulated from research and theoretical developments in testing knowledge. He reports that evidence of the status of test quality, as found in administration or technical manuals for tests, is often inadequate, and he contends test publishers are rewarded financially for test development by consumers who are, on the whole, psychometrically naive. If test sales are used as the guide, it appears that test users are, as a group, influenced by Madison-Avenue–type advertising and tests' promises and titles, and they are not functioning as informed consumers. The responsibility for naive behavior of test consumers is traced to education and communication failures of professionals in the fields of testing and measurement. Dr. Mitchell concludes his chapter with specific recommendations that he believes will upgrade the education level of the consumers of tests that in turn will result in requiring test developers to upgrade the quality of their test documentation and development.

The perceptions of tests, especially as they are influenced by attacks on tests by persons in the media or courts who are in positions to make recommendations or decisions without adequate psychometric training, is one central theme that recurs in the chapters of Section I. The "call to action," issued by Mitchell, is reverberated in all the chapters of the first section. Improvement of test construction and test usage, viewed from utilization, theoretical support for and from cognitive psychology, test validation, legal and social influences, or quality control, require communication channels to the ultimate users of test results—the public.

Section II

Section II contains three chapters that originally were presented in the 1982 American Psychological Association's State of the Art Symposium. The symposium was organized by Dr. Carol Dwyer and focused on testing issues. The first chapter in Section II is authored by Dr. Anne Anastasi and is titled "Aptitude and Achievement Tests: The Curious Case of the Indestructible Strawperson." Dr. Anastasi initially reviews the traditional distinctions between aptitude and achievement testing, specifying that aptitude testing has been conceived as measuring "innate capacity" independent of learning, whereas achievement testing presumably assesses the effects of learning. The historical antecedents of this view are traced from Franzen's (1920, 1922) description of AQ (achievement quotient), the components of which were identified as EQ (educational quotient) and IQ (intelligence quotient). Dr. Anastasi then recounts efforts of psychometricians to disband the AQ terminology, beginning with Kelley (1927), noting that investigators repeatedly have reported extensive overlap of information obtained from these two types of tests. Yet despite the attempts by psychometricians to establish similarity between aptitude and achievement tests, the distinction reappears continually in presentations and writings of psychologists and psychometricians. Progress is being made though, as test companies recognize and communicate to the consumers that the distinction between aptitude and achievement tests is essentially one of breadth versus specificity of test content and antecedent learning experience. The conclusion of her chapter contains a more detailed analysis of the continuum of developed abilities, a continuum on which she places both aptitude and achievement tests. Thus, the major thrust of Dr. Anastasi's chapter is that psychologists and measurement experts have been making steady progress in clarifying what aptitude and achievement tests measure; yet communication of this knowledge to test users, test takers, and the general public remains a problem.

Current issues in achievement testing is the topic of Dr. Robert Ebel's chapter, "Achievement Test Items: Current Issues." Dr. Ebel focuses his attention on the measurement of human characteristics and initially addresses the fundamental topic of the measurability of human characteristics. Within the domain of measuring human characteristics, Dr. Ebel considers the relative merits of various types of test items, such as: (1) essay and objective items; (2) realistic problem-solving items; and (3) alternate-choice items. Ebel concludes his chapter with a discussion of a technology of item writing. The major theme appears to be that any important human characteristic is necessarily measurable, and test items that focus on the basic components of knowledge are examples of an item-writing technology that has promise to yield highly reliable and valid assessments of human characteristics.

The final chapter in Section II, "Abilities and Knowledge in Educational Achievement Testing: The Assessment of Dynamic Cognitive Structures," is authored by Dr. Samuel Messick. The chapter begins by examining the question of what educational achievement tests are or ought to be. Both educational achievement and cognitive ability are viewed as constructs. The distinction between theoretical definitions and practical reality of assessment instruments is a major theme. Messick posits that educational achievement is a compound of developed abilities and knowledge structures. He then contrasts his view of what educational achievement tests are with that presented by Ebel, Anastasi, and others. Messick's conclusion is that theory, not empiricism, should guide the conceptualization and process of test development. He maintains that, to serve both theory and practice, new approaches to achievement measurement that are complex, dynamic, and cognitive need to be developed.

Each author in Section II conceptualizes aptitude and achievement testing differently. Anastasi elects to present aptitude and achievement testing on a single continuum, the distinction between them being one of specificity of a task and antecedents to the task. Ebel, on the other hand, considers aptitude as a special case of achievement and vice versa, establishing that intelligence, aptitudes, abilities, and achievements are synonymous. Messick believes the conceptual distinction between aptitude and achievement tests is flawed due to a reliance on empirical results obtained from using imperfect and variously contaminated tests. Thus, he discards the approach taken by Ebel, Anastasi, and others. His implication is that new approaches to appropriate measurement of aptitudes and achievement, which should be dynamic, cognitive, and complex, will enable a better assessment of what role cognitive abilities play or ought to play in educational achievement testing.

In summary, the authors in Section II focus on aptitude and achievement testing and debate social and technical issues pertaining to their application, meaning, and usage. Dr. Anastasi points out that, despite attempts by psychometricians to defeat the distinctions popularly held by the public about aptitude and achievement tests, the ''strawperson'' remains indestructible and hence is an excellent example of social influence on test interpretation and usage. Technical issues that influence test construction and usage are central to Ebel's and Messick's chapters, with Ebel postulating the existence of an item-writing technology and Messick imploring test developers to use a theoretical, not empirical, basis for test construction.

CONCLUSIONS

The assessment of human abilities and qualities by tests has become an integral part of decision making in modern society. Nearly everyone has taken or will take a test that has the potential to influence his or her life significantly. The public is becoming more aware of and concerned about testing, test quality, and appropriate test usage. Testing and measurement cannot be treated in isolation. They are not immune from criticisms and influences from the very people their work affects most—society. To survive and thrive, measurement and testing must continue to develop through both improved technology and interactions with society.

REFERENCES

Franzen, R. H. The accomplishment quotient, a school mark in terms of individual capacity. *Teachers College Record,* 1920, *21* 432–440.

Franzen, R. H. The accomplishment ratio: A treatment of the inherited determinants of disparity in school product. *Teachers College Contributions to Education,* 1922, No. 125.

Kelley, T. L. *Interpretation of educational measurements.* Yonkers, N.Y.: World Book Co., 1927.

SOCIAL AND TECHNICAL INFLUENCES

2 Struggles and Possibilities: The Use of Tests in Decision Making

Ellis Batten Page
Duke University

What a happy occasion it is to celebrate, as we do in this volume, the establishment of a national Buros Institute of Mental Measurements, located on the campus of the University of Nebraska, in Lincoln. What a culmination of many plans, hopes, and dreams! On such an occasion, we can take a quiet pride in our profession and in the life and accomplishments of one of our colleagues and friends, Oscar Krisen Buros, who with Luella Buros is leaving to us, and our posterity, an institution of integrity to foster the science and practice of testing.

How new all this field really is: According to Stanley and Hopkins (1972, p. 163), the first large-scale testing was done in the City of New York Survey, in 1911. Oscar Buros was 6 years old then, so we can think of most of the astonishing developments in measurement really happening during his lifetime. And the first machine for scoring of answer sheets, the old IBM 805, was developed when Oscar was 30. Many of us can remember, only 20 years ago, many clerical workers reading the dials from these machines and writing the scores as they might be estimated from this analog device. Then these tools also became obsolete as the field was overtaken by optical readers and computer scoring. So Oscar and Luella Buros have witnessed the explosion of testing into a central institution of education, of psychology, of all the social and behavioral sciences. But they have done much more than witness: Their publications have served as a steady center of this growth, and their independence has established a tradition of reputation and honor as a goal, if not always as a realization, of the profession and the practice of testing.

The establishment of such published symposia from the Buros Institute is an important further step. There is a major place for such a forum. I hope these symposia will represent a determined effort to stand apart from the testing giants, just as Buros did, and to remain independent of federal agencies as well. The Institute, and these symposia, should continue to sponsor solid, sometimes severe criticism of tests and test practices, also as Buros did. They should similarly stand apart from the political huckstering and trend riding, the cheap shots against testing, and apart from the constant distortion of what tests tell us about ourselves and our world.

Of course, the Institute should make full modern use of wordprocessing, automatic mailing, information retrieval, and all the present and future efficiencies of operation becoming available. But hopefully there will remain these steady principles that marked Buros' work, and a similar vision of mental measurement, of how it can help our society to be happier and more productive.

At such a historic time, it is a pleasure to remember the classic words of E. L. Thorndike (1918, p. 16), which serve as a kind of cornerstone for our whole professional and scientific development:

> Whatever exists at all exists in some amount. To know it thoroughly involves knowing its quantity as well as its quality. Education is concerned with changes in human beings; a change is a difference between two conditions; each of these conditions is known to us only by the products produced by it—things made, words spoken, acts performed, and the like. To measure any of these products means to define its amount in some way so that competent persons will know how large it is, better than they would without measurement. To measure a product well means so to define its amount that competent persons will know how large it is with some precision, and this knowledge will be conveniently recorded and used.

If we have, for our profession, an Apostle's Creed, surely Thorndike has here given it to us. And the last phrase echoes for us: ''so that this knowledge will be conveniently recorded and used.'' *And used.* Aye, there's the rub and the thrust of the testing movement. It is the *use* of testing that has caused its growth from academic curiosity to a billion-dollar industry and that makes it a battle ground today for conflictiong ideologies and the warring of powerful political alliances. In my opinion, technical people in testing cannot go on sidestepping these major battles. Sooner or later, we should recognize publicly what it is that we believe; we should state our beliefs openly for both colleagues and society; and we should counterattack the falsehoods about testing.

Who are these enemies? For one example, let us mention the recent storm of antitesting sentiment surrounding the publication of Gould's (1981) book, *The Mismeasure of Man.* This book follows in the tradition of Leon Kamin's (1973) *The Science and Politics of I.Q.,* the writing of the consumerists Nader and Nairn and of Lewontin, Layzer, and others. Once again, the major media have rushed to approve the new book by Gould and to endorse its claims. A recent New Yorker has an extended piece by one of their science popularizers, in which most test experts are implicitly denigrated and the founders of our discipline are derided and smeared. There are many echoes of these sentiments.

The major media of the Northeastern Seaboard are, of course, considerably more antitesting than is the American mainstream. What of the more conservative press? Although it is part of the conservative tradition to recognize and to accommodate large individual differences, the better-known conservative writers seem daunted by the name-calling and by the technical difficulty of the arguments. Both sides are handicapped by the recondite nature of many of the core proofs of testing. As Garrett Hardin recently commented during a visit at Duke, most opinion leaders and shapers who control our media, of whatever leaning, are highly literate but are "innumerate." Left or right, journalists fail to grasp our technicalities. They believe that our hard-won principles (the best body of theory in the social sciences) are purely a matter of opinion!

Then what about the "numerate" scientists concerned with tests? Those who do speak out often suffer for it and are frustrated again and again by the major media. Consider the experiences of one of our most productive and distinguished defenders of psychometrics, Arthur R. Jensen of Berkeley. Those who know him well can recount some of his harassment and defamation, which, by the way, is still going on. And Richard Herrnstein (1982) of Harvard has written a critique, much of it from his own unhappy treatment, about his efforts to be expressed properly in the major media. His forum is the *Atlantic Monthly,* an intellectual magazine that is highly respected and of general readership but that commands none of the publicity clout of CBS or of the *New York Times* and their multi-million audiences. Some of Herrnstein's (1982) accusation is worth reproducing here:

> Incurably addicted to quantification, I have now searched the daily and the Sunday *New York Times* from 1975 to November 1981 for all book reviews dealing with the IQ. The results speak for themselves. Of the 15 reviews that I found, every one denigrated IQ tests, often vitriolically. All but two of the books reviewed were anti-testing, as far as one can tell from the reviews, and were praised for their position. One exception was a book by Arthur Jensen [1980], which happened also to be the only book by a trained psychometrician (psychometrics is the psychological specialty concerned with testing). Jensen's book was panned by a philosopher with no detectable expertise in the subject.
>
> Except for Jensen's book, none of the other major works on testing written by professionals during the period was reviewed. Most remarkably, however, the *Times* published no review by a trained professional. Dozens of literate psychometricians might have commented on the shallowness of the books the *Times* usually chooses to review. But psychometrics is forbidden territory in the *Times*— its books are mostly unreviewed, its discoveries are unreported, and its experts are, from what gets published, unconsulted. Rarely, if ever, in more than a decade, has a specialist published a review of a book on testing in the *Times*, [or in] other national publications that occasionally comment on testing. For no other subject of public concern—not for economic policy, disarmament, welfare reform, nuclear power plants—has the professional outlook on a controversy been so shut off from a voice in the national press. Yet, while public policy on testing may not have the immediacy of a tax cut or a nuclear accident, it ultimately affects everyone [p. 69].

A DOUBLE STANDARD

Herrnstein's (1982) article is a good one, revealing for all concerned with testing and education. Its principal burden is the double standard of treatment of two cases of apparent malfeasance by testing researchers: One of these cases is known widely even to college students; the other is a nonevent, conveniently buried from public awareness. The first, so widely known, concerns the probable falsification of certain twin data by the late, brilliant Sir Cyril Burt. Herrnstein counted at least six stories about this apparent misconduct in the *New York Times* alone. However, as repeatedly noted by scholars of behavior genetics, nothing in Burt's estimates was very deviant from what has been found by other researchers since his reports. Burt's data are, in short, now redundant, and if he did fabricate some of his numbers, he ''apparently knew enough to guess correctly'' (Herrnstein, 1982, p. 70). But the attacks on him persist, endlessly, and are made central to denigrating not only behavior genetics but our entire field of mental measurement.

The other story will probably be new to many readers and will surely be new to most nonspecialists. In July 1981, Dr. Rick Heber, Director of the Waisman Center of the University of Wisconsin, Madison, and chief adviser to a U.S. president on mental retardation, was convicted in federal court of diverting funds to personal use and was sentenced to 3 years in prison. Heber, it will be remembered, was principal investigator of the much publicized miracle of the environmentalist movement, the ''Milwaukee Project.'' He had proved, he wrote, that it was possible to take 20 children of retarded parents and depressed homes and to raise their true IQs an average of over 30 points, from dull normal to superior in intelligence, by a massive preschool intervention.

What of his results themselves and their claim to scientific seriousness? Eight years before that trial, an article was published for fellow researchers (Page, 1972b), arguing that the Milwaukee Project was, for a number of technical reasons, not scientifically credible. And just before Heber's indictment, another article (Page & Grandon, 1981) carried an intensive criticism of the Project. In brief, we found that the Project, which had never been truly refereed, was extremely shaky, and the explanations of it shifted in ways quite unacceptable in scientific reporting. What evidence was available on follow-up data, moreover, suggested that there was no residual difference between the treatment and control groups on measures, such as school reading tests, which were outside the reach of Project management. The 30 points gain, if it ever existed, had apparently disappeared.

The point here, however, is not to resurrect the Milwaukee Miracle to slay it again but to draw attention to the way that psychometric questions are treated in the media. The earlier ''findings'' of the Milwaukee Project had been widely noted in the national media. The *Washington Post* believed that it might have ''settled once and for all'' (sic) the question of heredity versus environment for the intelligence of slum children. The *New York Times* had reported that the Project "has proved" that IQs could be raised more than 30 points by the methods of Heber and his associates (these quotes cited by Herrnstein, 1982). Wouldn't one suppose, therefore, that the disgrace of the Project leadership deserved some attention? After all, the Milwaukee work had been unique and widely acclaimed in its demonstration of such large environmental effects. And this demonstration had depended on faith in its leadership. Wouldn't the astonishing misconduct of the leadership, then, cast some shadow across such findings, which no one else had obtained?

Not at all. Not a word about the Heber scandal has appeared in the *Times*, the newsweeklies, *Science* magazine, or on national TV. To quote Herrnstein (1982) again,

> The media seem unwilling to publish anything that might challenge the certitude with which editors, politicians, judges, and others insist that we know how to increase measurable intelligence, or that test data "prove," to use *The New York Times*'s word, that a poor environment causes familial retardation [p. 710].

What is the cause of this remarkable double standard? Clearly, it is the ideology of the major media, warmly supportive even of falsehoods favorable to environmentalism, generally condemnatory of individual differences and hence of psychometrics, our field, which persistently and embarrassingly reiterates important and substantial differences in humankind.

Yes, we have our critics, and they have an extraordinary double standard; and they are in very strong positions, affecting the beliefs of everyone: of editors, educators, judges, legislators, federal officers, and the other countless millions who read the national press or listen to the national TV. If we believe in our discipline and its contributions to society, then we had better stand up for ourselves and our field. What, then, do we believe?

THE VALUE OF TESTING

Scientific Value.   In our own quiet way, and in our own private literature, there is a strong consensus among us concerning the persisting values of our science and our profession. In an excellent summary of this question, the scientific basis of testing was powerfully defended by Carroll and Horn (1981). They showed our growth to be following the earlier development of physics, in our gathering understanding of intelligence and our strengthening theory.

Poor Alternatives to Testing.   Many of our negative reactions to our critics and would-be reformers are similarly shared among ourselves. That the interference of the courts is often ignorant, confused, and damaging is noted by even the mildest of scientific commenters (Bersoff, 1981). And the reforms forced on testing by outside criticism have, we are largely agreed, been frequently "non-solutions" (Reschly, 1981). Such "unproductive changes" include the banning of intelligence tests (such as in California) and the use of "pluralistic norms" (such as SOMPA; cf. Mercer, 1977). Often aggressive counterattacks to our critics are slipped quietly into our thoughtful articles written for each other. Such a counterattack is well illustrated by the comment of two of our respected colleagues (Carroll & Horn, 1981): "Indeed, it seems clear to the present authors that far from being abused by overuse, the science of human abilities is underexploited in diagnosis, counseling, and evaluation [p. 1019]."

Fairness to Minorities. For a very important topic, the claim of racial unfairness, the view of experts was well summarized by Cole (1981), when she wrote - that "we have learned that there is not large-scale, consistent bias against minority groups in the technical validity sense in the major, widely used and widely studied tests [p. 1075]." This position has been strongly supported by a blue-ribbon panel on testing of the National Academy of Sciences. And a similar conclusion is widely understood for the question of bias in college admissions (Linn, 1982). Indeed, much of the claimed evidence against test validity, for example in employment, has apparently been misunderstood and improperly summarized (especially see Schmidt & Hunter, 1981).

IDEOLOGICAL AND SCIENTIFIC ISSUES

Through many arguments about test practice, however, run deeper currents of contemporary ideology, philosophical, political, and economic. Those who claim an exclusively societal or economic determinism are especially resentful of testing and psychometric research, and what these disciplines show us about the sources of human abilities and personality. In a candid account of the contemporary scene, then, we must not avoid the issue of what science and scientists say about family influences on these traits, both genetic and environmental.

Heritability of Intelligence

Surely we can now say that there is a scientific consensus for the heritability of intelligence, and we can reject the name-calling of those who would say that hereditary influence is a delusion or a hoax. If there is any scholar who honestly questions it, and sincerely seeks evidence, there is a direct solution: Such a person should read—or even just browse—in Fuller and Thompson's (1978) weighty volume, *Foundations of Behavior Genetics*. Absorb the stately march there from fundamental genetic principles to physiology, to neurobiology, to quantitative methods, to the genetics of cognitive and intellectual abilities, to personality and temperament, to mental illness. Loiter, for a while, in the 40 pages of bibliography with their 1500 references. And for those with quantitative curiosity, there are excellent works available (Falconer, 1960; Thompson & Thoday, 1979).

Or, if a scholar seeks further knowledge of the genetic evidence specific to mental measurements, give such a scholar Jensen's (1980) monumental book *Bias in Mental Testing.* Someday this may be more widely recognized as one of the best works ever written on testing, for the serious student of psychometrics. (For other informed appraisals of such evidences, see Bereiter, 1970; Cancro, 1971; Hébert, 1977. And for a nontechnical treatment of the issues, see Jensen, 1981.) But then, how should we convince the lay world outside of the large consensus on this matter of heritability? In 1972, more than 50 scholars from fields bearing on this question published a "Resolution on Scientific Freedom and Heredity," signing the emphatic statement that *"we believe such influences are very strong."* (Page, 1972c). Of the 50 signers, 60% were in *Who's Who in America,* and four were Nobel laureates. And their statement was published in the most prominent professional journal in psychology. But that testament, too, became a nonevent for the major media to ignore. The national press took no notice of this, nor did CBS when its special, "The IQ Myth," led by Dan Rather, managed, through distortion and omission, to make test scores seem a pure artifact of favored environments. One of the most common responses of informed psychologists and measurement experts is to avoid these questions or, if pressed, to state that these questions are not important for our major concern: the use of tests in decision making. On the contrary, I hope to persuade that such evasions, of such overpoweringly central questions, must lead to waste, futility, and dishonor in our testing field. Indeed, to some extent this has already happened.

Nonetheless, it is curious how blind the media are to this consensus among scientists about the heritability of intelligence. Even Gould's (1981) book, with its strong ideological loading, does not exactly dispute the existence of heritability, though taking exception to nearly every estimate of it. The device used by Gould, and by others before him, is to challenge the *precision* of such an estimate, as if some softness of numbers invalidated the whole pursuit. If a test score is not precise, they seem to affirm, it is useless. If a heritability estimate is not certain, then it is meaningless. One can only imagine the stultifying influence such perfectionism would have had on the growth of any of our sciences? But the clear fact, revealed even in the most polemical criticism to the careful reader, is that there is consensus about the large heritability of general intelligence.

Heritability of Special Abilities

Even among able psychometricians, however, there is much uncertainty about the heritability of specific abilities or achievement measures. To explore this question, a friend and I (Page & Jarjoura, 1979) obtained an unprecedented data set from one of the two major college testing programs, the respected American College Testing Program (ACT). Our results are briefly outlined here, as bearing on this important and neglected problem affecting many of the tests the schools have so widely adopted. If these measures, too, are loaded with heritability, we should take this fact carefully into consideration.

As is well known, the ACT has four achievement tests, in the four fields of English, Math, Social Studies, and Natural Sciences. From two different years of testing, 1976 and 1978, ACT gathered for us 6800 pairs of twins from the nearly 2 million students who used this excellent program to apply to colleges in those years. These twins were identified from the concordance of surname, birth date, and place of residence (or home phone). Even without knowing which pairs are fraternal or identical, it is possible to do some genetic analysis of such a wonder-fully large data base, as long as we are willing to make certain assumptions about same-sexed and opposite-sexed pairs (Scarr-Salapatek, 1971). Here there is little space for technical detail, but let us consider certain findings, displayed in Table 2.1.

Table 2.1 shows results from a factor analysis of the genetic components estimated from our methods (Page & Jarjoura, 1979, p. 115). First, we observe the sizable loadings of the four tests on the principal genetic factor. The heritability estimates of these four tests were all high, by the way, ranging from .64 to .84. That is, each of the four ACT achievement measures showed a substantial heritability in itself. The further question we raised, however, was the extent to which the measures were genetically unique and the extent to which they shared their genetic loadings with the others.

In Table 2.1, Part A shows these loadings of the four measures on the first, unrotated principal factor from the genetic correlations we generated. In Part B of the table, we observe the amount of each of the genetic correlations, which is explained by the principal component. And in Part C we see that there is also a genetic loading specific to each of the four tests (these loadings are in the major diagonal). What is thought provoking, and not often recognized among psycho-metricians, is that so much of the intercorrelation among such ability and achievement measures should have a unitary factor as its biological source. And it appears that G (genetic loading) and g (the always observed correlation among diverse mental measures) do indeed have much to do with each other. (See also kinship studies in Behrman, Hrubec, Taubman, & Wales, 1980; Loehlin, Lindzey, & Spuhler, 1975; Loehlin & Nichols, 1976; Martin, 1975.)

From this example, we can score some points against frequent criticisms. One of the repeated claims is that Burt's apparent defection destroyed the basis for any belief in heritability. But obviously, Burt's few disputed twin pairs played no role in this large analysis (nor in numerous other analyses in the United States or abroad). Another strawman from our critics is that we regard intelligence as a "single thing." This claim is clearly false. Here one sees that, even genetically, there are other influences distinct to each trait. Even so, however, here as in all

TABLE 2.1
Principal Factor Analysis of the Genetic Components of Twin Data[a]

Trait	English	Math	Soc. St.	Nat. Sci.
	(A) Loadings on principal genetic factor			
	.71	.65	.83	.84
	(B) Component "explained" by principal factor			
English	.50	.46	.59	.59
Math		.43	.54	.55
Soc. St.			.69	.70
Nat. Sci.				.71
	(C) Residual component			
English	.14	.02	−.02	.00
Math		.21	.00	−.02
Soc. St.			.15	.01
Nat. Sci.				.01

[a]From Page & Jarjoura, 1979, p. 115.
[b]Of the total genetic matrix, 81.5% of the variance was explained by the single factor.

matrices of mental measures we see the ubiquitous positive component underlying the whole matrix, which in this analysis is genetic. "Single thing" it is not; indeed, by all estimates, it is based on many gene loci. And psychologically there are surely various subabilities that contribute to it. Still, whatever its nature, g does appear, to a greater or lesser extent, in virtually all mental tests.

Still another charge hurled at testers, but denied by our analysis, is that we believe that "genetics is all." Our Table 2.1 clearly rejects any such conclusion, as does the research of everyone else known to us. Indeed, it is the power of behavior genetics that it can best expose those influences that are, indeed, environmental. For example, we may consider the simple declaration that variance of a test is the sum of the genetic variance, the environmental variance, and error:

$$Var(test) = Var(G) + Var(E) + error. \qquad (1)$$

Then it is possible to regard a test score in the way suggested by Fig. 2.1.

For students of testing, this figure seems a most familiar one. From any test, we might infer that the shaded curve represents the variance expectable from error around some true score X''. But let us alter the meaning: Let X' now represent the genotype, and the shaded figure represent the variation expected in the phenotype, through the operation of a combination of environment and errors of measurement. What such a perspective makes us realize is that, in each one of our mental test scores, we are indeed looking at a genotype, plus other influences. That is, we may consider the individual score to consist of genotype "true" score, the environmental variations around such a genotype, and of course a residual error variance. Indeed, given the enormous amount of research on these matters, we may assert that, for the individual student, most of the

however, there has been little recognition of its importance to educational psychology and its kindred disciplines, and few investigators have applied it to our most serious problems of educational choice.

Decision Analysis.   For easy understanding, the science of decision making is often expressed in the notation of *decision analysis,* and the notation is that of an upside-down tree, as shown in Fig. 2.2. The best-known writer in this field is undoubtedly Howard Raiffa (1968), whose approach can be appreciated without extensive mathematics, and can be applied directly in practical situations.

In Fig. 2.2, let us suppose that there is a career choice at stake, such as whether to pursue a premedical career or some other. In this drastically simplified representation, as in many more complex ones, there are just four aspects of choice:

1. Decisions to be made (in squares).
2. Probabilities to be estimated (in circles).
3. Values of the outcomes (numbers at dots).
4. Costs of the choices (small tollgates).

Let us assume that the values of the outcomes are estimated in the same units as the costs at the tollgate. Then such a tree may be automatically solved by applying recursively two rules, beginning at the bottom of the tree and working up:

1. *Probability nodes are averaged,* by multiplying each value by its associated probability, summing across the branches, and carrying the weighted mean up to the node.
2. *Decision nodes are maximized,* by selecting that branch that carries the highest net value. (Costs are subtracted from the value of the relevant branch.)

Tests for Individual Decisions.   Decision analysis, then, like most methods used in operations research, suggests our optimal choice, under the assumption of the correctness of our data.

But where do we obtain the number themselves? They are based on some sort of data, either objective or subjective. And the role of tests in forecasting should be closely tied to the probabilities shown. The probabilities of various outcomes, once a decision is taken, must depend on all appropriate information about these outcomes: the experiences of others and the chooser's own abilities, past achievements, economic needs, and the like. For example, suppose that the choice of Plan B is for premedical training, where the payoff ($100,000 a year?) is high but where the general probability of success is only 1 in 5. In the individual case, this probability should be adjusted to the person concerned. Once again, test scores should play an important role in such adjustment, consid-

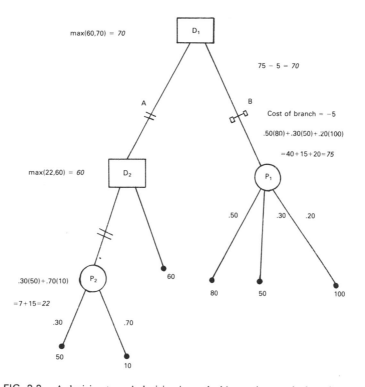

max(60,70) = *70*

D_1

75 − 5 = *70*

A

B

Cost of branch = −5

.50(80) + .30(50) + .20(100)

= 40 + 15 + 20 = *75*

max(22,60) = *60*

D_2

P_1

.50   .30   .20

.30(50) + .70(10)

P_2

60

= 7 + 15 = *22*

80   50   100

.30   .70

50

10

FIG. 2.2. A decision tree. A decision is reached by tracing out the branches as far as possible, assigning values to each terminal node, and probabilities to each branch from a P node. P nodes are then solved (working from the bottom up), by averaging out the branches. And D nodes are solved by folding back all but the most valuable branch as evaluated below each D. For vocations, the probability values are determined by knowledge of both the world and self, as are also the terminal values. Technical procedures can be applied to aid all such determinations. (*Source:* Page, 1974b, p. 71. Reprinted with permission.)

ered together with the background information about others who have gone before.

Consider, then, what great damage is done to decision making, if tests are discredited and not used or if they are eliminated from the tools of decision makers by court order or administrative uncertainty. It is not only the testers who have much at stake in such mistaken elimination of tests; the biggest losers are the students and those who would guide and select them.

From even such a simple model, an immediate realization is that such decision trees become complex, requiring computer assistance in their solution—just as life decisions are indeed complex, yet made quite haphazardly today, without mathematical help. We still await truly competent, computerized advisory systems for such choices, though we have been aware of the need for some years

(Page, 1974b), and some working research models were established in the past (Katz, 1966).

Tests for Program Decisions.   Let us look at Fig. 2.2 from another viewpoint, as though we were administrators and the decision were between two programs, here labeled A and B. Suppose Program B seems to produce higher average values, where these are measured in terms of test scores, but our data are from a national study, where there is confounding of tests with school practices and with the SES variables of the communities. What we face, again, is that decision sciences must depend not on naive correlational data but on *production functions* of the treatment variables. If this seems an obvious point, then it has been seriously neglected in the social planning of the past several decades, and its neglect has led us to one disillusionment after another in the world of educational research and development (cf. Page, 1972a).

Scores as Production Functions.   In our desire to use tests in planning, we are often blocked when we must choose among educational programs. Choosing a criterion test then becomes troubled. Suppose one program relies more on a textbook and the other more on films. Then it will be very difficult to construct a test that will not be biased toward one outcome or the other. Quite understandably, in such a situation, we often wisely choose tests that are not so close to the programs. We may, rather, choose a selection of standardized tests of global ability or achievement: in English, for example, or in math, social studies, or natural sciences. But wait, these are the very tests we found to be heavily loaded on the same g factor (general ability). Even more disturbingly, they are loaded on the same G factor (general *genetic* ability). And when we employ pre–post testing with such measures, the change scores have well-known problems. Are we really expected to detect the effects of programs through such measures of general (and even genetic) ability?

Yes, in general we must, for there seem to be few defensible alternatives. We have mentioned the experimental bias of tests designed explicitly for the comparisons, and these (even where available) have many problems beyond such built-in program biases. Tests that are called "criterion referenced" frequently exhibit these problems. We have long seen much literature for and against such criterion referencing, and some excellent consideration and debate have occurred (for example, by Julian Stanley, Robert Ebel, Roger Lennon, and Frank Womer). For an extended period Dr. Womer directed the massive National Assessment of Educational Progress, which was dedicated, at least originally, to the criterion-referencing philosophy (also see Page, 1982, on this philosophy). For research questions about programs, such issues have a special bite.

Special Versus General Tests of Achievement.   Let us briefly summarize our dilemma: On one hand, it is fairly easy to write tests that measure some very limited body of knowledge (e.g., the new vocabulary taught in a specific lesson). Here indeed we can show marked change from before an instruction to after. On the other hand, a small handful of words will have practically no visible effect on one's ability to read general matter—and this is the goal we really cherish for major decisions. If we test only the explicit program content, we may be acting out something like the ''drunkard's search,'' which the philosopher Abraham Kaplan used to tell us about at UCLA. The drunkard was feeling around under a lamppost and was asked what he was looking for. ''I dropped my key.'' Where did you drop it? ''Over there.'' But if you dropped it over there, why are you looking for it over here, under the lamppost? ''This is where the light is.''

We can, after all, develop a test for the lesson just past, which may show us how we improved. That is where the light is. But the most important outcomes of education often seem like the lost key, beyond our reach, over there in the dark.

Is there a way out of this problem? Yes, if we have sufficient numbers and sufficient random assignment and accurate enough predictive control variables, then our standard errors of the means will be small enough to permit comparisons that are meaningful for such standard testing programs. Such conditions, however, hold in probably less than 1% of the evaluation situations that face the psychometric researcher.

Showing Environmental Effect.   The problem is not hopeless. If we have, indeed, important variables, sufficient cases, and solid models, we may be able to show these important environmental influences in a helpful light. Let us consider two findings from recent research on the applied issue of private and public schooling.

Our first case illustrates the danger of failing to provide for large individual differences (in *g* or in *G*). Coleman, Hoffer, and Kilgore (1981) had claimed very prominently that, even after ''controlling'' for effects of family, they found a striking superiority of the private schools in the United States in the educational achievement of the huge sample from High School and Beyond. In a reanalysis of the data, however, this time including six brief subtests of mental ability (mostly nonverbal and relatively school-free), we found that any residual effect of private school was less than 0.5% of the variance in student achievement (Page, 1981; Page & Keith, 1981). Thus a claimed environmental effect largely disappeared when student input was weighed into the test. This is, of course, a common enough result when such variables are included—which has apparently led some to wish to avoid measuring intelligence in such research.

The second findings, from the same debate, had a more optimistic outcome, as shown in Fig. 2.3. In Fig. 2.3, we observe some major student variables, such as family background, race, and general ability, which are understandably loaded with parental influences, both genetic and environmental, and largely beyond the control of the school system. But here we also introduced the amount of homework the student did, as a causal variable for the general achievement of

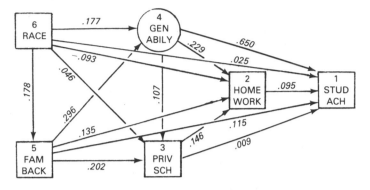

FIG. 2.3. Explaining student achievement of students in private and public high
schools. After allowing for background variables, homework still explains 3% of
test achievement. (*Source:* Page & Keith, 1981. Reprinted with permission.)

reading and math. Clearly, from the paths shown, our major background variables were fundamental in explaining test achievement; and the special control of
"general ability" (a factor score made from two short vocabulary tests and four
nonverbal tests) was the most influential of all. Yet the homework does shine
through, explaining 3% of the variance in achievement even after controlling for
background variables. The eternal verities of educational psychology still stand:
After ability, time spent on task does make the most difference, and our standard
tests, even loaded as they are with heritability, *can* show that such time matters.
Indeed, in this case of school comparison, homework also helps explain about
half of the tiny effect of private schools.

Tim Keith and I believe that homework, then, is a major variable that all
schools should emphasize, one that could truly improve performance. Keith's
(1982) separate article shows this homework effect even more clearly for student
grades: There is, in fact, a possible compensation for low ability shown in this
study of grades, with the low-ability hard worker actually catching up with the
high-ability nonworker in such school performance. Keith's remarkable graph is
shown in Fig. 2.4.

But another problem of practical decision making is illustrated in this homework question. I have talked about these results with various groups of policy
people: school boards, legislators, practicing administrators, equal opportunity
officials, teachers, and even governors active in education. The idea of increasing homework seems to have no lobbies! To the contrary, there is often an
embarrassed silence (and the facts are indeed embarrassing, with the average
senior doing less than 4 hours of homework each week, in all classes combined).
Some educators have even denigrated the homework question altogether, speaking of "meaningless drill" and the like. Clearly, far more than our psychometric
research enters into educational policy! But this case does illustrate how test

information may improve our knowledge of basic issues, and our understanding, if not always our application, of practical issues.

Heritability and Program Research.   Our general neglect of heritability has led to research handicaps that may unfortunately hinder our understanding of some policy issues. In order to guide curricular change, we should know which variables are relatively more influenced by family variables and which more influenced by schools. But our usual research strategies, with no kinship controls, do not often permit this distinction. Given large samples of twins and siblings, however, and item information across achievement tests, we could do heritability analysis on *each item.* Or, if zygosity were not known for the twin pairs, we could analyze which items were more influenced by home or school, and various analyses of these results could in turn illuminate areas for greater curricular attention in those schools showing such deficits.

Still another application of such techniques could be in matters of national assessment, where we seek to track the national performance of student generations and to study the changes from one generation to another. For example, there remain large questions about the causes of the decline of standardized test scores over the past 15 years or so. One real possibility—that declines were caused by shifting ability levels of parents—was never really explored. Yet item analysis of the SAT scores, using the huge available samples of twins, might cast

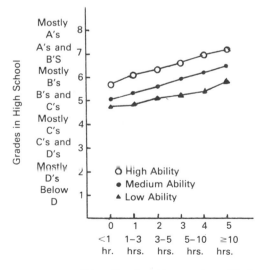

FIG. 2.4.   Mean grades in high school as a function of time spent on homework and of ability. (*Source:* Keith, 1982. Reprinted with permission.)

some light on the question, through the following reasoning: Reused items may be measured at two points in time and their gain or loss reported. The twin correlations of such reused items may be also discovered. Then if the more family-influenced items are those in which there is greatest decline, the inference would be that the decline was more likely caused within the home than within the school; and the conclusions would be quite different from those in the contrary case. Conceivably, this exploration would not be very productive (we would soon find out), but it would open a major line of investigation. And it was a thesis that would be very easy and inexpensive to explore. A major cluster of hypotheses remained unstudied. Once again, our psychometric understandings are frustrated by our current political and ideological commitments. And we have failed to make adequate use of the psychometric information available to us in our search for improved social strategies.

Decision Making and Ratio Scales.   One apparent problem of test scores for decision making is the following: Most scientific strategies for optimizing decisions require that benefits be measured on some *absolute scale of values.* In many decision techniques (such as certain kinds of dynamic programming), one develops a ratio of costs and benefits for each alternative choice, a ratio that makes no sense unless both costs and benefits have some recognized zero points. Even in simple decision trees like that in Fig. 2.2, where costs are used there must be some way of equating costs and benefits; they must be translated to the same scale. But in mental measurement, we take most of our test scores to be interval scaled, not ratio scaled. How may this difficulty be overcome, so that the most important outcomes of education may be appropriately studied?

This question has been considered elsewhere, but some general answers may be suggested here. Any time we consider *change in scores* then we have, indeed, a ratio scale, for no change will be zero; two points will be twice the value of one point, etc. Now, as we know, change scores have their own problems, because the error variances are additive, whereas the subtraction of one score from the other eliminates from the result most of the variance in the true scores. But if we use *group* change scores, as we often will in program decisions, then indeed the errors of measurement are made very small as the number of observations grows large; and our analysis may proceed.

Often, of course, we will not have repeated measures on the same group but will have some other groups that may be regarded as controls for comparison purposes in our multivariate studies. Here, again, a zero point may be established as the mean made by the relatively ''untreated'' control, and a production function may be estimated as a relation between possible alternatives and the growth in such means. This should not give the impression that all such questions of zero points are easily resolved but that they can become tractable for many practical purposes in scientific decision making. And we are currently taking little advantage of such strategies.

TEST SCORES AND DEEPER VALUES

Test scores, we have assumed, measure those outcomes for which we most depend on our schools. The scores, then, stand for social values that we highly esteem. Yet strangely little attention has been given to the placing of these test values in some higher framework.

Suppose we ask the simplest curricular question: For example, should we double the time for mathematics in a certain grade, at the expense of some other course of study, such as history? How could we obtain evidence to help guide us in this decision? It is striking that, after 70 years of using test scores and a century of behavioral science, we still have no commonly accepted way of combining such test scores or of trading them off against each other.

The Bentee.   A decade ago, some of us studied this question, with the concern of being able to use test scores as production functions (Page, 1972d, 1973, 1974a, 1976, 1980; Page & Breen, 1974a, 1974b). In this work, we felt it necessary to invent a unit of measurement of educational benefit, called the *bentee,* for *benefit T-score.* An illustration of the bentee is shown in Fig. 2.5.

In this figure, we note that the bentee represents the highest educational value, and the branches beneath it stand for seven major branches of educational gain, ranging from the verbal, quantitative, social sciences, and natural sciences through esthetic learning, matters of the body (such as sports, health) to the "personality" (which may include citizenship and moral and spiritual learning where these are deemed appropriate). Each of these major branches may be itself divided into subdivisions. In the present figure, only one, *verbal,* has been divided into seven exhaustive areas. And one of these in turn, *literature,* has been divided. And the tree branches down through *poetic analysis* and *poetic meter,* to *iambic pentameter,* the great verse metric that has been the medium of Shakespeare and of many of our greatest English poets. Recognition of iambic pentameter, then, may be an explicit goal of instruction for good English students; it would be a suitable topic for a test item or for an operational objective in instruction. In these steps, we observe that the tree reaches from the highest philosophical and social values, through only a few steps, to the lowliest and most concrete behavioral objective. Surprisingly, climbing down this tree, the educational philosopher may actually be able to converse (chatter?) with the educational psychologist, who may be occupied with behavior modification techniques.

But how is the actual "evaluation" carried on? Having investigated two methods, we believe that a "token" method may be suitable for most curricular purposes: In this method, appropriate judges, acting individually, apportion 100 tokens (such as poker chips) among the half-dozen divisions at each branch. The method may be applied recursively, at any level of the tree, and by judges chosen as appropriate to that level. At the top, it might be educational leaders or simply

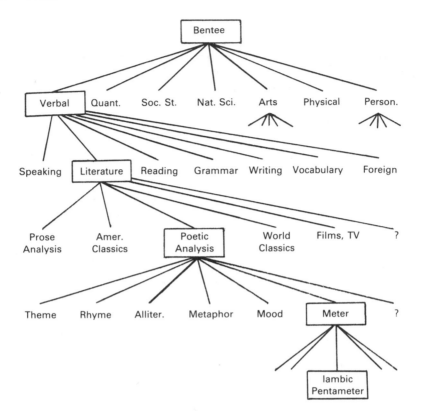

FIG. 2.5.   The recursive nature of the bentee method. As analysis moves from the general to the specific, a shift is made from societal to expert opinion and from value space to test space. (*Source:* E. B. Page, 1974. Reprinted with permission.)

informed citizens. At the lower levels, it might be subject matter specialists or future employers (in training situations). These trees may be adapted for any new program of study with its own nodes and branches.

Such a tree has a fairly clear relation to the use of test scores in decision making. Where we have test scores for the various branches (such as English, math, social studies, natural sciences), we may apportion our tokens according to our beliefs in the relative benefits of these accomplishments. And our weightings may vary with the individual concerned (the general student may have a different weighting vector from the premed) or with the program under study. But once such judgments are established, then we may proceed to *evaluate* the educational accomplishment of individuals, of groups, and of programs. By adopting changes in such bentees as our objectives, we may plot our production functions as a relation between decision alternatives and the values that we seek to optimize. Given such methods, we may employ much more frequently the well-developed techniques of the decision sciences in our own studies of policy. (The reader is directed to related literature: For a technical approach different from the bentee, see Dalkey, 1969. For a deeper understanding of means-end analysis, see Churchman, 1961. For a classic treatment of personnel decisions and test scores, see Cronbach & Gleser, 1965; and for the most advanced general treatment of multiple objectives, see Keeney & Raiffa, 1976.)

PRODUCTION FUNCTIONS AND CAUSAL RESEARCH

We have already noted that "production functions" must involve more than incidental relationships between variables. When we seek to "optimize" some benefits from our decisions, we must depend on the assumption of a *causal relation* between the decision alternatives and the desired benefit. For example, suppose we note, as many researchers have, a recurring agreement between child intelligence and family income. If we believe that this relation is causal, then we naturally predict that when we change family income, we will correspondingly change child intelligence, at least to some limited degree. Programs to eliminate poverty, therefore, according to this reasoning, should have a strong influence on reducing school failure.

Or if we believe that such intelligence is a causal outcome of time spent with the child by a well-intentioned adult, then we will predict that programs such as Head Start will have a clearly beneficial effect on future performance of participating children. Many programs of recent decades have, in fact, been constructed on the assumption that observed correlations of this sort represented strong causal relations. The disappointment about such programs results from the ambiguous and debatable outcomes actually observed. (For a sharp disappointment in a major experiment, see Page, 1972a.) We do not need to resolve these issues themselves to understand the need for some improved methods of policy study. The most important improvement seems to be this: We must routinely seek out data that will permit us to establish *causal models* explaining the maximum amount of variance possible of those variables that we wish to optimize. This means, in the first place, that we indeed have such models and, in the second, that we systematically collect the information that will maximize our knowledge. The first requirement implies that we must turn to *path analysis* to make explicit our causal models. Figure 2.3 shows such a model for exactly such a purpose, here seeking a causal influence of homework time on test achievement. The second requirement implies that we should emphasize the use of comprehensive data sets, rich with the correlates, whether from school, society, or family, that most aid in causal explanation of our outcomes of interest. In Fig. 2.3, then, we truly wish to know the effect of homework time on achievement; but we do not wish to be deceived by the correlates of race, SES, or other school variables in establishing our "production function." But if we did not collect these background characteristics (including intelligence) or if we did not combine them properly into our causal model, we would be utterly deceived about the effect of homework (just as Coleman, as mentioned earlier, was deceived in his claimed effect of private schools).

Path Analysis.   As a testing profession, then, interested in policy decisions, we must turn to the rich discipline that is now the center for policy research in most social sciences. This is the field of path analysis, introduced by Sewall Wright (1921) some 6 decades ago. In its wandering route, it has come from genetics, to economics, to sociology, to education and psychology and is now found at the heart of many of the research journals in these fields. The number of textbooks about path analysis has rapidly increased in recent years, and these have improved in complexity and quality (Aigner & Goldberger, 1977; Blalock, 1971; Duncan, 1975; Heise, 1975; Kenny, 1979; Kerlinger & Pedhazur, 1973, ch. 11; Li, 1975; Pedhazur, 1982, chs. 15–16; Taubman, 1977).

There is excellent research discipline in using these models. Because they are explicitly causal, their use forces us to specify our hypotheses about the presence and direction of causal influences and strongly encourages us to employ in our models whatever variables we have available that may illuminate our interests. Drawing and publishing such a model, moreover, forces us to put ''up front'' our assumptions about these influences. If we have left out measures of intelligence, say, or family influence, then this will be apparent in our model. Or if we have placed variables in the wrong order, thus distorting the influences, this too will be apparent to our readers, whether they are allies or critics. These considerations, clearly, have huge meanings for debates about policy decisions. Indeed, without such considerations of background influences, it would be difficult, if not impossible, to plot out any ratios for costs versus anticipated benefits.

Comprehensive Data Sets.   The second major requirement for such causal reasoning is the availability and use of large data sets containing the information necessary for causal inference and estimation. High School and Beyond is probably the most pertinent and available data set for many current concerns. It will be still more valuable as the follow-ups are completed and distributed in 1983 and beyond (current tapes are available through the National Center for Education Statistics, U.S. Department of Education, Washington, D.C.). A splendid data set is also available in the predecessor to HSB, the National Longitudinal Study of 1972, with its four follow-ups (also available from the NCES in Washington). Still another valuable set of tapes may be obtained from the U.S. Department of Labor, dealing more with work and later life and less with the high school years. But each of these data sets lacks something of great importance in family background and many other matters that might be of large interest for many particular policy questions.

Still, such data sets are much more powerful than many realize, even when they appear to lack certain variables of prime concern. Advanced path techniques involving *unmeasured variables* or *latent variables* can often generate new factors much closer to the variables of real concern. For instance, we generated a relatively school-free "mental ability" from factor analyzing a set of short mental tests (Page & Keith, 1981). Others have similarly constructed factors of "self-concept" from a collection of items about attitude. HSB already supplies an excellent SES scale from a weighted sum of many relevant questions about education, occupation, home, and other factors. In general, then, a rich data set can be much more than the simple sum of its parts.

CONCLUSIONS

From this analysis, there are some strong inferences to draw about the use of tests in decision making, and we briefly summarize them here:

1. Test professionals and test users should stop being placed on the defensive by ill-informed and polemical critics. We should reassert, firmly and publicly, the many virtues of testing and the superiority of making decisions using tests, compared with those made without tests.

2. We should insist that psychometricians and others depending on tests be heard in the major media when tests are discussed.

3. We should stop being apologetic about the reality that tests do, in part, show genetic influences and other family influences as well as social environmental influences. These are in fact part of their purpose.

4. We should cite frequently the research on the alleged biases of the most widely used standardized tests of ability and achievement. In general, the conclusions are similar to those of the blue-ribbon National Academy of Sciences panel: When properly used, *tests are not biased against English-speaking U.S. minority groups.*

5. The measurement of intelligence is one of the greatest achievements in all behavior science. The attempts to eliminate it from consideration at many decision points (such as selection for certain programs, schools, colleges, and professions) are not in the best interests of education nor of society as a whole.

6. When using tests in research on achievement, we should often lean toward the available standardized instruments, especially when these may be treated securely.

7. In such research situations, we should commonly control for the entering ability of the students. It is often fallacious to make program selection without such controls and may lead us to wasteful and disillusioning programs.

8. To assist in making decisions, test researchers should become more familiar with methods from the decision sciences, which permit technical analysis of projected costs and benefits.

9. To make use of such decision models, test researchers should translate scores, where necessary, into useful *values* to serve as production functions.

10. But to use such production functions, we must look closely at the underlying causal relations of the variables (such as achievement) that we wish to optimize. We should design these relations into explicitly causal models in path analysis.

11. If researchers look only at the variables of narrow interest, they will often be deceived by what Simon called "spurious correlation." Rather, the explanatory variables must be expanded to control, as much as possible, for background correlates of both programs and outcomes.

12. Many of such correlates will be found strongly active in family influences. To study such family influences, wherever possible researchers should look to twin pairs and other sibling and kinship relations, together with their degree of kinship (e.g., if known, whether twins are identical or fraternal).

13. It is important that government agencies, large testing corporations, and other collectors of data recognize the explanatory power of such family information and collect such variables into data sets wherever feasible.

14. And it is, finally, important that data sets be made inexpensively available to researchers, so that the causal study of human achievement may proceed in as open and active and public an environment as we can create.

Now it should be evident why this chapter is called *Struggles and Possibilities*. Testing is struggling under attacks by many enemies, operating from many motives and conceptions, often incorrect. And testing is also under constant criticism from its friends. It is friendly criticism, of course, that most characterizes the scientific enterprise and the tradition of Oscar Buros, as editor and model for this Institute that we celebrate in this volume. It is this ferment of friendly and informed criticism that has fostered the splendid growth of our field in its theoretical structure and in the construction and use of tests. These too are struggles, and they are essential to the continuing evolution of testing. Surely, the Buros Institute will continue this tradition of sharp and searching criticism by its most knowledgeable friends.

We must call upon ourselves, as well, to defend our field firmly against the defamations and uninformed assaults by its enemies. If we are faithful to the scientific tradition of open scientific debate and self-criticism, then testing will continue to grow and flourish, just as it has during the Buros' shared lifetime of work. But let us, and the Institute, firmly and courageously *take sides*.

Our field, after all, is probably the soundest structurally of any in the social and behavioral sciences. It is probably the most useful for decision making, for individuals and for social programs. For its past accomplishments, it probably has the smallest amount of apology to make—though it will surely be transformed in each succeeding generation as more is learned. Let us celebrate the field as we celebrate the Buros Institute. Perhaps the Institute might prominently display on its wall those famous lines from Shakespeare, now as applicable to our discipline as to ourselves as individuals:

> This above all: To thine own self be true,
> And it must follow, as the night the day,
> Thou canst not then be false to any man.

REFERENCES

Aigner, D. J., & Goldberger, A. S. (Eds.). *Latent variables in socioeconomic models.* Amsterdam: North-Holland, 1977.

Anderson, G. E., Jr. Operations research: A missing link. *Educational Researcher,* March 1970, *21,* 1–3.

Banghart, F. *Educational systems analysis.* Toronto: Collier-Macmillan, 1969.

Behrman, J. R., Hrubec, Z., Taubman, P., & Wales, T. J. *Socioeconomic success: A study of the effects of genetic endowments, family environment, and schooling.* Amsterdam: North-Holland, 1980.

Bereiter, C. Genetics and educability: Educational implications of the Jensen debate. In J. Hellmuth (Ed.), *Disadvantaged child* (Vol. 3). New York: Brunner-Mazel, 1970.

Bersoff, D. N. Testing and the law. *American Psychologist,* 1981, *36*(10), 1047–1056.

Blalock, H. M., Jr. (Ed.). *Causal models in the social sciences.* Chicago: Aldine, 1971.

Cancro, R. (Ed.). *Intelligence: Genetic and environmental influences.* New York: Grune & Stratton, 1971.

Carroll, J. B., & Horn, J. L. On the scientific basis of ability testing. *American Psychologist,* 1981, *36*(10), 1012–1020.

Churchman, C. W. *Prediction and optimal decisions: Philosophical issues of a science of values.* Englewood Cliffs, N.J.: Prentice-Hall, 1961.

Churchman, C. W., Ackoff, R. L., & Arnoff, S. L. *Introduction to operations research.* New York: Wiley, 1957.

Cole, N. S. Bias in testing. *American Psychologist,* 1981, *36*(10), 1067–1077.

Coleman, J., Hoffer, T., & Kilgore, S. *Public and private schools.* A report to the National Center for Education Statistics by the National Opinion Research Center. University of Chicago, March 1981.

Cronbach, L. J., & Gleser, G. *Psychological tests and personnel decisions* (2nd ed.). Urbana: University of Illinois Press, 1965.

Dalkey, N. Analyses from a group opinion study. *Futures,* December 1969, *1,* 541–551.

Duncan, O. D. *Introduction to structural equation models.* New York: Academic, 1975.

Eaves, L. J., Last, K., Martin, N. G., & Jinks, J. L. A progressive approach to non-additivity and genotype-environmental covariance in the analysis of human differences. *British Journal of Mathematical and Statistical Psychology,* 1977, *30,* 1–42.

Edwards, W., Guttentag, M., & Snapper, K. A decision-theoretic approach to evaluation research. In E. L. Struening, & M. Guttentag (Eds.), *Handbook of evaluation research* (Vol. 1). Beverly Hills, Calif.: SAGE, 1975. Ch. 8, pp. 139–182.

Falconer, D. S. *Introduction to quantitative genetics.* New York: Ronald Press, 1960.

Fuller, J. L., & Thompson, W. R. *Foundations of behavior genetics.* St. Louis, Mo.: Mosby, 1978.

Gould, S. J. *The mismeasure of man.* New York: Norton, 1981.

Hamburg, M. *Statistical analysis for decision making.* New York: Harcourt, Brace & World, 1970.

Hébert, J. P. *Race et intelligence.* Paris: Copernic, 1977.

Heise, D. R. *Causal analysis.* New York: Wiley, 1975.

Herrnstein, R. J. *IQ in the meritocracy*. Boston: Little, Brown, 1973.

Herrnstein, R. J. IQ testing and the media. *Atlantic*, August 1982, 68–74.

Hillier, F. S., & Lieberman, G. J. *Introduction to operations research* (2nd ed.). San Francisco: Holden-Day, 1974.

Jensen, A. R. *Bias in mental testing*. New York: Macmillan-Free Press, 1980.

Jensen, A. R. *Straight talk about mental tests*. New York: Macmillan–Free Press, 1981.

Johnstone, J. N. Mathematical models developed for use in educational planning: A review. *Review of Educational Research*, 1974, *44*(2), 177–201.

Kamin, L. *The science and politics of IQ*. New York: Wiley, 1973.

Katz, M. R. A model of guidance for career decision-making. *Vocational Guidance Quarterly*, September 1966, 2–10.

Kaufman, R. *Educational system planning*. Englewood Cliffs, N.J.: Prentice-Hall, 1972.

Keeney, R. L., & Raiffa, H. *Decisions with multiple objectives: Preferences and value tradeoffs*. New York: Wiley, 1976.

Keith, T. Z. Time spent on homework and high school grades: A large-sample path analysis. *Journal of Educational Psychology*, 1982, *74*, 248–253.

Kenny, D. A. *Correlation and causality*. New York: Wiley–Interscience, 1979.

Kerlinger, F. N., & Pedhazur, E. J. *Multiple regression in behavioral research*. New York: Holt, Rinehart & Winston, 1973.

Layzer, D. Heritability analyses of IQ scores: Science or numerology? *Science*, 1974, *183*, 1259–1266.

Levin, H. M. Cost-effectiveness analysis in evaluation research. In M. Guttentag & E. L. Struening (Eds.), *Handbook of evaluation research* (Vol. 2). Beverly Hills, Calif.: SAGE, 1975. Ch. 5, pp. 89–122.

Li, C. C. *Path analysis: A primer*. Pacific Grove, Calif.: Boxwood, 1975.

Linn, R. L. Admissions testing on trial. *American Psychologist*, 1982, *34*(3), 279–291.

Loehlin, J. C., Lindzey, G., & Spuhler, J. N. *Race differences in intelligence*. San Francisco: Freeman, 1975.

Loehlin, J. C., & Nichols, R. C. *Heredity, environment, and personality: A study of 850 sets of twins*. Austin: University of Texas Press, 1976.

Martin, N. G. The inheritance of scholastic abilities in a sample of twins: II. Genetical analysis of examination results. *Annals of Human Genetics, London*, 1975, *39*, 219–229.

McNamara, J. F. Mathematical programming models in educational planning. *Review of Educational Research*, 1971, *41*(5), 419–446.

Mercer, J. R. *Labelling the mentally retarded*. Berkeley: University of California Press, 1977.

Novick, M. R., & Jackson, P. H. *Statistical methods for educational and psychological research*. New York: McGraw-Hill, 1974.

Page, E. B. How we all failed in performance contracting. *Educational Psychologist*, 1972, *9*, 40–42. (a)

Page, E. B. Miracle in Milwaukee: Raising the I.Q. *Educational Researcher*, 1972, *1*(10), 8–15. (b)

Page, E. B. Resolution on scientific freedom and heredity. *American Psychologist*, 1972, *27*(7), 660–661. (c)

Page, E. B. Seeking a measure of general educational advancement: The bentee. *Journal of Educational Measurement*, 1972, *9*(1), 33–43. (d)

Page, E. B. Effects of higher education: Outcomes, values, or benefits. In L. C. Solmon & P. Taubman (Eds.), *Does college matter? Some evidence on the impacts of higher education*. New York: Academic, 1973. Pp. 159–172.

Page, E. B. 'Top-down' trees of educational values. *Educational and Psychological Measurement*, 1974, *34*(3), 573–584. (a)

Page, E. B. Problems and perspectives in measuring vocational maturity. In D. E. Super (Ed.), *Measuring vocational maturity for counseling and evaluation.* Washington, D. C.: Monograph of the National Vocational Guidance Association, 1974. (b)

Page, E. B. Heritability of intelligence: Methodological questions. Technical comment, *Science,* 13 June 1975, *188*(4193), 1126–1128.

Page, E. B. The optimization of educational values in Navy curriculum design. *Proceedings of the American Statistical Association: Social Statistics,* Part II: 1976, 655–659.

Page, E. B. Should educational evaluation be more objective or more subjective? More objective! *Educational Evaluation and Policy Analysis,* 1978, 1(1), 5–6

Page, E. B. Tests and decisions for the handicapped: A guide to evaluation under the new laws. Special issue: A monograph, *Journal of Special Education,* Winter 1980, *14*(4)

Page, E. B. The media, technical analysis, and the data fcast: A response to Coleman. *Educational Researcher,* 1981, *10*(7), 21–23.

Page, E. B. *Rethinking the principles of national assessment: Towards a more useful and higher quality knowledge base for education.* Report commissioned by the National Institute of Education. In ERIC, 1982.

Page, E. B., & Breen, T. F., III. Educational values for measurement technology: Some theory and data. In W. E. Coffman (Ed.), *Frontiers in educational measurement and information processing.* Boston: Houghton-Mifflin, 1974. Ch. 3, pp. 13–30. (a)

Page, E. B., & Breen, T. F., III. Factor analysis of educational values across two methods of judgment. *Proceedings of the 15th Interamerican Congress of Psychology* (Bogotá, Colombia), 1974, pp. 106–107. (b)

Page, E. B., & Canfield, J. *Design of Navy course structure through a dynamic programming algorithm.* Report for the U.S. Navy Personnel R. & D. Center, San Diego, Calif., June 1975.

Page, E. B., & Grandon, G. M. Massive intervention and child intelligence: The Milwaukee Project in critical perspective. *Journal of Special Education,* 1981, *15*(2), 239–256.

Page, E. B., & Jarjoura, D. Seeking the cause of correlations among mental abilities: Large twin analysis in a national testing program. Special issue on Intelligence, *Journal of Research and Development in Education,* 1979, *12*(2), 108–117.

Page, E. B., Jarjoura, D., & Konopka, C. Curriculum design through operations research. *American Educational Research Journal,* 1976, *13*(1), 31–49.

Page, E. B., & Keith, T. Z. Effect of U.S. private schools: A technical analysis of two recent claims. *Educational Researcher,* August 1981, *10*(7), 7–17.

Pedhazur, E. J. *Multiple regression in behavioral research: Explanation and prediction* (2nd ed.). New York: Holt, Rinehart & Winston, 1982.

Raiffa, H. *Decision analysis: Introductory lectures on choice under uncertainty.* Boston: Addison-Wesley, 1968.

Reschly, D. J. Psychological testing in educational classification and placement. *American Psychologist,* 1981, *36*(10), 1094–1102.

Scarr-Salapatek, S. Race, social class, and IQ. *Science,* 1971, *174*, 1285 1295.

Schmidt, F. L., & Hunter, J. E, Fmploymont testing: Old theories and new research findings. *American Psychologist,* 1981, *36*(10), 1128–1137.

Stanley, J. C., & Hopkins, K. D. *Educational and psychological measurement and evaluation.* Englewood Cliffs, N.J.: Prentice-Hall, 1972.

Taubman, P. (Ed.). *Kinometrics: Determinants of socioeconomic success within and between families.* Amsterdam: North-Holland, 1977.

Thompson, J. N., Jr., & Thoday, J. M. (Eds.). *Quantitative genetic variation.* New York: Academic, 1979.

Thorndike, E. L. The nature, purposes, and general methods of measurements of educational products. *The 17th Yearbook of the National Society for the Study of Education,* Part II. 1918.

Tillett, P. I. Optimization of secondary teacher assignments using operations research. *Socio-Economic Planning Sciences* (London), 1975, *9*, 101–104.

Trueman, R. E. *An introduction to quantitative methods for decision making.* New York: Holt, Rinehart & Winston, 1974.

VanDusseldorp, R. A., Richardson, D. W., & Foley, W. J. *Educational decision-making through operations research.* Boston: Allyn & Bacon, 1971.

Wagner, H. M. *Principles of operations research: With applications to managerial decisions.* Englewood Cliffs, N.J.: Prentice-Hall, 1969.

Winkler, R. L., & Hays, W. L. *Statistics: Probability, inference, and decision* (2nd ed.). New York: Holt, Rinehart & Winston, 1975.

Wright, S. Correlation and causation. *Journal of Agricultural Research,* 1921, *20,* 557–585.

3 What Cognitive Psychology Can (and Cannot) Do for Test Development

Robert J. Sternberg
Yale University

Whenever research is launched under a new paradigm for studying an old set of mental phenomena, researchers joining the new armada of explorers hope, at best, to discover new uncharted mental territories and, at worst, to provide new mental maps of previously charted territories that amend errors of the old maps. This has been, I believe, the experience of cognitive psychologists studying mental abilities. Although they may not have revolutionized our map of the mind (yet), neither have they left the old maps standing. What is critical is that at least the flaws and incompletenesses of the new methods are different from those of the old. One can therefore be provided with some new insights about the mental phenomena being studied. Consider an analogy to polar and Cartesian coordinates: Each provides a different and useful view of a world that is not quite so simple as either coordinate system would have us believe. Seeing the mental world in two ways can tell us more than seeing it in just one way. In the language of Garner, Hake, and Eriksen (1956), we have provided "converging operations" to view a unitary phenomenon.

I have divided my analysis of the contribution of cognitive psychology to test construction into four main parts dealing, respectively, with the contributions of cognitive psychology to: (1) content for construction of tests; (2) validation of tests; (3) scoring and interpretation of tests; and (4) modification of tests. Before discussing these contributions, however, let me say just what are the characteristics that define "cognitive psychology" and what psychologists do in the cognitive–psychological investigation of intelligence.

WHAT IS COGNITIVE PSYCHOLOGY?

Cognitive psychology is the study of the mind in terms of the mental (cognitive) representations and processes that underlie observable behavior. In particular, I find that cognitive researchers tend to address five main questions:

1. What are the mental processes that constitute intelligent task performance?
2. How rapidly and accurately are these processes performed?
3. Into what strategies for task performance do these mental processes combine?
4. Upon what forms of mental representation do these processes and strategies act?
5. What is the knowledge base that is organized into these forms of representation, and how does it affect and become affected by the processes, strategies, and representations that individuals use?

These questions have been asked of performance on a rather wide range of cognitive tasks.

Cognitive Versus Psychometric Approaches

The cognitive approach is often contrasted with the psychometric one, perhaps because historically it has seemed easy enough to separate the psychometricians of a given time from the experimental psychologists of that time (many of whom now call themselves "cognitive" psychologists). However, I think it worth mentioning and even emphasizing that the distinction has never been as clear as Cronbach's (1957) paper on "the two disciplines of scientific psychology" or as the conventional wisdom (which may in part be based upon Cronbach's paper) might have one believe. Many of the great experimental or "cognitive" psychologists in the history of psychology have also been psychometricians and vice versa, and it often seems almost arbitrary to identify a given individual as one or the other. Consider some examples.

Sir Francis Galton invented the correlational method and yet was an avid experimentalist. Alfred Binet invented the prototype for the most widely used psychometric intelligence test, and yet a close reading of his writings will show his often neglected theorizing to be as "cognitive" as any we find today. Charles Spearman invented factor analysis, and yet his 1923 treatise on the "principles of cognition" was a cognitive monograph and the basis for much cognitive theorizing today, particularly in the domain of inductive reasoning. Edward Thorndike is most well known for his experimental work in animal learning and yet was the author of a major book on the subject of psychometrically measured intelligence. Clark Hull, another famous learning theorist, wrote his first book on the subject of aptitude testing. Louis Thurstone, a psychometrician if ever there was one, advocated factorial methods as preliminaries to experimental ones, not as replacements for them. Finally, J. P. Guilford, clearly identified as a psychometrician, has also proposed a theory of intelligence in which one of the three facets describes the processes of intelligence.

The list could go on and on, but I think the point by now should be clear: Even before Cronbach's (1957) paper, there was already a substantial connection between psychometric and cognitive lines of endeavor. I do not believe they were ever quite so separate as Cronbach's paper suggested, and for all the overwhelming positive contribution the paper clearly made, it may have served the slightly negative function of tending to underscore the points of friction rather than the points of smooth contact. Today, I believe (in part because of the positive contribution of Cronbach's paper) that the distinction between psychometricians and cognitive psychologists, at least in the research domain of intelligence, is fuzzier than ever. People like Jack Carroll, Earl Hunt, Robert Glaser, Susan Whitely, Richard Snow, and myself, among others, could perhaps as easily be classified as falling into one camp as into the other.

If the line between psychometrics and cognitive psychology is so unclear, just what is it that is distinctive about the cognitive approach? Certainly it is not just the questions asked, in that the questions listed earlier would also be quite relevant to the interest of many psychometricians theorizing about intelligence. Nor is it, really, the emphasis of the questions upon stimulus rather than subject variation. Psychometric methods, like factor analysis, really can be used to study either source of variation (although they are most commonly used to study subject variation), and experimental methods can also be used to study either stimulus or subject variation (although they are most commonly used to study stimulus variation).

The critical difference, I believe, is a sociological one and resides primarily (but not exclusively) in the professional identification of the investigator and of the methods he or she uses. A number of contemporary investigators, including this author, use multiple regression in modeling of test performance; for whatever reason, this methodology today seems more to belong to the ''cognitive camp,'' despite the fact that multiple regression can certainly be and has been viewed as a psychometric method. Susan Whitely does a highly similar (although by no means identical) kind of modeling using latent-trait analysis and tends to be viewed more in the psychometric camp. Users of exploratory factor analysis, like Raymond Cattell and John Horn, tend to be identified with the psychometric camp, whereas users of confirmatory factor analysis, like Carl and John Frederiksen, tend more to be identified with the experimental camp. The lines between camps are certainly not clearly drawn, although they can be inferred to some extent by the conventions one attends and by the journals in which one publishes as well as by the methods one uses. The rationale for placing someone in one or the other camp is certainly not clear-cut.

I have tried in several ways to make the basic point, one that I have come to believe only recently. This point is that the lines that have been drawn between the psychometric and cognitive approaches to intelligence are often arbitrary and even capricious. If I speak in this chapter of the contribution of cognitive psychology to the psychometric tradition of mental test development, I am speaking of boundaries between traditions that I think have much more to do with the sociology of science than with its substantive concerns.

Cognitive–Psychological Approaches to the Study of Mental Abilities

How do cognitive psychologists go about studying mental abilities? Cognitive psychologists are highly similar in their emphasis on intensive task analysis. The idea is to take performance on a single task and then to study it in great depth. One then constructs an information-processing model of performance in the given task, a model that specifies in considerable detail just how subjects solve the task. Only after the task has been intensively analyzed is an attempt made to generalize the results of the task analysis to related tasks as well.

One can carve up the field in many different ways, as people in fact have (Pellegrino & Glaser, 1979; Sternberg, 1977, 1981c). I have loosely classified these different approaches into four different categories, but it should be understood that these categories are neither mutually exclusive nor exhaustive with respect to current research approaches in cognitive psychology. I now briefly describe what each approach is, what its goals are, what kinds of research it has generated, and what its implications for test construction are.

Cognitive Correlates. In this approach to understanding mental abilities, subjects are tested in their ability to perform tasks that contemporary cognitive psychologists believe measure basic human information-processing abilities. (Information processing is generally defined as the sequence of mental operations and their products involved in performing a cognitive task.) Such tasks include, among others, the Posner and Mitchell (1967) letter-matching task, in which subjects are asked to state as quickly as possible whether the letters in a pair such as "A a" constitute a physical match (which they don't) or (in another condition) a name match (which they do), and the S. Sternberg (1969) memory-scanning task, in which subjects are asked to state as quickly as possible whether a target digit or letter, such as 5, appeared in a previously memorized set of digits or letters, such as 3 6 5 2. Individuals are usually tested either via tachistoscope (a machine that provides rapid stimulus exposures) or via a computer terminal, with the principal dependent measure of interest being response time.

The proximal goal in this research is to estimate parameters (characteristic quantities) representing the durations of performance for the information-processing components constituting each task and then to investigate the extent to which these components correlate across subjects with each other and with scores on measures commonly believed to assess intelligence (e.g., Raven's Progressive Matrices test). Most commonly, correlations between parameter estimates and measured intelligence are statistically significant but moderately low—usually around .3 (Hunt, Frost, & Lunneborg, 1973; Hunt, Lunneborg, & Lewis, 1975). The distal goal of cognitive-correlates research is to integrate individual-differences research and mainstream cognitive–psychological research—in particular, by providing a theoretical grounding from cognitive psychology for differential research (Hunt et al., 1973). Thus, instead of trying to draw theoretical conclusions by correlating scores on one empirically derived test (e.g., reasoning) with scores on another empirically derived test (e.g., vocabulary), as differential researchers have done, cognitive-correlates researchers draw theoretical conclusions by correlating scores on an empirically derived test with parameters generated by a cognitive model of some aspect of mental functioning (e.g., memory scanning).

Cognitive-correlates researchers would be most likely to supplement psychometric tests with information-processing tests based on standard laboratory information-processing tasks such as the memory-scanning and letter-matching tests mentioned earlier. Rose (1978) has actually constructed and tested an information-processing assessment battery based on standard laboratory tasks. Using this battery, one can isolate latency scores for a variety of different information-processing components. Rose's battery is an impressive one, although correlations across tasks are relatively low, and correlations of the information-processing tasks and parameters with psychometric tests or various types of real-world performance have yet to be reported.

Cognitive Components. In this approach to understanding mental abilities, subjects are tested for their ability to perform tasks of the kinds actually found on standard psychometric tests of mental abilities—for example, analogies, series completions, mental rotations, and syllogisms. Subjects are usually tested via a tachistoscope or a computer terminal, and response time is usually the principal dependent variable, with error rate and pattern of response choices as secondary dependent variables. These latter dependent variables are of more interest in this approach than in the cognitive-correlates approach because the tasks tend to be more difficult and thus more susceptible to erroneous responses.

The proximal goal in this research is first to formulate a model of information processing in performance on IQ-test types of tasks; second, to test the model at the same time as parameters for the model are estimated; and, finally, to investigate the extent to which these components correlate across subjects with each other and with scores on standard psychometric tests. Because the tasks that are analyzed are usually taken directly from IQ tests, or else are very similar to tasks found on IQ tests, the major issue in this kind of research is not whether there is any correlation at all between cognitive task and psychometric test scores. Rather, the issue is one of isolating the locus or loci of the correlation that is obtained. One seeks to discover what components of information processing in task performance are the critical ones from the standpoint of the theory of intelligence.

Cognitive-components researchers would be most likely to supplement psychometric tests with information-processing tests based on the psychometric ones, but with test items administered in a computer-controlled setting that would enable the examiner to decompose test performance into its information-processing constituents. An information-processing analysis of a subject's inductive reasoning performance, for example, would assess skills such as the individual's ability: (1) to encode stimuli; (2) to infer relations between stimulus terms; (3) to map higher-order relations between relations; (4) to apply previously inferred relations to new settings; (5) to compare alternative answer options in terms of their similarities and differences; (6) to justify one answer as preferred but not necessarily ideal; (7) to respond; (8) to combine these components into a strategy that results in efficient item solution; and (9) to represent information in a way that facilitates operations on the data base stored in long-term memory (Sternberg & Gardner, 1982).

Cognitive Training.   This approach to understanding mental abilities can be used in conjunction with either the cognitive-correlates approach or the cognitive-components approach, or in conjunction with some other approach. The essense of this approach is aptly described by Campione, Brown, and Ferrara (1982). Essentially, the approach seeks to infer the identities of cognitive processes through an analysis of effects of training. The cognitive-training approach has been used widely in a variety of domains. For example, Belmont and Butterfield (1971), Borkowski and Wanschura (1974), and Campione and Brown (1978) have used the approach in investigations of learning and memory. Feuerstein (1979), Holzman, Glaser, and Pellegrino (1976), and Linn (1973) have used it in investigations of reasoning and problem solving. One conclusion has emerged with striking regularity in many studies by many different investigators: To attain both durability and generalizability of training, it seems to be necessary to train both at the level of metacomponents (or executive processes) and at the level of performance components (or lower-order processes used to carry out the orders of the executive processes—see, e.g., Belmont, Butterfield, & Ferretti, 1982; Feuerstein, 1979, 1980).

Cognitive-training researchers might follow any of a number of paths to testing depending on their choice of what to train and how to train it. One of the more interesting approaches to testing among such investigators is that of Feuerstein (1979), who has devised a "learning potential assessment device" that he believes measures cognitive modifiability, or what Vygotsky (1978) referred to as the "zone of potential development." Modifiability is assessed by giving examinees guided instruction in solving problems that the examinees are initially unable to solve and by evaluating the examinees' ability to profit from instruction.

Cognitive Contents.   Recently, a new approach to research has emerged on the cognitive–psychological scene that has yet to be applied directly to the study of mental abilities but that seems to provide a good entree into such research. The approach seeks to compare the performances of experts and novices in complex tasks such as the solution of physics problems (Chi, Feltovich, & Glaser, 1981; Chi, Glaser, & Rees, 1982; Larkin, McDermott, Simon, & Simon, 1980a, 1980b), the selection of moves and strategies in chess and other games (Chase & Simon, 1973; DeGroot, 1965; Reitman, 1976), and the acquisition of domain-related information by groups of people at different levels of expertise (Chiesi, Spilich, & Voss, 1979; Spilich, Vesonder, Chiesi, & Voss, 1979). Research on expert–novice differences in a variety of task domains suggests that the way information is stored in and retrieved from long-term memory can largely account for the substantial differences in performance between experts and novices. This view would suggest that a possible locus of differences between more and less mentally able people is in their ability to organize information in long-term memory in a way that makes it readily accessible for a variety of purposes (Egan & Greeno, 1973). Presumably, information stored in such a flexible way is maximally available for transfer from old to new problem situations.

Because the cognitive-contents approach has not yet been directly applied to the investigation of differences in mental abilities, it is impossible to evaluate its utility for purposes of such investigation. But the approach seems to supply a valuable new inroad for mental-abilities research, and I expect it will be only a matter of time before it is used for this purpose.

Cognitive-contents researchers might supplement psychometric tests with complex-learning or problem-solving tasks that elicit an examinee's knowledge base and the way in which knowledge is mentally represented. Such researchers would be particularly interested in the features of problems to which examinees attend. It has been found, for example, that less skilled physics problem solvers tend to pay more attention to surface features of physics problems, whereas more skilled problem solvers tend to pay more attention to deep structural features (Chi et al., 1981, 1982). Cognitive-contents tests might also supplement cognitive-components tests, with the former assessing knowledge deficiencies and the latter assessing processing deficiencies.

Cognitive psychologists studying mental abilities differ markedly in the tasks they have chosen to study, in the dependent variables they use to study these tasks, in the kinds of theories that motivate their research, and in their concern with individual differences. Because I have more to offer later about differences in task content, I pass over this source of differences now. The kinds of dependent variables that cognitive psychologists use include reaction time, percentage correct, breakdown of response choices, protocol analysis, and output of computer simulations. Although choice of one (or more) dependent variable(s) may not seem like a major issue to many psychologists, the history of cognitive psychology up to the present has been marked by active (and at times explosive) debates regarding the relative merits of various dependent measures (see, e.g., Ericsson & Simon, 1980; Nisbett & Wilson, 1977; Pachella, 1974; Sternberg, 1977; S. Sternberg, 1969). Cognitive psychologists also differ in the scope of the theories that motivate their research, with scope ranging from quite narrow (Egan, 1976) to very broad (Anderson, 1976). The optimal scope of a motivating theory of intelligence has also been a subject of intense debate among cognitive psychologists (Anderson, 1976; Sternberg & Davidson, 1982). Finally, cognitive psychologists differ greatly in their concern with individual differences. In the past decade, cognitive psychologists have progressed from little or no concern to an increasingly broad concern with this issue.

COGNITIVE PSYCHOLOGY AND TEST CONSTRUCTION

Cognitive psychologists studying mental abilities have investigated a wide range of tasks, some of which have been used in test construction. The tasks they have investigated differ in a multitude of ways, but it is convenient and, I believe, accurate to array them along a single dimension of task complexity, from simple and choice reaction time at one extreme to complex logic and mathematics at the other extreme. The tasks along this continuum differ in the apparent "level" of mental processing required.

At the simple end of the continuum, Furneaux (1956), Jensen (1979), and Lunneborg (1977) have used simple and choice reaction time tasks to test the hypothesis that individual differences in mental ability can be understood largely in terms of individual differences in sheer speed of mental functioning. Hunt (1978; Hunt et al., 1975) has studied mental speed as well but at a somewhat higher level of processing. He has suggested that individual differences in mental abilities, especially verbal ones, can be understood in terms of differences in people's speed of access to lexical information in long-term memory. In sharp contrast to Furneaux, Jensen, and Lunneborg, he has preferred to hold constant simple or choice reaction time divorced from lexical access so as not to confound his measurement of access speed. Pellegrino and Glaser (1979, 1980), Snow (1979), and I (Sternberg, 1977, 1980c, 1981c), among others, have claimed that the level of mental processing studied by Hunt and his colleagues is still low and have preferred instead to study performance on tasks at a level of complexity equal to that of intelligence-test items. Like those cited earlier, these researchers have emphasized speed of processing, but particularly speed in solving relatively complex tasks such as analogies and syllogisms. Finally, investigators such as Greeno (1980); Chi et al. (1982); and Larkin (1981) have suggested, if only by implication, that even the intelligence-test items are at too low a level of processing and have studied instead performance in very complex mathematics and physics problems.

In sum, the range of tasks studied by cognitive psychologists investigating intelligence is at least as broad as that studied by psychometricians. Indeed, the range in levels of complexity is probably greater: Whereas most psychometricians seem to have resolved the Galton–Binet dispute regarding test content to their satisfaction, cognitive psychologists seem not to have done so.

Even if cognitive psychologists did display more agreement regarding the kinds of task performance that should be studied under the rubric of intelligence, it is not at all clear that they would have much to contribute to psychometricians by way of useful feedback regarding test content, because when cognitive psychologists have used reference measures at all for external criteria for their tasks and theories, they have used intelligence tests and subtests rather than the behaviors these tests were themselves intended to predict (such as school grades and job success). Their use of psychometric tests as (obviously proximal) criteria for their own tasks and tests has made it impossible to use their data to modify the tests. One can use the criteria to suggest changes in the predictor but not the other way around!

My message regarding the contribution of cognitive psychology to selection of test content is not a wholly pessimistic one, however. Some recent cognitive research has suggested promising lines of endeavor that I believe are now ready for at least pilot attempts in psychometric tests. I think three suggestions are clearly forthcoming, albeit from experiments using IQ-test items as criteria.

First, there is good evidence that performance on the Clark and Chase (1972) sentence–picture verification task, which requires the examinee rapidly to indicate whether a sentence representation (such as ''The star is above the plus.'') agrees with a pictorial representation (such as $^*_+$), can provide a quick estimate of a person's general level of intelligence (Hunt et al., 1975) and even, possibly, of their proclivity for verbal versus spatial strategies for problem solving (MacLeod, Hunt, & Mathews, 1978; Mathews, Hunt, & MacLeod, 1980). The task is easy to administer and usable for examinees over a wide range of ages, ability levels, and mental conditions.

Second, there is strong evidence to suggest value in measuring fluid intelligence by using novel tasks employing novel kinds of concepts (Snow, 1980; Sternberg, 1981a). The important thing appears to be not the particular task or concepts used but their relative novelty for the examinees performing them. By *novelty*, I refer not only to a difference in content but to a difference in kind from conventional kinds of test items.

Third, substantial evidence has now been accumulated for the considerable value in measuring crystallized, or verbal, intelligence of a task requiring examinees to learn and then define previously unfamiliar words presented in natural written contexts (Sternberg, Powell, & Kaye, 1982). Such a task appears to tap at least one major aspect of the antecedents of developed individual differences in verbal skills and knowledge.

To conclude this section, cognitive psychology has probably not been at its best in suggesting to test developers the kinds of content they might profitably use in test construction. There is almost no resolution among cognitive psychologists as to what kinds of test contents best measure intellectual functioning, and experiments have not been designed in ways that would be particularly informative with regard to suggested content even if cognitive psychologists could agree as to what kinds of contents to employ. Nevertheless, a few suggestions have emerged from cognitive research regarding several kinds of contents that might be beneficially employed in future testing.

COGNITIVE PSYCHOLOGY AND TEST VALIDATION

Whereas cognitive psychology has probably made its weakest contribution to test development in the realm of test content, it has probably made its strongest contribution in the realm of test validation and, in particular, construct validation. There is perhaps some irony in the fact that the paradigm that was perhaps hoped by some to provide a replacement for the psychometric paradigm has instead provided converging evidence to support its major findings. Let me elaborate.

Whereas psychometricians have generally attempted to understand mental abilities through the construct of the "factor," cognitive psychologists have generally attempted to understand mental abilities through the construct of the "process" and, to a lesser extent, the "mental representation" of information. Through successive refinements, cognitive psychologists have developed techniques that seem to be quite successful in the isolation of mental processes (Ericsson & Simon, 1980; Newell & Simon, 1972; Pachella, 1974; Siegler, 1976; Sternberg, 1977; S. Sternberg, 1969). A few of the cognitive psychologists, such as Carroll (1976, 1981) and myself (Sternberg, 1980a), have explicitly addressed the question of the extent to which the structural factors of psychometricians deal, at some deep level, with the same latent abilities as the processes of cognitive psychologists. We have concluded that both sets of investigators are, in fact, looking at the same underlying entities, albeit in different ways.

I disagree with Carroll's (1981) position that factors are in some interesting sense more "basic" than are processes, and I also disagree with my own earlier position (Sternberg, 1977) that processes are in some interesting sense more basic than factors. So far as I can tell, there exists no empirical means to determine which is more basic, nor is it even clear what, conceptually, "more basic" means. If there is some basic molar unit in terms of which mental abilities are organized, we probably do not know what it is; even more discouraging, perhaps, we wouldn't know we knew if we did, in fact, know. At this point, therefore, I regard arguments regarding basic-level mental units as nonfruitful and believe we should probably be quite pleased that constructs from the psychometric and cognitive, as well as from other approaches (Sternberg, 1981b), have converged as well as they have in suggesting how mental abilities might be organized.

What, exactly, are these points of convergence? I believe there are three main ones.

First, there appears to be some (if you wish, higher-order) general factor or source of individual differences that is common to performance on a strikingly wide range of cognitive tasks (Holzinger, 1938; Jensen, 1980; Spearman, 1927; Thurstone, 1938; Vernon, 1971). Individual differences in this general ability, or *g,* appear to derive in large part from differences in the functioning of (higher-order) executive processes—such as solution planning, monitoring, and control—that regulate most mental functions (Butterfield & Belmont, 1977; Campione & Brown, 1978; Snow, 1979; Sternberg, 1979).

Second, there appear to be at least two, and possibly several more, broad constellations of skills that operate in fairly broad ranges of tasks but not, by any means, in all tasks. The two most prominent constellations, which have been referred to by many names but here will be referred to by the names of "fluid" and "crystallized" abilities (Horn & Cattell, 1966), encompass reasoning kinds of tasks on the one hand and verbal kinds of tasks on the other (Cattell, 1971; Horn, 1968; Vernon, 1971). Individual differences in these abilities appear to be traceable to present and past functioning of lower-order performance and learning processes, as well as to the interactions of these processes with the higher-order executive ones (Sternberg, 1980c).

Finally, for however they may interact, it is important to separate speed from power aspects of performance (Carroll, 1981; Egan, 1976; Guyote & Sternberg, 1981; Sternberg, 1977, 1980b). Speed and power appear to be differentiable aspects of mental skill, and confounding them can lead to misleading or even downright incorrect conclusions (Sternberg, 1980b).

To conclude this section, I would argue that cognitive psychology has provided a valuable complementary way of investigating pretty much the same constructs psychometricians have been studying all along. The contribution of cognitive psychology goes beyond a merely salutary or congratulatory one. Cognitive psychology has provided insights into the processes underlying the products studied by psychometricians and has told us what happens in real time to generate these products. The process models of cognitive psychologists, and the theoretical and metatheoretical schemes underlying them, have provided important insights into mental abilities that previously had been lacking.

COGNITIVE PSYCHOLOGY, TEST SCORING, AND TEST INTERPRETATION

Using a cognitive approach, one would derive and interpret a set of test scores quite different from that derived and interpreted via a psychometric approach. The major difference in scoring would be the isolation, in cognitive analysis, of subscores based on processes rather than actual or alleged factors.

Consider, for example, the rather global construct of reasoning ability. It would not be at all surprising to discover that individuals believed, for one reason or another, to be of low intelligence score below the average on tests of reasoning ability. But exactly what does this tell us? Does it tell us what it is that leads to the subject's low intelligence? Does it tell us what kinds of interventions might be indicated to increase the individual's level of intellectual functioning? Does it even tell us that the individual is low in reasoning ability as opposed, say, to encoding the terms of the problem so that the reasoning operations can be performed? I would argue that the answer to each of these questions is negative; in short, that the low score in reasoning provides relatively little by way of diagnostic or prescriptive information.

A cognitive analysis of the bases of performance on one or more reasoning tests would seek to go "inside" the reasoning factor—to elicit for each individual a measure of performance on each of the processes theorized in combination to constitute reasoning performance. In my own theory of inductive reasoning, for example (Sternberg, 1977, 1980c), separate component scores might be estimated for processes such as encoding, inference, application, and response. Other cognitive theories would yield somewhat different sets of process scores, just as alternative factorial theories yield somewhat different sets of factor scores. At the very least, any of the "reasonable" theories of cognitive processing would permit a separation between performance on the encoding, pure reasoning, and response aspects of task performance.

These process scores not only permit a finer diagnosis of strengths and weaknesses in congitive skills but permit as well the construction of a process-based training program. It is difficult to conceive of training something as ill-defined as "reasoning" but relatively easy to conceive of training a specific skill such as inferring relations. The relative ease of conceiving and actually of preparing such a training program should not, however, desensitize one to the considerable difficulty that can be involved in instantiating transfer of training in the individuals exposed to the program of instruction.

The theoretical basis now exists not only for analyzing processing skills in reasoning tasks but for analyzing processing skills in other kinds of tasks as well, such as spatial, verbal, and numerical tasks. Yet, I do not recommend our actually implementing the theory in practice at this time. There are several reasons for my reluctance to what I view as premature implementation.

First, obtaining reliable estimates of process scores for individuals requires very lengthy testing, usually via a computer terminal or comparable device. Thus, the technology does not yet exist for implementing theory in an expeditious way. We need much more research aimed simply at enabling efficient measurement of process parameters of test performance.

Second, the differential validity of process scores in predicting interesting criterion performances has yet to be demonstrated. At present, such differential validity is available as a promissory note rather than as a demonstrated accomplishment.

Third, although we have the means for isolating lower-order processes of performance (i.e., those processes used in strategy implementation), we do not yet have adequate means for isolating higher-order executive processes (i.e., those processes used in strategy planning, monitoring, and control). Yet, these latter processes are the ones I believe most crucial to understanding the bases of individual differences in intelligence. Until we have a feasible technology for isolating these more interesting processes, I am reluctant to advocate rapid implementation of process analysis in mental-ability testing.

To conclude this section, I believe we now have a theoretical basis for the scoring and interpretation of ability tests but that the practical basis has lagged behind. In some ways, this situation is a welcome contrast to what has been the typical one in abilities research, where theory has tended to lag behind practice. I believe that process analysis will eventually become both feasible and desirable in the scoring and interpretation of ability tests; the time has not yet come.

COGNITIVE PSYCHOLOGY AND TEST MODIFICATION

What are the implications of the previous discussion for the modification of ability tests? The answer depends on the time frame into which one puts it. At present, I think they are modest. None of the cognitive research that has been done has come up with any alternative test that is clearly better than the best of the ability tests we now have. But there have been interlaced throughout this discussion a number of promising notes that I would like to summarize here, because I believe they will, eventually, result in test modification. First, with regard to test content, I feel the research to date suggests the importance of using measurements based upon performance on novel tasks comprising novel task content. Second, with regard to construct validation, I think cognitive research has shown that current tests can be understood in terms of their measurement of process constructs. Third, with regard to test scoring and interpretation, I believe it will eventually be possible to measure executive and performance processes in technically feasible ways and that such measurements will provide new bases for diagnosis and training that are currently unavailable. Finally, I feel that cognitive psychology will continue to provide a basis for the questioning of some of our assumptions regarding the nature of mental abilities and how they can be measured.

Let me give three specific examples of some dubious assumptions regarding the nature of mental abilities that are entrenched in mental testing, and let me show how these assumptions are being added into question by information-processing research.

Dubious Assumption 1. To be smart is to be fast. The assumption that "smart is fast" permeates our entire society. When we refer to someone as "quick," we are endowing them with one of the primary attributes of what we perceive an intelligent person to be. Indeed, in a recent study of people's conceptions of intelligence, when we asked people to list behaviors characteristic of intelligent persons, behaviors such as "learns rapidly," "acts quickly," "talks quickly," and "makes judgments quickly" were commonly listed (Sternberg, Conway, Ketron, & Bernstein, 1981). It is not only the man in the street who believes that speed is associated with intellect: Several prominent contemporary theorists of intelligence base their theories in large part upon individual differences in the speed with which people process information (Hunt, 1978; Jensen, 1979).

The assumption that more intelligent people are rapid information processors also underlies the overwhelming majority of tests, including creativity as well as intelligence tests. It is rare to find a test that is not timed or a timed test that virtually all examinees are able to finish by working at a comfortable rate of problem solving. I would argue that this assumption is a gross overgeneralization: It is true for some people and for some mental operations but not for all people or all mental operations. Blind, across-the-board acceptance of the assumption is not only unjustified—it is wrong.

Almost everyone knows people who, although often slow in performing tasks, perform the tasks at a superior level of accomplishment. Moreover, we all know that snap judgments are often poor ones. Indeed, in our study of people's conceptions of intelligence, "does not make snap judgments" was listed as an important attribute of intelligent performance. Evidence for the dubiousness of the "smart is fast" assumption extends, however, beyond intuition and everyday observation. A number of findings from carefully conducted psychological research undermine the validity of assumption. I will cite four such findings, which are only examples from a wider literature on the subject.

First, it is well known that, in general, a *reflective* rather than an *impulsive* style in problem solving tends to be associated with more intelligent problem-solving performance (see Baron, 1981, 1982, for reviews of this literature). Jumping into problems without adequate reflection is likely to lead to false starts and erroneous conclusions. Yet, timed tests often force the examinee to solve problems impulsively. It is often claimed that the strict timing of such tests merely mirrors the requirements of our highly pressured and productive society. But ask yourself how many significant problems you encounter in your work or personal life that allow no more than the 15 to 60 seconds allowed for a typical test problem on a standardized test; you will probably be hard pressed to think of any such problems.

Second, in a study of the role of planning behavior in problem solving, it has been found that more intelligent persons tend to spend relatively more time than do less intelligent persons on global (higher-order, up-front) planning and relatively less time on local (problem-specific, lower-level) planning. In contrast, less intelligent persons show the reverse pattern, emphasizing local rather than global planning (relative to the more intelligent persons) (Sternberg, 1981a). The point is that what matters is not total time spent but distribution of this time across the various kinds of planning one can do.

Third, in studies of reasoning behavior in children and adults, it has been found that although greater intelligence is associated with more rapid execution of most components of information processing, problem encoding is a notable exception to this trend. The more intelligent individuals tend to spend relatively more time encoding the terms of the problem, presumably to facilitate subsequent operations on these encodings (Mulholland, Pellegrino, & Glaser, 1980; Sternberg, 1977; Sternberg & Rifkin, 1979). Similar outcomes have been observed in comparisons of expert versus novice problem solvers confronted with difficult physics problems (Chi et al., 1982).

Finally, in a study of people's performance in solving insight problems (arithmetical and logical problems whose difficulty resided in the need for a nonobvious insight for problem solution rather than in the need for arithmetical or logical knowledge), a correlation of .75 was found between the amount of time people spent on the problems and measured IQ. The correlation between time spent and score on the insight problems was .62 (Sternberg & Davidson, 1982). Note that, in these problems, individuals were free to spend as long as they liked solving the problems. Persistence and involvement in the problems was highly correlated with success in solution: The more able individuals did not give up; nor did they fall for the obvious, but often incorrect, solutions.

The point of these examples is simple: Sometimes speed is desirable; sometimes it is not. Whether it is desirable or not depends on the task, the particular components of information processing involved in solution of the task, and, most likely, the person's style of problem solving. Blind imposition of a strict time limit for a test, or even a not-so-strict one, is theoretically indefensible and practically self-defeating.

Dubious Assumption 2. Intelligence is last year's achievement. At first glance, this would appear to be an assumption few people would accept. Indeed, doesn't almost everyone make a clear distinction between intelligence and achievement? But if one examines the content of the major intelligence tests, one will find that they measure intelligence as last year's (or the year before's, or the year before that's) achievement. What is an intelligence test for children of a given age would be an achievement test for children a few years younger. In some test items, like vocabulary, the achievement component is obvious. In others, it is more disguised, for example, verbal analogies or arithmetic problems. But virtually all tests commonly used for the assessment of intelligence place heavy achievement demands on the students tested.

The achievement-testing orientation exhibited in intelligence tests may be acceptable and even appropriate when the tests are administered to children who have had fully adequate educational opportunities in reasonably adequate social and emotional environments. But for children whose environments have been characterized by deprivation of one kind or another, the orientation may lead to invalid test results. There is no fully adequate solution to the problem of identification of the gifted among such youngsters, especially if the youngsters will have to function in the normal sociocultural milieu. A common solution to the problem, exclusive use of nonverbal tests, is almost certainly an inadequate solution: First, one is measuring only a subset of important intellectual skills; second, and perhaps more importantly, nonverbal tests actually show, on the average, greater differences in scores across sociocultural groups than do verbal ones (Jensen, 1980; Lesser, Fifer, & Clark, 1965). An alternative solution to the problem is to ask what abilities one is really interested in measuring by the achievement-saturated tests and then to attempt to measure these abilities more directly and in ways that reduce the achievement load. This is the path we have followed. Consider two examples.

Consider first one of the most common types of items on intelligence tests—vocabulary. It is well known that vocabulary is one of the best predictors, if not the best single predictor, of overall IQ score (Jensen, 1980; Matarazzo, 1972). Yet, few tests have higher achievement load than does vocabulary. Can one measure the latent ability tapped by vocabulary tests without presenting children with what is essentially an achievement test? I believe one can.

There is reason to believe that vocabulary is such a good measure of intelligence because it measures, albeit indirectly, children's ability to acquire information in context (Jensen, 1980; Sternberg, Powell, & Kaye, 1982, 1983; Werner & Kaplan, 1952). Most vocabulary is learned in everyday contexts rather than through direct instruction. Thus, new words are usually encountered for the first time (and subsequently) in textbooks, novels, newspapers, lectures, and the like. More intelligent people are better able to use surrounding context to figure out the words' meanings. As the years go by, the better decontextualizers acquire the larger vocabularies. Because so much of one's learning (including learning other than vocabulary) is contextually determined, the ability to use context to add to one's knowledge base is an important skill in intelligent behavior. Is there any way of measuring this skill directly rather than relying on indirect measurement (vocabulary testing) that involves a heavy achievement load? We have attempted to measure this skill directly by presenting children with paragraphs written at a level well below their grade level. Embedded in the paragraphs are one or more unknown words. The children's task is to use the surrounding context to figure out the meanings of the unknown words. Note that, in this testing paradigm, differential effects of past achievement are reduced by using reading passages that are easy for everyone but target vocabulary words that are unknown to everyone. We have found that quality of children's definitions of the unknown words is highly correlated with overall verbal intelligence, reading comprehension, and vocabulary test scores (about .6 in each case). Thus, one can measure an important aspect of intelligence directly and without heavy reliance on achievement rather than indirectly and with heavy reliance on past achievement.

Consider second another common type of intelligence test—arithmetic word problems (and at higher levels, algebra and geometry word problems as well). Again, performance on such problems is heavily dependent on one's mathematical achievements and, indeed, opportunities. Can one measure the main skills tapped by such tests without creating what is essentially an achievement test? We believe we have done so through the insight problems mentioned earlier. Consider two typical examples of such problems:

1. If you have black socks and brown socks in your drawer, mixed in the ratio of 4 to 5, how many socks will you have to take out to make sure of having a pair the same color?
2. Water lilies double in area every 24 hours. At the beginning of the summer there is one water lily on a lake. It takes 60 days for the lake to become covered with water lilies. On what day is the lake half-covered?

Solutions of problems such as these requires a fair amount of insight but very little in the way of prior mathematical knowledge. In most problems such as these, a common element in successful solution is selective encoding—knowing what elements of the problem are relevant to solution and what aspects are irrelevant. Performance on such problems is correlated .66 with IQ. Thus, it is possible to use word problems that are good measures of intelligence but that require very little in the way of prior arithmetical knowledge (Sternberg & Davidson, 1982). Moreover, it is unnecessary to time problem administration. As mentioned earlier, higher performance is associated with more, not less, time spent on the problems.

To summarize: We need not measure intelligence as last year's achievement. It is probably impossible to rid intelligence tests of achievement load entirely. Indeed, it may not even be desirable to do so. But the load can be substantially reduced by asking oneself what intellectual skills one wishes to measure and then by seeking to measure these directly through the use of items that tap the skills rather than their by-products.

Dubious Assumption 3.   Testing needs to be conducted in a stressful, anxiety-provoking situation.   Few situations in life are as stressful as the situation confronting the examinee about to receive (and then receiving) a standardized test. Most examinees know that the results of the test are crucial for the examinees' future and that 1 to 3 hours of testing may have more impact on the future than years of school performance. The anxiety generated by the testing situation may have little or no effect on some examinees and even a beneficial effect on other examinees. But there is a substantial proportion of examinees—the test anxious—whose anxiety will cripple their test performance, possibly severely. Moreover, because the anxiety will be common to standardized testing situations (although often not to other testing situations), the error in measurement resulting from a single testing situation will be compounded by error in measurement in other testing situations. With repeated low scores, a bright but test-anxious individual may truly appear to be stupid. What is needed is some kind of standardized assessment device that is fair to the test anxious, as well as to others, and that does not impose a differential penalty on individuals as a function of a form of state anxiety that may have no counterpart in situations other than that of standardized testing. I believe that we have at least two promising leads in this direction.

The first lead is testing based on the notion of intelligence as in part a function of a person's ability to profit from incomplete instruction (Resnick & Glaser, 1976). A measure of this ability is now provided by Feuerstein's (1979) Learning Potential Assessment Device (LPAD), which although originally proposed as an assessment device for retarded performers, can be used for performers at varying levels of performance, including advanced ones. The device involves administration of problems with graded instruction. The amount of instruction given depends on the examinee's needs. Moreover, the test is administered in a supportive, cooperative atmosphere, where the examiner is actually helping the examinee solve problems rather than impassively observing the examinee's success or failure. The examiner does everything he or she can do to allay anxiety (rather than to create it!). Feuerstein has found that children who are cowed by and unable to perform well on regular standardized tests can demonstrate high levels of performance on his test. Moreover, their performance outside the testing situation appears to be predicted better by the LPAD than by conventional intelligence tests (Feuerstein, 1979).

The second lead is based on the notion that intelligence can be measured with some accuracy by the degree of resemblance between a person's behavior and the behavior of the "ideally" intelligent individual (Neisser, 1979). Sternberg et al. (1981) had a group of individuals rate the extent to which each of 250 behaviors characterized their own behavioral repertoire. A second group of individuals rated the extent to which each of the 250 behaviors characterized the behavioral repertoire of an "ideally intelligent" person. The investigators then computed the correlation between each person's self-description and the description of the ideally intelligent person (as provided by the second group of individuals). The correlation provided a measure of degree of resemblance between a real individual and the ideally intelligent individual. The claim was that this degree of resemblance is itself a measure of intelligence. The facts bore out the claim: The correlation between the resemblance measure and scores on a standard IQ test was .52, confirming that the measure did provide an index of intelligence as it is often operationally defined. And doing self-ratings involved minimal stress.

The behaviors that were rated had previously been listed by entirely different individuals as characterizing either "intelligent" or "unintelligent" persons. The intelligent behaviors were shown (by factor analysis) to fall into three general classes: problem-solving ability (e.g., "reasons logically and well," "identifies connections among ideas," and "sees all aspects of a problem");

verbal ability (e.g., "speaks clearly and articulately," "is verbally fluent," and "reads with high comprehension"); and social competence (e.g., "accepts others for what they are," "admits mistakes," and "displays interest in the world at large"). (No attempt was made to classify the unintelligent behaviors, which were not the object of interest in the study.)

I would not propose the behavioral checklist, or the LPAD, for that matter, as replacements for standard intelligence tests. Certainly, there is not enough validity information yet to make such a proposition. But I think that they deserve to be considered as supplements to standard tests. They are much less stress provoking than standard intelligence tests and may well be more accurate, at least for individuals who fall to pieces when confronted with standardized tests. Persons who scored high on these new indices but low on conventional indices would merit further follow-up before writing them off as weak or even average performers. Such measures carry the potential of identifying gifted individuals who are being lost for no reason other than their high levels of test anxiety.

To conclude, although cognitive psychology has not yet provided (and may never provide) a basis for replacing existing psychometric tests, it has made and is continuing to make contributions that I believe will result in some important reconceptualizations of the nature of intelligence and its measurement. I think cognitive psychologists have made substantial progress toward this goal during the past decade, and I see no reason to believe that this progress will not continue.

REFERENCES

Anderson, J. R. *Language, memory, and thought.* Hillsdale, N.J.: Lawrence Erlbaum Associates, 1976.

Baron, J. Reflective thinking as a goal of education. *Intelligence,* 1981, *5,* 291–309.

Baron, J. Personality and intelligence. In R. J. Sternberg (Ed.), *Handbook of human intelligence.* New York: Cambridge University Press, 1982.

Belmont, J. M., & Butterfield, E. C. Learning strategies as determinants of memory deficiencies. *Cognitive Psychology,* 1971, *2,* 411–420.

Belmont, J. M., Butterfield, E. C., & Ferretti, R. To secure transfer of training, instruct self-management skills. In D. K. Detterman & R. J. Sternberg (Eds.), *How and how much can intelligence be increased?* Norwood, N.J.: Ablex, 1982.

Borkowski, J. G., & Wanschura, P. B. Mediational processes in the retarded. In N. R. Ellis (Ed.), *International review of research in mental retardation* (Vol. 7). New York: Academic Press, 1974.

Butterfield, E. C., & Belmont, J. M. Assessing and improving the executive cognitive functions of mentally retarded people. In I. Bialer & M. Sternlicht (Eds.), *The psychology of mental retardation: Issues and approaches.* New York: Psychological Dimensions, 1977.

Campione, J. C., & Brown, A. L. Toward a theory of intelligence: Contributions from research with retarded children. *Intelligence,* 1978, *2,* 279–304.

Campione, J. C., Brown, A. L., & Ferrara, R. Mental retardation and intelligence. In R. J. Sternberg (Ed.), *Handbook of human intelligence.* New York: Cambridge University Press, 1982.

Carroll, J. B. Psychometric tests as cognitive tasks: A new "structure of intellect." In L. B. Resnick (Ed.), *The nature of intelligence*. Hillsdale, N.J.: Lawrence Erlbaum Associates, 1976.

Carroll, J. B. Ability and task difficulty in cognitive psychology. *Educational Researcher*, 1981, *10*, 11–21.

Cattell, R. B. *Abilities: Their structure, growth, and action*. Boston: Houghton-Mifflin, 1971.

Chase, W. G., & Simon, H. A. The mind's eye in chess. In W. G. Chase (Ed.), *Visual information processing*. New York: Academic Press, 1973.

Chi, M. T. H., Feltovich, P. J., & Glaser, R. Representation of physics knowledge by experts and novices. *Cognitive Science*, 1981, *5*, 121–152.

Chi, M. T. G., Glaser, R., & Rees, E. Expertise in problem solving. In R. J. Sternberg (Ed.), *Advances in the psychology of human intelligence* (Vol. 1). Hillsdale, N.J.: Lawrence Erlbaum Associates, 1982.

Chiesi, H. L., Spilich, G. J., & Voss, J. F. Acquisition of domain-related information in relation to high and low domain knowledge. *Journal of Verbal Learning and Verbal Behavior*, 1979, *18*, 257–273.

Clark, H. H., & Chase, W. G. On the process of comparing sentences against pictures. *Cognitive Psychology*, 1972, *3*, 472–517.

Cronbach, L. J. The two disciplines of scientific psychology. *American Psychologist*, 1957, *12*, 671–684.

DeGroot, A. D. *Thought and choice in chess*. The Hague: Mouton, 1965.

Egan, D. E. *Accuracy and latency scores as measures of spatial information processing* (Report No. 1224). Pensacola, Fla.: Naval Aerospace Medical Research Laboratories, 1976.

Egan, D. E., & Greeno, J. G. Acquiring cognitive structure by discovery and rule learning. *Journal of Educational Psychology*, 1973, *64*, 85–97.

Ericsson, K. A., & Simon, H. A. Verbal reports as data. *Psychological Review*, 1980, *87*, 215–251.

Feuerstein, R. *The dynamic assessment of retarded performers: The learning potential assessment device, theory, instruments, and techniques*. Baltimore, Md.: University Park Press, 1979.

Feuerstein, R. *Instrumental enrichment: An intervention program for cognitive modifiability*. Baltimore, Md.: University Park Press, 1980.

Furneaux, W. D. *The Nufferno manual of speed and level tests*. Slough, England: National Foundation for Educational Research, 1956.

Garner, W. R., Hake, H. W., & Eriksen, C. W. Operationism and the concept of perception. *Psychological Review*, 1956, *63*, 149–159.

Greeno, J. G. Trends in the theory of knowledge for problem solving. In D. T. Tuma & F. Reif (Eds.), *Problem solving and education: Issues in teaching and research*. Hillsdale, N.J.: Lawrence Erlbaum Associates, 1980.

Guyote, M. J., & Sternberg, R. J. A transitive-chain theory of syllogistic reasoning. *Cognitive Psychology*, 1981, *13*, 461–525.

Holzinger, K. J. Relationships between three multiple orthogonal factors and four bifactors. *Journal of Educational Psychology*, 1938, *29*, 513–519.

Holzman, T. G., Glaser, R., & Pellegrino, J. W. Process training derived from a computer simulation theory. *Memory & Cognition*, 1976, *1*, 349–356.

Horn, J. L. Organization of abilities and development of intelligence. *Psychological Review*, 1968, *75*, 242–259.

Horn, J. L., & Cattell, R. B. Refinement and test of the theory of fluid and crystallized general intelligences. *Journal of Educational Psychology*, 1966, *57*, 253–270.

Hunt, E. B. Mechanics of verbal ability. *Psychological Review*, 1978, *85*, 109–130.

Hunt, E. B., Frost, N., & Lunneborg, C. E. Individual differences in cognition: A new approach to intelligence. In G. Bower (Ed.), *The psychology of learning and motivation* (Vol. 7). New York: Academic Press, 1973.

Hunt, E. B., Lunneborg, C., & Lewis, J. What does it mean to be high verbal? *Cognitive Psychology*, 1975, *7*, 194–227.

Jensen, A. R. *g:* Outmoded theory or unconquered frontier? *Creative Science and Technology*, 1979, *2*, 16–29.

Jensen, A. R. *Bias in mental testing.* New York: Free Press, 1980.

Larkin, J. Enriching formal knowledge: A model for learning to solve textbook physics problems. In J. R. Anderson (Ed.), *Cognitive skills and their acquisition.* Hillsdale, N.J.: Lawrence Erlbaum Associates, 1981.

Larkin, J. H., McDermott, J., Simon, D. P., & Simon, H. A. Expert and novice performance in solving physics problems. *Science*, 1980, *208*, 1335–1342. (a)

Larkin, J. H., McDermott, J., Simon, D. P., & Simon, H. A. Models of competence in solving physics problems. *Cognitive Science*, 1980, *4*, 317–345. (b)

Lesser, G. S., Fifer, G., & Clark, D. H. Mental abilities of children from different social-class and cultural groups. *Monographs of the Society for Research in Child Development*, 1965, *30*, No. 4.

Linn, M. C. The role of intelligence in children's responses to instruction. *Psychology in the Schools*, 1973, *10*, 67–75.

Lunneborg, C. E. Choice reaction time: What role in ability measurement? *Applied Psychological Measurement*, 1977, *1*, 309–330.

MacLeod, C. M., Hunt, E. B., & Mathews, N. N. Individual differences in the verification of sentence-picture relationships. *Journal of Verbal Learning and Verbal Behavior*, 1978, *17*, 493–507.

Matarazzo, J. D. *Wechsler's measurement and appraisal of adult intelligence.* Baltimore: Williams & Wilkins, 1972.

Mathews, N. N., Hunt, E. B., & MacLeod, C. M. Strategy choice and strategy training in sentence-picture verification. *Journal of Verbal Learning and Verbal Behavior*, 1980, *19*, 531–548.

Mulholland, T. M., Pellegrino, J. W., & Glaser, R. Components of geometric analogy solution. *Cognitive Psychology*, 1980, *12*, 252–284.

Neisser, U. The concept of intelligence. In R. J. Sternberg & D. K. Detterman (Eds.), *Human intelligence: Perspectives on its theory and measurement.* Norwood, N.J.: Ablex, 1979.

Newell, A., & Simon, H. A. *Human problem solving.* Englewood Cliffs, N.J.: Prentice-Hall, 1972.

Nisbett, R., & Ross, L. *Human inference: Strategies and shortcomings of social judgment.* Englewood Cliffs, N.J.: Prentice-Hall, 1980.

Nisbett, R. E., & Wilson, T. D. Telling more than we can know: Verbal reports on mental processes. *Psychological Review*, 1977, *84*, 231–259.

Pachella, R. G. The interpretation of reaction time in information-processing research. In B. H. Kantowitz (Ed.), *Human information processing: Tutorials in performance and cognition.* Hillsdale, N.J.: Lawrence Erlbaum Associates, 1974.

Pellegrino, J. W., & Glaser, R. Cognitive correlates and components in the analysis of individual differences. In R. J. Sternberg & D. K. Detterman (Eds.), *Human intelligence: Perspectives on its theory and measurement.* Norwood, N.J.: Ablex, 1979.

Pellegrino, J. W., & Glaser, R. Components of inductive reasoning. In R. E. Snow, P.-A. Federico, & W. Montague (Eds.), *Aptitude, learning, and instruction: Cognitive process analyses of aptitude* (Vol. 1). Hillsdale, N.J.: Lawrence Erlbaum Associates, 1980.

Posner, M. I., & Mitchell, R. Chronometric analysis of classification. *Psychological Review*, 1967, *74*, 392–409.

Reitman, J. S. Skilled perception in go: Deducing memory structures from inter-response times. *Cognitive Psychology*, 1976, *8*, 336–356.

Resnick, L. B., & Glaser, R. Problem solving and intelligence. In L. B. Resnick (Ed.), *The nature of intelligence.* Hillsdale, N.J.: Lawrence Erlbaum Associates, 1976.

Rose, A. M. *An information processing approach to performance assessment.* (NR 150-391 ONR Final Technical Report). Washington, D.C.: American Institutes for Research, 1978.

Siegler, R. S. Three aspects of cognitive development. *Cognitive Psychology,* 1976, *8,* 481–520.

Snow, R. E. Theory and method for research on aptitude processes. In R. J. Sternberg & D. K. Detterman (Eds.), *Human intelligence: Perspectives on its theory and measurement.* Norwood, N.J.: Ablex, 1979.

Snow, R. E. Aptitude processes. In R. E. Snow, P.-A. Federico, & W. E. Montague (Eds.), *Aptitude, learning and instruction: Cognitive process analyses of aptitude* (Vol. 1). Hillsdale, N.J.: Lawrence Erlbaum Associates, 1980.

Spearman, C. *The nature of 'intelligence' and the principles of cognition.* London: Macmillan, 1923.

Spearman, C. *The abilities of man.* New York: Macmillan, 1927.

Spilich, G. J., Vesonder, G. T., Chiesi, H. L., & Voss, J. F. Text processing of domain-related information for individuals with high and low domain knowledge. *Journal of Verbal Learning and Verbal Behavior,* 1979, *18,* 275–290.

Sternberg, R. J. *Intelligence, information processing, and analogical reasoning: The componential analysis of human abilities.* Hillsdale, N.J.: Lawrence Erlbaum Associates, 1977.

Sternberg, R. J. The nature of mental abilities. *American Psychologist,* 1979, *34,* 214–230.

Sternberg, R. J. Factor theories of intelligence are all right almost. *Educational Researcher,* 1980, *9,* 6–13, 18, (a)

Sternberg, R. J. A proposed resolution of curious conflicts in the literature on linear syllogisms. In R. Nickerson, (Ed.), *Attention and performance VIII.* Hillsdale, N.J.: Lawrence Erlbaum Associates, 1980. (b)

Sternberg, R. J. Sketch of a componential subtheory of human intelligence. *Behavioral and Brain Sciences,* 1980, *3,* 573–584. (c)

Sternberg, R. J. Intelligence and nonentrenchment. *Journal of Educational Psychology,* 1981, *73,* 1–16. (a)

Sternberg, R. J. Nothing fails like success: The search for an intelligent paradigm for studying intelligence. *Journal of Educational Psychology,* 1981, *73,* 142–155. (b)

Sternberg, R. J. Testing and cognitive psychology. *American Psychologist,* 1981, *36,* 1181–1189. (c)

Sternberg, R. J., Conway, B. E., Ketron, J. L., & Bernstein, M. People's conceptions of intelligence. *Journal of Personality and Social Psychology: Attitudes and Social Cognition,* 1981, *41,* 37–55.

Sternberg, R. J., & Davidson, J. E. The mind of the puzzler. *Psychology Today, 16,* June 1982, 37–44.

Sternberg, R. J., & Gardner, M. K. A componential interpretation of the general factor in human intelligence. In H. J. Eysenck (Ed.), *A model for intelligence.* Munich: Springer-Verlag, 1982.

Sternberg, R. J., Powell, J. S., & Kaye, D. B. The nature of verbal comprehension. *Poetics,* 1982, *11,* 155–187.

Sternberg, R. J., Powell, J. S., & Kaye, D. B. Teaching vocabulary-building skills: A contextual approach. In A. C. Wilkinson (Ed.), *Communicating with computers in classrooms: Prospects for applied cognitive science.* New York: Academic Press, 1983.

Sternberg, R. J., & Rifkin, B. The development of analogical reasoning processes. *Journal of Experimental Child Psychology,* 1979, *27,* 195–232.

Sternberg, S. The discovery of processing stages: Extensions of Donders' method. *Acta Psychologica,* 1969, *30,* 276–315.

Thurstone, L. L. *Primary mental abilities.* Chicago: University of Chicago Press, 1938.

Vernon, P. E. *The structure of human abilities.* London: Methuen, 1971.

Vygotsky, L. *Mind in society.* Cambridge, Mass.: Harvard University Press, 1978.

Werner, H., & Kaplan, E. The acquisition of word meanings: A developmental study. *Monographs of the Society for Research in Child Development,* 1952, No. 51.

4 The Status of Test Validation Research

Lyle F. Schoenfeldt
Texas A & M University

More than any other area, validation research is where the "rubber meets the road" in test construction and test usage. The very term *validation* implies the assessment or measurement of individuals and the relationship of this assessment to some criterion of performance. The success of a test validation effort, or the lack thereof, has implications for the value of the assessment and for the utility of the procedures.

In today's environment, whether the validation is intended for employee selection, educational decisions, or personal counseling, there is an increasing probability that the outcomes of research will have legal implications. In the past, a testing program could be set up in terms of professional judgment without including the experimental validation of the procedures. If the individuals involved in establishing the test program were knowledgeable, it was quite possible the tests, although unvalidated, would make a practical contribution in terms of the goals intended. In the absence of a formal validation, however, one would never know the extent to which the testing program was successful or superior to another assessment procedure. A testing program that does not involve validation research is at best an unknown and at worst may be an outright fraud. In either case, the likelihood that testing procedures will have to be defended, including the possibility of legal action, has increased dramatically.

The purpose of the present review is to look carefully at the current status and future directions of test validation research. It will be of value to look at what we know, some of the problems with the process by which tests have been validated up to now, what needs to be learned, and how we will move ahead in the area of test validation research. Finally, it will be important to consider test validation research as a vehicle for improving test construction and test usage.

61

Test Validation: A Definition

In the context of this discussion a *test* is defined as any measure, combination of measures, or procedure used to evaluate differences among people. In this manner, the term *tests* includes the full range of assessment techniques from traditional paper and pencil tests to performance assessments, and includes such things as training programs (e.g., school achievement), situational assessment, and probationary tryouts. In other words, a test is any formal or informal assessment from which an inference is drawn. For example, if a student transferring into a middle school were to be given a series of paper and pencil assessments as a basis for determining course assignments, few would disagree that these assessments constitute a test. On the other hand, the same decisions could be made on the basis of an interview between a school counselor, the student, and parents. Because inferences about readiness for various courses result from the counselor–student interaction, one could consider that this is also a test.

Validity is the degree to which inferences from scores on tests or other assessments are supported or justified on the basis of actual evidence. Validity is not a characteristic of a test; rather it is a characteristic of inferences that result from a test, assessment, or observation. Thus, validation determines the degree of relatedness between inferences made and actual events.

History of Test Validation

The history of measurement and validation is at least as old as Plato's *Republic*. Various summaries of the important events surrounding modern mental measurements have been well documented (Linden & Linden, 1968). In his review of the role of tests in personnel selection, Guion (1976) developed a series of tenets that summarize the "orthodox" history of validation research. These tenets, as adapted from Guion (1976), are summarized in Table 4.1. As seen, the emphasis is on developing a singular predictor–criterion relationship as the basis for determining validity. The dates in the table suggest that the tenets were well established early in this century. Further, these values would not be wide of the mark in the 1980s for an investigator interested in a traditional validation project.

TRADITIONAL APPROACHES TO TEST VALIDATION

Criterion Related

Traditionally, the criterion-related approach has dominated validation research. The "tenets" of criterion-related research are essentially those described by Guion (1976) and summarized in Table 4.1. It is possible to distinguish two alternate approaches within the criterion-related procedure. Concurrent validation involves the relationship of tests to criterion measures obtained at the same

TABLE 4.1
Guion's Historical Tenets of Orthodox Validation Research[a]

Tenet	Comments
1. The purpose of validation is to predict future performance.	"It is . . . essential to know whether the scores are in any useful sense predictive of subsequent success [Bingham, 1937, p. 216]."
2. Predictors and criteria should be selected on the basis of job analysis.	"the tests which are to be experimented with can be chosen only on the basis of some more or less plausible relationship between particular tests and the sort of duties performed [Kornhauser & Kingsbury, 1924, p. 47]."
3. Measuring instruments must be standardized.	"In order for measurements of persons taken at varying times to be comparable, the procedure of the test must be uniform [Freyd, 1923, p. 232]."
4. Tests should be empirically validated.	No test has any significance before it is tried out (Link, 1924).
5. Validation is situation-specific.	"if maximum value is to be attached to test scores the conditions under which the . . . [examinees performed] with the use of tests should reproduce in general the conditions under which they . . . [performed] when the tests were evaluated [Freyd, 1923, p. 381]."
6. More than one test should be used.	To quote Guion (1976, p. 783), "Hull (1928) insisted that a battery of four or five tests or more must be developed if the criterion in all its complexity was to be predicted with maximum efficiency."
7. Only one criterion should be used.	Freyd (1923, p. 223) described the process by which "a criterion" should be selected.
8. Tests are preferred over nontest assessments.	"The experimenter will not limit himself to any particular type of measuring instrument, but those in which he will be most interested are tests and questionnaires [Freyd, 1923, p. 231]."
9. Individual differences should be recognized in evaluating tests.	"If men and women are both . . . [involved in the validation research] it will be necessary to examine the results for sex differences, and if need be, to evaluate the test separately for the two sexes [Freyd, 1923, p. 225]."

[a]Adapted from Guion (1976). Copyright © 1976 by John Wiley & Sons, Inc. Used by permission.

time as the test data. Predictive validity involves the assessment of individuals followed by the collection of criterion information at some subsequent time. In some designs, the time factor can be an important consideration, whereas in other situations it is not. For example, in predicting job success, concurrent validation inevitably involves existing employees whose motives for performing well on the test may differ from the motivation of applicants. In other fields, such as psychometrics, concurrent validity is used to demonstrate, for example, that a paper and pencil assessment is an adequate substitution for a more cumbersome, painful, or inefficient assessment procedure. In both cases, though, the goal is to develop and to test a hypothesis and (hopefully) to assert validity on the bases of a demonstrated relationship between individual characteristics and measures of performance.

Criterion-related validity has traditionally been the most frequently used approach to test validation. In any instance of criterion-related validity, most attention is usually given to the decision about the selection of the criterion variables. Given that the validation process is one of inferences from test scores, the definition of the criterion or standard to be inferred looms large as a possible limitation in the criterion-related approach.

The fact that two relatively recent review articles dealt with this subject (James, 1973; Smith, 1976) emphasizes the attention that criteria selection is receiving. Although the orthodox tenets of the traditional approach focus on a single criterion, which often is a weighted combination of several criteria or a succession of single measures, the emphasis of these two reviews is on a more complex approach to the development of criteria. Mention is made in these reviews of various models including the ultimate criterion (Thorndike, 1949), the complete final goal of a particular type of selection or training; multiple criteria approaches (Dunnette, 1963; Ghiselli, 1956; Guion, 1961; Wallace, 1965) (as exemplified by the model shown in Fig. 4.1 and discussed later); and general criterion models (as exemplified by the models shown in Figs. 4.2 and 4.3 and discussed in a later section).

Content Oriented

Another traditional approach to the validation of tests is the content-oriented procedure. This approach is applicable when empirical investigation is not possible and involves validation on the basis of assumed or hypothesized relationships. The legitimacy of the content-oriented procedure lies in the degree to which the hypothesis itself is well grounded in carefully controlled observations and prior research results (Guion, 1976). Although mentioned in various texts and in the *Standards for Educational and Psychological Tests* (American Psychological Association, 1974), content-oriented validation has always been the stepchild of testing. Until quite recently information about procedures for demonstrating content-oriented validity has been perfunctory, contradictory, or un-

TABLE 4.2
Steps in Content Validation

1. Task analysis
2. Definition of performance domain
3. Survey of performance domain
4. Development of items
5. Demonstration that items constructed are representative of the performance domain
6. Development of cut-off score

available. The emergence of content-oriented validity has been largely a result of a series of conferences (Guion, 1974a; *Proceedings,* 1975), articles (Guion, 1974b, 1977; Schoenfeldt, Schoenfeldt, Acker, & Pearlson, 1976; Tenopyr, 1977), and manuals (American Psychological Association, 1974, 1975, 1980; Mussio & Smith, 1973). The steps involved in a study of content-oriented validity are summarized in Table 4.2.

Perhaps the criticism of these two approaches to validation has been best exemplified by Loevinger's (1957) belief that criterion-related validities are "ad hoc" and that content-oriented validity relies too much on the judgment of the investigator and is thus nongeneralizable. Loevinger believes that ad hoc arguments are scientifically of minor importance if not actually inadmissible and terms both approaches to validation as "administrative" as her way of implying a lack of scientific basis.

CONSTRUCT VALIDATION

Definition of Construct Validity

Construct validity is concerned with understanding the underlying dimensions or attributes being measured through any test or observation process. This type of validation is less concerned with specific performance inferences but instead considers the relationship of test scores to possible underlying attributes.

Many researchers have conducted validation studies but tend to show little concern for construct validity. Construct validity is more in the nature of determining the scientific basis of a particular measure and frequently does not concern practitioners. Evidence of construct validity is often found in a well-developed manual accompanying a particular test or is obtained by pulling together the results of studies dealing with a particular instrument. With regard to the latter, *The Eighth Mental Measurements Yearbook* (Buros, 1978) lists over 5000 references to the Minnesota Multiphasic Personality Inventory (MMPI). Undoubtedly, the totality of this massive body of research provides much valuable information about relationships to other tests, to criteria, and (through various multivariate analytic procedures) to numerous constructs.

On the basis of relating particular measures to a wide variety of possible performance outcomes or other test scores, a network of research data is developed from which inferences could be drawn about the nature of the original test and the constructs that underlie it. Large-scale studies of construct validity are done and form the basis for new scientific learning about specific measures in particular and human differences in general. More than with other approaches to validation, a successful study of construct validity suggests and encourages further research.

History of Construct Validity

Construct validation has always existed, at least at an implicit level, but was only formally defined and extensively discussed in the mid- to late 1950s. A quote from Cronbach and Meehl (1955) best summarizes the early articulation of this conceptualization:

> Validation of psychological tests has not yet been adequately conceptualized, as the APA Committee on Psychological Tests learned when it undertook (1950–54) to specify what qualities should be investigated before a test is published. In order to make coherent recommendations the Committee found it necessary to distinguish four types of validity, established by different types of research and requiring different interpretation. The chief innovation in the Committee's report was the term *construct validity*. This idea was first formulated by a subcommittee (Meehl and R. C. Challman) studying how proposed recommendations would apply to projective techniques, and later modified and clarified by the entire Committee. . . . The statements agreed upon by the Committee (and by committee of two other associations) were published in the *Technical Recommendations*. . . .
>
> Identification of construct validity was not an isolated development. Writers on validity during the preceding decade had shown a great deal of dissatisfaction with conventional notions of validity, and introduced new terms and ideas, but the resulting aggregation of types of validity seems only to have stirred the muddy waters. Portions of the distinctions we shall discuss are implicit in Jenkins' paper, "Validity for what?" (1946), Gulliksen's "Intrinsic validity" (1950), Goodenough's distinction between tests as "signs" and "samples" (1950), Cronbach's separation of "logical" and "empirical" validity (1949), Guilford's "factorial validity" (1946), and Mosier's papers on "face validity" and "validity generalization" (1947, 1951). Helen Peak (1953) comes close to an explicit statement of construct validity as we shall present it [p. 281].

Further discussions by Loevinger (1957), Bechtoldt (1959), Campbell (1960), and Ebel (1961) followed, and all contributed in refining of the definition of construct validity as well as in compiling evidence necessary to substantiate its existence.

Multitrait–Multimethod Approach

In terms of providing a methodology to verify construct validity, the article with by far the greatest impact was "Convergent and Discriminant Validation by the Multitrait–Multimethod Matrix" by Campbell and Fiske (1959). In this seminal work, Campbell and Fiske (1959) advocated a procedure for triangulating a construct, utilizing a matrix of intercorrelations among tests representing at least two traits, each measured by at least two methods. Construct validity is the degree to which measures of the same trait correlate higher with each other than they do with measures of different traits involving separate methods.

The importance of the multitrait–multimethod (MTMM) procedure is in the provision of a conceptualization of construct validity that could be readily operationalized by researchers. Interestingly, few articles or dissertations were published in the 1960s using the MTMM approach. The rate of diffusion of the technology was understandably slow. However, the MTMM procedure has come into its own in the 1970s and 1980s. An extensive computer review of the validity literature revealed that 10 articles/dissertations were published in 1979 and another 12 were published in 1980, using the MTMM approach. This is exemplary of how standard the procedure has become in the establishment of construct validity.

There have been both extensions and critiques of the MTMM. Werts, Joreskog, and Linn (1972) suggested that the MTMM approach may be treated as a problem in confirmatory factor analysis and that the MTMM is subsumed by the general model for analysis of covariance structure. Other authors have proposed further innovative factor analytic applications (Golding & Seidman, 1974; Jackson, 1975; Kenny, 1976; Levin, 1974; Ray & Heeler, 1975). Other extensions have been in the application of nonparametric statistics (Hubert & Baker, 1978) and path analytic procedures (Schmidt, 1978). Limitations of the MTMM have been discussed by Kalleberg and Kluegel (1975).

Other Approaches to Construct Validity

The multitrait–multimethod procedure has clearly become a standard for the establishment of construct validity. At the same time, given the definition of construct validity discussed previously, it is obvious that researchers are not limited in the number of procedures employed to establish its existence. In fact, given the nature of content validity, it is somewhat heretical to focus on methods rather than models, although to a large extent the two are closely linked in the context of this topic.

Historically, factor analysis has been associated with the establishment of constructs. Many applications of factor analysis are in the nature of data reduction, and as such the results have little in the way of implications for the establishment of construct validity. However, in conjunction with an appropriate model, factor analysis can play a valuable role in the validation of constructs. Guilford's (1967; Guilford & Hoepfner, 1971) extensive work on the structure of intellect is one of many examples that could be cited illustrating how a model and appropriate factor analytic procedures can come together in the establishment of construct validity.

Another method receiving recent recognition as a vehicle for its contribution to the establishment of construct validity are latent-trait models (LTM). Several recent studies by Whitely (1980a, 1980b) provide an example of the potential contribution of LTM to the study of intelligence. LTM resolve several measurement problems in studies of intellectual change, including ability modification and life-span development. LTM contribute to construct validity in their capability to represent an individual differences model of cognitive processing on ability test items.

Construct Validity: State of the Science

Although specific procedures play an important role in the demonstration of construct validity, the more important priority should be the research design. With regard to the latter, some of the most recent work was discussed in a conference on *Construct Validity in Psychological Measurement* (U.S. Office of Personnel Management, 1980). This conference involved several important themes. First was a call for more clearly defined professional standards for construct validity. Second was a discussion of the realization of the role construct validity plays, in conjunction with criterion-related and content-oriented validity, in the assessment of human differences. Included in this theme was the singularly unique application of a construct model in the validation of the Federal Government's Professional and Administrative Career Examination (PACE), as reported by McKillip and Wing (1980).

A third theme of the conference involved a review of thinking and progress in several important areas of assessment by several recent contributors in each area. Carroll (1980) discussed background and progress in his assessment of abilities. Sternberg examined different approaches to the construct validity of aptitude tests in the context of an information-processing assessment (Sternberg, 1980). Jackson (1980) reviewed construct validity and personality assessment, concluding "that through a judicious combination of psychological analysis of dispositional variables and psychometric and multivariate procedures, progress in personality assessment is possible [p. 79]." Frederiksen (1980) and Messick (1980), in different presentations, discussed research models for construct validation.

In his conference review, Dunnette (1980) developed a number of integrating thoughts with respect to construct validity. One of his main points was that, as a part of a scientific undertaking, the study of constructs should be pursued by diverse research strategies. Certainly anyone present at the conference or familiar with the proceedings would be impressed with the diversity of approaches taken and with the state of the art with respect to scientific knowledge about intelligence, aptitude, and personality constructs.

MULTIVARIATE VALIDATION MODELS

Psychologists and measurement specialists have been interested in predicting human behavior over a long period of time, although the shape and form of this interest has changed. Traditional interest was largely empirical and has been based on linear methods of prediction. Typical results have been disappointing. For example, Ghiselli (1966) has summarized 107 validity coefficients calculated to predict training and proficiency criteria. The mean validity coefficients in five major aptitude areas are shown in Table 4.3. As seen, coefficients are relatively modest, with the overall average correlation to predict training success being .30 and to predict the more important criterion of job performance, .19. These results have spurred many researchers to experiment with various multivariate models over the last 15 years.

Person–Process–Product Models

One class of approaches might be termed *person–process–product* models in that they attempt to examine behavior as a complex outcome of interactions between individual attributes and organizational requirements within the setting in which the behavior occurs. Figure 4.1 is a schematic portrayal of a prediction model adapted from one suggested by Guetzkow and Forehand (1961). It was designed in an effort to take into account complex interactions that may occur among various predictor combinations, different groups or types of individuals, different behaviors, and the consequences of these behaviors. As Dunnette (1963) indicated, the model permits the possibility of predictors being differentially useful for predicting the behaviors of different subsets of individuals. Also evident is the fact that similar behaviors may be predictable by different patterns of interaction between groupings of predictors and individuals or even that the same level of performance on predictors can lead to substantially different patterns of behavior for different people. Also, incorporated into the model is the fact that the same or similar behaviors can lead to quite different outcomes depending on the situation.

A similar model, couched in terms of predicting job performance, is shown in Fig. 4.2 (Campbell, Dunnette, Lawler, & Weick, 1970). In this model, job performance is viewed as a product of the person impacting with various organizational forces. The individual is represented as a configuration of abilities, special skills, interest, personality traits, attitudes, expectancies, and reward preferences.

TABLE 4.3
Comparison of Validity Coefficients for Training and Proficiency
Criteria by Type of Test[a]

	Mean Validity Coefficient		No. Pairs of
	Train.	Prof.	Coefficients
Intellectual abilities	.35	.19	38
Intelligence	.34	.21	16
Immediate memory	.23	.15	5
Substitution	.27	.23	4
Arithmetic	.42	.15	13
Spatial and mechanical abilities	.36	.20	28
Spatial relations	.38	.19	13
Location	.24	.17	6
Mechanical principles	.41	.24	9
Perceptual accuracy	.26	.23	15
Number comparison	.25	.24	4
Name comparison	.24	.29	3
Cancellation	.58	.19	1
Pursuit	.18	.17	4
Perceptual speed	.30	.27	3
Motor abilities	.18	.17	24
Tracing	.18	.15	4
Tapping	.15	.13	6
Dotting	.15	.14	4
Finger dexterity	.16	.20	7
Hand dexterity	.24	.22	2
Arm dexterity	.54	.24	1
Personality traits	.05	.08	2
Interest	.05	.08	2
All tests	.30	.19	107

[a]From Ghiselli, 1966.

Looking at the model from the individual's point of view, a job involves task demands that are objective lists of expectancies or priorities imposed upon the individual in an attempt to alter behavior in specified ways. Due to this, an individual's behavior consists entirely of emitted responses and performance on the job that includes those aspects of behavior related to organizational climate. The result or product of the individual's effort is a contribution to the organization, the generalized result of performance.

The models shown in Figs. 4.1 and 4.2 are two of several that summarized the relationship between individual characteristics and outcomes. The implications are significant. Behavior is seen as a complex product of cognitive, noncognitive (including motivational tendencies), and stylistic abilities. Expenditures of ener-

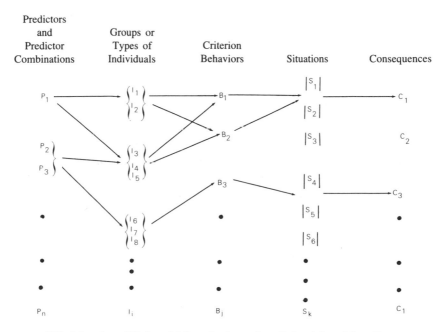

FIG. 4.1. A modified model for selection and prediction (adapted from Dunnette, 1963, p. 319).

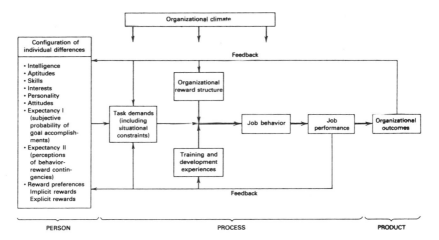

FIG. 4.2. Model for the prediction of job effectiveness (from Campbell, Dunnette, Lawler, and Weick, 1970, p. 475).

gy are the product of motivational forces. The level of motivation determines whether goal-oriented behavior occurs or not. Once an individual is motivated, the effectiveness of performance is determined by the cognitive capabilities, stylistic tendencies, and other attributes of the individual.

Moderator Validation

A study by Berdie (1961) suggested that persons differing in intraindividual trait variation (on measures of mathematics proficiency) might be differentially predicted to be successful or unsuccessful in engineering studies. Thus, intraindividual trait variation was thought to "modify" performance predictions. Other efforts to discover moderators in predictions were given in studies by Fiske (1957) and Fiske and Rice (1955), both of which were similar to the Berdie (1961) study. In addition, studies by Cleary (1966), Frederiksen and Melville (1954), Ghiselli (1956, 1960a, 1960b), Lee (1961), and Rock (1969) are relevant. In each case, the dominate theme has been an effort to identify persons who are consistently more (or less) predictable using particular sets of predictors or subgroups of persons requiring different prediction procedures.

The procedures described are statistical in that they all involve variations of frequently employed prediction procedures. Although some of the procedures are more difficult to implement than others, unlike the models shown in Figs. 4.1 and 4.2, all have been attempted in one or several studies.

Recently it has become apparent that moderated prediction approaches are not much better than traditional linear methods of prediction. Zedeck (1971), for example, showed that initially favorable results usually failed to maintain their superiority upon cross validation. In discussing such statistical strategies, Dunnette and Borman (1979) concluded that:

> Selection research must devote increased effort toward reducing sources of both variable error (measurement and sampling error) and constant error (such as perceptional biases) in the development of instruments and in the design of studies. Non-linear models may some day once again warrant attention but not until such errors have been reduced significantly to overcome the inherently superior robustness of the simple linear model [p. 495].[1]

Aptitude by Treatment Interactions

In 1957, Cronbach wrote of "The Two Disciplines of Scientific Psychology," the one concerned with correlation and the other, through experimentation, with the sequence of events. General discussions of the importance of combining the

---

[1]Reproduced with permission, from the *Annual Review of Psychology,* Volume 30. © 1978 by Annual Reviews, Inc.

"two disciplines," as Cronbach (1957) has been recommending, have been published by, among others, Owens (1968, 1971) and Vale and Vale (1969). More recently Cronbach (1975) and Cronbach and Snow (1977) have published comprehensive and penetrating reviews examining the background into the nature of the problem as well as the rationale for the aptitude by treatment (ATI) procedure they advocated as an alternate validation model for enhanced prediction.

The results of the ATI approach to date have not been impressive. Evidence for significant interactions is scarce and fragmentary. Second- or third-level interactions tend to cloud any simple person–performance relationships, or at least render relationships inconsistent from sample to sample. In Cronbach's (1975) words:

> The line of investigation I advocated in 1957 no longer seems sufficient. Interactions are not confined to the first order; the dimensions of the situation and the person enter into complex interactions. . . . Taking stock today, I think most of us judge theoretical progress to have been disappointing [p. 116].

Later in the same article, Cronbach (1975) states:

> When ATIs are present, a general statement about a treatment effect is misleading because the effect will come or go *depending on the kind of person treated.* When ATIs are present, a generalization about aptitude is an uncertain basis for prediction because the regression slope will depend on the treatment chosen. . . . An ATI result can be taken as a general conclusion only if it is not in turn moderated by further variables. If Aptitude × Treatment × Sex interact, for example, then the Aptitude × Treatment effect does not tell the story. Once we attend to interactions, we enter a hall of mirrors that extends to infinity. However far we carry our analysis—to third order or fifth order or any other—untested interactions of a still higher order can be envisioned (emphasis added) [p. 199].

Thus, in Cronbach's own words, the ATI path he has walked in an effort to infer future performance better has not been fruitful. Gains were made, as reported in the 1975 publication, but these were of less magnitude than had been hoped might materialize. These reservations have led Cronbach (1975) to propose abandonment of the ATI approach as a potential explanatory model for predicting performance behavior.

Assessment–Classification Model

Although the list of approaches that have been attempted to improve the inferential or validation process could extend ad infinitum, one further procedure, namely the Assessment–Classification model described by Schoenfeldt (1974), is worthy of mention. The Dunnette (1963) model, and virtually all the approaches discussed in this section, sought to improve the quality of inferences made on the basis of the assessment data by identifying subsets of persons for whom predictors were differentially useful, for whom situational factors varied, and so forth. On the basis of these concerns, as well as in the interest of an alternative to the ATI model, Owens (1968, 1971) suggested his developmental–integrative model. The Assessment–Classification model, shown in Fig. 4.3, is the logical extension of the Owens' developmental–integrative approach

Individual Assessment   **Job Structure**

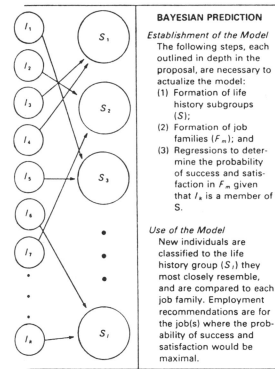

BAYESIAN PREDICTION

Establishment of the Model
The following steps, each outlined in depth in the proposal, are necessary to actualize the model:
(1) Formation of life history subgroups (S);
(2) Formation of job families (F_m); and
(3) Regressions to determine the probability of success and satisfaction in F_m given that I_k is a member of S.

Use of the Model
New individuals are classified to the life history group (S_i) they most closely resemble, and are compared to each job family. Employment recommendations are for the job(s) where the probability of success and satisfaction would be maximal.

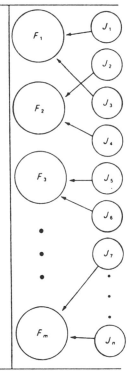

| Individual Antecedent Behavior | Life History Subgroups | | Job Families | Job Activities |

Biographical questionnaire to classify individuals (I_k) to subsets (S_i) homogeneous with respect to important dimensions of life experience.

Predictor set to estimate job success and satisfaction given that I_k is a member of S_i and is performing job J_n which is a member of family F_m.

Position Analysis Questionnaire to classify jobs (J_n) to job families (F_m) homogeneous with respect to important activities.

FIG. 4.3.   Assessment-Classification model of manpower utilization.

and the version most compatible with the models shown in Figs. 4.1 and 4.2. Thus, it incorporates the evaluation of person, process, and product (as suggested by the models in Figs. 4.1 and 4.2) with the subgroup conceptualization formulated by Owens (1968).

The specific process involved in actualizing the Assessment–Classification model consists of providing separate categorizations of the predictor and criteria sets. In dealing with the predictor set, two steps are needed. The first step involves identifying standard predictors found to be related logically to the criteria in question. The individual differences variables of the Campbell et al. (1970) model provide an example of predictor variables that might be used. The second step requires implementation of the procedures described by Owens (1968), that is, formulating subgroups with respect to the major dimensions of antecedent behavior and relating the subgroups to relevant criteria. This entails administering a background questionnaire to assess the antecedent behaviors. On the basis of responses to this questionnaire, individuals would then be classified into subgroups that are homogenous with respect to important dimensions of life behavior. In other words, the subgroups are constructed on the basis of bringing together individuals who have reported similar background patterns.

The other aspect of the Assessment–Classification model concerns the structuring of the criteria domain, the jobs (in the case of Fig. 4.3), but with other criteria for other situations. In Fig. 4.3, the structuring of jobs into families homogeneous with respect to their performance requirements and desirable configurations of attributes is illustrated. Also, several instruments have been developed and found to be of use for measuring or structuring jobs in terms of the psychological demands required for successful performance (Cunningham, 1969; McCormick, Jeanneret, & Mecham, 1969). Other procedures would be used for structuring the criteria domain in educational or clinical settings.

Unlike the conceptual models in Figs. 4.1 and 4.2 that do not lend themselves to statistical evaluation or the statistical models that have been tried and found lacking, the results with the Assessment–Classification model have been positive. Schoenfeldt (1974) examined the validity of the model with a large sample of students ($N = 1934$) working toward college degrees. Subgroups formed on the basis of previous behavioral data collected during the freshman year differed with respect to criterion (major, grade point average, and so forth) measurements taken 4 years later. More importantly, the subgroups differed with respect to the curricular paths taken during college. The result indicated that it was possible to differentiate people in meaningful ways (i.e., to subgroup individuals and to match these subgroups with similar structuring of the criteria domain).

Two industrial applications using the Assessment–Classification model have been reported. In the first, Morrison (1977) tested the model's efficacy in making placement decisions in an industrial setting with nonexempt employees. Eight developmental-interest dimensions describing life choices, values, and interests of 438 blue-collar workers were formulated. Job analysis identified two clusters of positions that were homogenous within and differentiated between each other on relevant job attributes. One cluster composed of 102 incumbents with more than 6 months service consisted of process operator positions. The other cluster was composed of heavy equipment operator positions and had 148 incumbents. A discriminate function was calculated on a validation group of incumbents in an effort to develop a linear combination of the life history factors that maximinally differentiated the two job families. Cross validation demonstrated that three psychologically meaningful dimensions discriminated among the groups at both statistical and practical levels of significance. The process operators were more likely to be raised in an urban environment, to have a more favorable self-image, and to prefer standardized work schedules than the heavy equipment operators.

The second study was by Brush and Owens (1979) and utilized a total of 1987 nonexempt employees of a U.S. oil company. Each employee completed an extensive biographical inventory. Hierarchical clustering of the resulting biographical profiles produced 18 subgroups of employees such that, within any one subgroup, background experience and interest were similar, and yet among subgroups they were different. A similar methodology was applied to job analysis data in creating a structure of 19 job families for 939 office and clerical jobs. Significant relationships were found between biodata subgroups and other variables, such as sex, educational level, termination rate, job classification, and (most important) performance rating.

VALIDITY GENERALIZATION

One of the tenets of the traditional criterion-related validity model has been belief in the situational nature of the results. For more than 50 years, researchers have believed that the results of criterion-related validity studies were applicable only to the situation on which the study was based. This is understandable because research, such as that by Ghiselli (1966), has clearly demonstrated results of using the same predictors to predict similar criteria using different subjects in comparable (different) settings varied over a wide range. The empirical results of Ghiselli (1966) demonstrated considerable variability in validity coefficients even when predictors and criteria were essentially identical.

On the basis of findings by Ghiselli (1966) and other investigators over a long period of years, the profession has concluded that validity generalization was essentially impossible (Ghiselli, 1966, p. 228; Guion, 1965, p. 126). This conclusion even has been incorporated into professional standards (American Psychological Association, 1975) and government regulations (U.S. Equal Opportunity Commission, 1978). In fact, Guion (1976) indicated that the problem of limited validity generalization was perhaps the most serious limitation of personnel psychology.

Bayesian Validity Generalization

Change in the belief of limited generalizability was seen in the mid-1970s and the years followed through the work of Schmidt and Hunter along with their colleagues. The initial article by Schmidt, Hunter, and Urry (1976) attacked the problem of small numbers typically used in validity studies. As pointed out in the Schmidt et al. (1976) article, it typically has been believed that sample sizes of 30 to 50 individuals were adequate to make criterion-related validity studies technically feasible. To quote Schmidt and Hunter (1980):

> When sample sizes are in the 30–50 range statistical power is typically in the .25 to .50 range. That is, if the test is in fact valid, such studies will correctly detect the validity only 25–50% of the time. Sample sizes required to produce statistical power of .90 are much larger, often ranging above 200 or 300 [p. 43].

In further articles, Schmidt and Hunter (1977) and Schmidt, Hunter, Pearlman, and Shane (1979, pp. 260–261) identified seven artifactual sources that would explain the fact that different validity coefficients would result when identical predictors and criteria were studied within the context of the same job. The seven sources of variance that might lead to different results were as follows:

1. Differences between studies in criterion reliability.
2. Differences between studies in test reliability.
3. Differences between studies in range restriction.
4. Sampling error (i.e., variance due to $N < \infty$).
5. Differences between studies in amount and kind of criterion.
6. Computational and typographical error.
7. Slight differences in factor structure between tasks of a given type (e.g., arithematic reasoning test).

Schmidt, Hunter, Pearlman, and Shane (1979) proposed that a researcher with, say, 100 validity coefficients relating tests of perceptual speed to clerical proficiency compute the variance of the validity coefficient distribution and subtract variance due to each of the artifactual sources from this total. The Schmidt and Hunter (1977) article, as well as other articles by these authors, included computational procedures associated with the first four of the seven artifactual sources given previously. It is proposed that if the remaining variance is zero or near zero, validity generalization has been achieved, because the observed variation in validity results has been shown to be entirely a result of statistical artifacts. Further, as Schmidt and Hunter (1977) have pointed out: "in cases in which the mean of the corrected distribution is too low and/or the variance too great to allow conclusions [as to the generalizability of the validity], the corrected distribution will still be useful—as the prior distribution in a Bayesian study of the test's validity [p. 530]." The procedures and results of such a Bayesian study are described in the Schmidt, Hunter, Pearlman, and Shane (1979) article.

Schmidt and Hunter, along with their colleagues, have diligently demonstrated the generalizability of results from numerous small studies covering several test–job relationships. In their initial publication (Schmidt & Hunter, 1977), they examined 114 validity coefficients relating tests of mechanical principles to performance of mechanical repairmen, 191 tests of finger dexterity related to performance of bench workers, 72 intelligence tests related to performance of general clerks, and 99 studies of spatial relations correlated with performance as machine tenders. In the Schmidt, Hunter, Pearlman, and Shane (1979) article these results were extended through the examination of generalizability of various tests related to performance in two families of clerical jobs and the job of first-line supervisor. With respect to clerical jobs, the criterion–performance relationships of 11 tests were examined, with the number of validity coefficients ranging from 53 to 321. In their most recent report (Schmidt, Hunter, & Caplan, 1981), the generalizability of validities were established for four types of cognitive tests and a weighted biographical information blank, five measures in all, in relation to performance in two petroleum industry job groups.

The results of Schmidt and Hunter's investigations have been nothing short of a revolution with respect to validation research. In essence, they have sorted through the confusing and varying results of a 50-year period to show that a "true" validity can be established. They are of the belief that these estimates are far more meaningful than the results of typical studies with small samples for individual scientists and that validities are possible even when they are not technically feasible in the context of a particular predictor criterion relationship.

Meta-Analysis

The term *meta-analysis* comes from the work of Glass (1976, 1977) and involves integrating findings across studies. The idea is similar to that advanced by Schmidt and Hunter (1977), namely to bring together results from numerous small studies into an integrated study. Glass (1976) was seeking a way of organizing and depicting results from numerous studies as an alternative to the traditional narrative review. Again, the most definitive work in the area is by Hunter, Schmidt, and Jackson (1982) and describes both quantitative and qualitative procedures for integrating findings across studies. The methods are similar to those in validity generalization, namely one of removing sources of artifactual variance. However, the range of possibilities is far greater than just the simple correlation coefficients considered in the validity generalization work. Hunter et al. (1982) deal with the possibility that results of the several studies to be integrated might be presented in terms of diverse statistical procedures, such as regression, canonical correlation, or multivariate analysis of variance. In addition, procedures were considered for identifying moderator variables or interactions that are indicative of findings that might be selected to be integrated.

Meta-analysis has clearly been an innovation whose time has come. Although the original introduction of the method by Glass was 1976–1977, there have already been extensive publications using meta-analysis procedures. An extensive computer review of the validity literature for 1980 and 1981 indicated 11 and 10 articles/dissertations, respectively. This is extremely rapid diffusion, equivalent to the current diffusion of the multitrait–multimethod matrix after 20 years.

PRODUCTIVITY ANALYSIS

New attention has been focused on procedures that have been available for over 30 years to estimate work force productivity on the basis of validity information. Some of the original work can be traced to Brogden (1949) and the well-known publication by Cronbach and Gleser (1965), *Psychological Tests and Personnel Decisions.* More recently Schmidt, Hunter, McKenzie, and Muldrow (1979) have suggested simplified procedures that make the previously cumbersome productivity analysis approach within the range of possibilities in most situations.

The goal in productivity analysis is to estimate the dollar impact that would be realized in using a valid test to select individuals for a particular job. In the past the practical value of a selection procedure has been estimated in terms of the increase in the percentage of "successful" workers through expectancy table analysis or some equivalent procedure. Seldom have these estimates been in terms of the economic implications of the valid selection procedure on work force productivity.

The basic formula for overall gain in utility from use of a test is:

$$\Delta U = N_s r_{xy} SD_y \bar{z}_x - \frac{N_s C}{p}$$

where

N_s = number of selectees
C = cost of testing one applicant
p = selection ratio
$\bar{z}_x$ = average standard score on the test of those selected (in applicant group standard score units)
r_{xy} = test validity
SD_y = standard deviation of job performance in dollar terms among randomly selected employees.

As shown by Schmidt and Hunter (1980), the first four items of information are easily determined. In the past it was believed that the standard deviation of job performance dollars (SD_y) could only be estimated using cost accounting procedures that were both complex and uncertain. Schmidt and Hunter (1980) have shown how SD_y could be estimated by supervisors of the job under study using a questionnaire procedure. In the Schmidt and Hunter (1980) study, budget analysis supervisors were given the following instructions:

> Now, based on your experience with agency budget analysts, we would like for you to estimate the yearly value to your agency of the products and services produced by the average budget analyst. Consider the quality and quantity of output typical of the average budget analyst in the value of this output. In placing an overall dollar value on this output, it may help to consider what the costs would be of having an outside consulting firm provide these products and services [pp. 55–56].

Following an appropriate opportunity to provide that estimate, the supervisors were instructed:

> We would now like you to consider the "superior" budget analyst. Let us define a "superior" performer as a budget analyst who is at the 85th percentile. That is, his performance is better than that of 85 percent of his fellow budget analysts and only 15 percent of budget analysts turn in better performances. Consider the quality and quantity of the output typical of the "superior" budget analyst. Then estimate the value of these products and services. In placing an overall dollar value in this output, it may again help to consider what the costs would be of having an outside consulting firm perform these products and services [p. 56].

Schmidt and Hunter (1980) were able to use these estimates to obtain final estimates for SD_y and were able to estimate the value of productivity gains from the use of a test in hiring 2000 budget analysts at over 32 million dollars.

These fairly innovative procedures for estimating the component of an important equation (SD_y) should make feasible the analysis of the productivity impact of selection procedures. As Schmidt and Hunter (1980) concluded: "the results of these analyses will convince many who are currently skeptical that good selection is critical to organizational success [p. 57]."

IMPLICATIONS FOR TEST CONSTRUCTION AND TEST USAGE

It is worth reemphasizing that validity speaks to the ultimate value of a test by affirming, or denying if that be the case, the inferential value of the score in a particular circumstance. As such, validity evidence has obvious implications for the worthiness of a test's construction and the appropriateness of its usage.

Problems with the Process of Validation Research

Despite the importance of validity evidence, validation research has not always been of the nature that one could point to with pride. The initial half of this century could be characterized as relying most heavily on criterion-related evidence of validity, often in a way that represented "blind empiricism" at its worst. To be sure, the methods of factor analysis popularized in the 1930s encouraged the development of constructs, but the methods were somewhat prohibitive until the commercial availability of the electronic computer in the mid-1950s. Until rather recently, validity research meant a predictor–criterion correlation to the average practitioner. Even worse, as evidenced by the intial court cases on employment discrimination, tests had a half-life of their own and often enjoyed widespread use without concomitant validity evidence. In retrospect, it was clear that validation, as the feedback loop to test construction and test usage, could not operate effectively if not undertaken.

Changes in Validation Research

Change was rapid and proceeded along several fronts. The formalization of construct validation, more than anything else, legitimized validation research as a scientific undertaking rather than as a practitioner art. The definition of construct validity began in the mid-1950s and has continued in a steady, albeit slow, progression ever since. Certainly the 1979 conference discussed at length earlier showed that much progress has been made and that work continues using the diverse research strategies recommended.

There can be no doubt that Title VII of the Civil Rights Act of 1964 has been a profound stimulus in validation research. Although there was a latency period of 6 or 7 years before the *Griggs v. Duke Power Co.* (1971) case communicated in clear and forceful terms that tests had to measure the person for the job and not the person in the abstract, the effect has been profound.

The initial flurry of activity, at least at the practitioner level, involved efforts to validate existing tests. Implications for test usage were immediate as validation efforts failed and test programs for employee selection were discontinued. At the same time, work was initiated on alternate validation strategies. Those alternatives included such diverse approaches as attempts to define and refine further content-oriented validity along with application of several of the multivariate validation models discussed previously. The obvious capstone to these many efforts has been the validity generalization research by Frank Schmidt, John Hunter, and their colleagues.

The Future of Validation Research

The future of validation research is promising. There has been more progress in the last decade than in the previous quarter century. Extending this trajectory will undoubtedly lead to new learning about the inferential value of tests in predicting and understanding behavior.

Obviously the work on validity generalization will continue. The profession has had only a short time to adjust to these fairly unique notions. Perhaps the recency of the research is best exemplified by the fact that virtually all the work has been by Schmidt and Hunter, along with their students. Ultimately their work should render as obsolete the need for the empirical validation that has so characterized the research to date. Practitioners and researchers will only need to analyze jobs or situations of concern and, on the basis of these circumstances, consult tables of generalized validities from the numerous previous studies using various predictors in similar circumstances. This work is still in its infancy, and the implications are yet to be felt.

The inferential value of any single assessment or combination of measures is *at best* such to explain half the criterion variance. This is not a problem that will be addressed by the ongoing work on validity generalization or utility concepts. Instead, the multivariate validation models hold the single best hope of improving the inferential value of assessments. By seeking to incorporate information about the types of individuals and types of behaviors with organizational consideration and consequences, these models hold the best hope of improving the level of predictions. As we have seen (Owens & Schoenfeldt, 1979), these multivariate procedures can bridge the construct and empirical validity procedures. On the other hand, the procedures are complex, and progress has been slow. The hope of the future is being unshackled from the necessity of endless small studies of empirical validity with efforts being directed to the multivariate procedures.

REFERENCES

American Psychological Association. American Educational Research Association, & National Council on Measurement in Education. *Standards for educational and psychological tests.* Washington, D.C.: American Psychological Association, 1974.

American Psychological Association. Division of Industrial–Organizational Psychology. *Principles for the validation and use of personnel selection procedures.* Dayton, Ohio: Author, 1975.

American Psychological Association. Division of Industrial–Organizational Psychology. *Principles for the validation and use of personnel selection procedures (2nd ed.).* Berkeley, Calif.: Author, 1980.

Bechtoldt, H. P. Construct validity: A critique. *American Psychologist,* 1959, *14,* 619–629.

Berdie, R. F. Intra-individual variability and predictability. *Educational and Psychological Measurement,* 1961, *21,* 663–676.

Bingham, W. V. *Aptitudes and aptitude testing.* New York: Harper, 1937.

Brogden, H. E. When testing pays off. *Personnel Psychology,* 1949, *2,* 171–184.

Brush, D. H., & Owens, W. A. Implementation and evaluation of an assessment–classification model for manpower utilization. *Personnel Psychology,* 1979, *32,* 369–384.

Buros, O. K. (Ed.). *The eighth mental measurements yearbook.* Highland Park, N.J.: Gryphon, 1978.

Campbell, D. T. Recommendations for APA test standards regarding construct, trait, or discriminant validity. *American Psychologist,* 1960, *15,* 546–553.

Campbell, D. T., & Fiske, D. W. Convergent and discriminant validation by the multitrait–multimethod matrix. *Psychological Bulletin,* 1959, *56,* 81–105.

Campbell, J. P., Dunnette, M. D., Lawler, E. E., III, & Weick, K. E., Jr. *Managerial behavior performance, and effectiveness.* New York: McGraw-Hill, 1970.

Carroll, J. B. Measurement of ability construct. In U.S. Office of Personnel Management & Educational Testing Service, *Construct validity in psychological measurement: Proceedings of a colloquium on theory and application in education and employment.* Princeton, N.J.: Educational Testing Service, 1980.

Cleary, T. A. An individual differences model for multiple regression. *Psychometrika,* 1966, *31,* 215–224.

Cronbach, L. J. *Essentials of psychological testing.* New York: Harper, 1949.

Cronbach, L. J. The two disciplines of scientific psychology. *American Psychologist,* 1957, *12,* 671–684.

Cronbach, L. J. Beyond the two disciplines of scientific psychology. *American Psychologist,* 1975, *30,* 116–127.

Cronbach, L. J., & Gleser, G. C. *Psychological tests and personnel decisions* (2nd ed.). Urbana: University of Illinois Press, 1965.

Cronbach, L. J., & Meehl, P. E. Construct validity in psychological tests. *Psychological Bulletin,* 1955, *52,* 281–302.

Cronbach, L. J., & Snow, R. E. *Aptitudes and instructional methods.* New York: Irvington, 1977.

Cunningham, J. W. A conceptual framework for the study of job similarities. In J. W. Cunningham (Ed.), The job-cluster concept and its curricular implications. *Center for Occupational Education Monograph,* 1969 (no. 4).

Dunnette, M. D. A modified model for test validation and selection research. *Journal of Applied Psychology,* 1963, *47,* 317–323.

Dunnette, M. D. Summary and integration. In U.S. Office of Personnel Management & Educational Testing Service. *Construct validity in psychological measurement: Proceedings of a colloquium on theory and application in education and employment.* Princeton, N.J.: Education Testing Service, 1980.

Dunnette, M. D., & Borman, W. C. Personnel selection and classification systems. In L. Porter (Ed.), *Annual Review of Psychology.* Palo Alto, Calif.: Annual Reviews, Inc., 1979.

Ebel, R. L. Must all tests be valid? *American Psychologist,* 1961, *16,* 640–647.

Fiske, D. W. The constraints of intra-individual variability in test response. *Educational and Psychological Measurement,* 1957, *17,* 317–337.

Fiske, D. W., & Rice, L. Intra-individual response variability. *Psychological Bulletin,* 1955, *52,* 217–250.

Frederiksen, N. Research models for exploring constructs. In U.S. Office of Personnel Management & Educational Testing Service. *Construct validity in psychological measurement: Proceedings of a colloquium on theory and application in education and employment.* Princeton, N.J.: Education Testing Service, 1980.

Frederiksen, N., & Melville, S. D. Differential predictability in the use of test scores. *Educational and Psychological Measurement,* 1954, *14,* 647–656.

Freyd, M. Measurement in vocational selection: An outline of research procedure. *Journal of Personnel Research,* 1923, *2,* 215–249, 268–284, 377–385.

Ghiselli, E. E. Dimensional problems of criteria. *Journal of Applied Psychology,* 1956, *40,* 1–4.

Ghiselli, E. E. The prediction of predictability. *Educational and Psychological Measurement,* 1960, *20,* 3–8. (a)

Ghiselli, E. E. Differentiation of tests in terms of the accuracy with which they predict for a given individual. *Educational and Psychological Measurement,* 1960, *20,* 675–684. (b)

Ghiselli, E. E. *The validity of occupational aptitude tests.* New York: Wiley, 1966.

Glass, G. V. Primary, secondary and meta-analysis of research. *Educational Researcher,* 1976, *5,* 3–8.

Glass, G. V. Integrating findings: The meta-analysis of research. *Review of Research in Education,* 1977, *5,* 351–379.

Golding, S. L., & Seidman, E. Analysis of multitrait–multimethod matrices: A two step principal components procedure. *Multivariate Behavioral Research,* 1974, *9,* 479–496.

Goodenough, L. *Mental testing.* New York: Rinehart, 1950.

Griggs v. Duke Power Co., 401 U.S. 424(1971).

Guetzkow, H., & Forehand, G. A. A research strategy for partial knowledge useful in the selection of executives. In R. Taguiri (Ed.), *Research needs in executive selection.* Boston: Harvard Graduate School of Business Administration, 1961.

Guilford, J. P. New Standards for test evaluation. *Educational and Psychological Measurement,* 1946, *6,* 427–439.

Guilford, J. P. *The nature of human intelligence,* New York: McGraw-Hill, 1967.

Guilford, J. P., & Hoepfner, R. *The analysis of intelligence.* New York: McGraw-Hill, 1971.

Guion, R. M. Criterion measurement and personnel judgments. *Personnel Psychology,* 1961, *14,* 141–149.

Guion, R. M. *Personnel testing.* New York: McGraw-Hill, 1965.

Guion, R. M. Content validity conference. *The Industrial-Organizational Psychologist,* 1974, *12*(1), 18. (a)

Guion, R. M. Open a new window: Validities and values in psychological measurement. *American Psychologist,* 1974, *29,* 287–296. (b)

Guion, R. M. Recruiting, selection and job placement. In M. D. Dunnette (Ed.), *Handbook of industrial and organizational psychology.* Chicago: Rand McNally, 1976. (Copyright © 1976 by J. Wiley & Sons, Inc.)

Guion, R. M. Content validity—the source of my discontent. *Applied Psychological Measurement,* 1977, *1,* 1–10.

Gulliksen, H. Intrinsic validity. *American Psychologist,* 1950, *5,* 511–517.

Hubert, L. J., & Baker, F. B. Analyzing the multitrait–multimethod matrix. *Multivariate Behavioral Research,* 1978, *13,* 163–179.

Hull, C. L. *Aptitude testing.* Yonkers, N.Y.: World Book, 1928.

Hunter, J. E., Schmidt, F. L., & Jackson, G. B. *Advanced meta-analysis: Quantitative methods for cumulating research findings across studies.* San Francisco: Sage, 1982.

Jackson, D. N. Multimethod factor analysis: A reformulation. *Multivariate Behavioral Research,* 1975, *10,* 259–275.

Jackson, D. N. Construct validity and personality assessment. In U.S. Office of Personnel Management & Educational Testing Service. *Construct validity in psychological measurement: Proceedings of a colloquium on theory and application in education and employment.* Princeton, N.J.: Education Testing Service, 1980.

James, L. R. Criterion models and construct validity for criteria. *Psychological Bulletin,* 1973, *80,* 75–83.

Jenkins, J. G. Validity for what? *Journal of Consulting Psychology,* 1946, *10,* 93–98.

Kalleberg, A. L., & Kluegel, J. R. Analysis of the multitrait–multimethod matrix: Some limitations and an alternative. *Journal of Applied Psychology,* 1975, *60,* 1–9.

Kenny, D. A. An empirical application of confirmatory factor analysis to the multitrait–multimethod matrix. *Journal of Experimental Social Psychology,* 1976, *12,* 247–252.

Kornhauser, A. W., & Kingsbury, F. A. *Psychological tests in business.* Chicago: University of Chicago Press, 1924.

Lee, M. C. Interactions, configurations, and nonadditive models. *Educational and Psychological Measurement.* 1961, *21,* 797–805.

Levin, J. A rotational procedure for separation of trait, method and interaction factors in multi-trait–multimethod matrices. *Multivariate Behavioral Research,* 1974, *9,* 231–240.

Linden, K. W., & Linden, J. D. *Modern mental measurement: A historical perspective.* Boston: Houghton Mifflin, 1968.

Link, H. C. *Employment psychology.* New York: Macmillan, 1924.

Loevinger, J. Objective test as instruments of psychology theory. *Psychological Reports* (monograph Supp. 9), 1957, 635–694.

McCormick, E. J., Jeanneret, P. R., & Mecham, R. C. *The development and background of the Position Analysis Questionnaire (PAQ).* Occupational Research Center, Purdue University, June 1969.

McKillip, R. H., & Wing, H. Application of a construct model in assessment of employment. In U.S. Office of Personnel Management & Educational Testing Service. *Construct validity in psychological measurement: Proceedings of a colloquium on theory and application in education and employment.* Princeton, N.J.: Educational Testing Service, 1980.

Messick, S. Constructs and their vicissitudes in educational and psychological measurement. In U.S. Office of Personnel Management & Educational Testing Service. *Construct validity in psychological measurement: Proceedings of a colloquim on theory and application in education and employment.* Princeton, N.J.: Education Testing Service, 1980.

Morrison, R. F. A multivariate model for the occupational placement decision. *Journal of Applied Psychology,* 1977, *62,* 271–277.

Mosier, C. I. A critical examination of the concepts of face validity. *Educational and Psychological measurement,* 1947, *7,* 191–205.

Mosier, C. I. Problems and designs of cross-validation. *Educational and Psychological Measurement,* 1951, *11,* 5–12.

Mussio, S. J., & Smith, M. K. *Content validity: A procedural manual.* Chicago: International Personnel Management Association, 1973.

Owens, W. A. Toward one discipline of scientific psychology. *American Psychologist.* 1968, *23,* 782–785.

Owens, W. A. A quasi-actuarial prospect for individual assessment. *American Psychologist,* 1971, *26,* 992–999.

Owens, W. A., & Schoenfeldt, L. F. Toward a classification of persons. *Journal of Applied Psychology Monographs,* 1979, *65,* 569–607.

Peak, H. Problems of objective observation. In L. Festinger & D. Katz (Eds.), *Research methods in the behavioral sciences.* New York: Dryden Press, 1953.

Proceedings of Content Validity II. Bowling Green, Ohio: Bowling Green State University, 1975.

Ray, M. L., & Heeler, R. M. Analysis techniques for exploratory use of the multitrait–multimethod matrix. *Educational and Psychological Measurements,* 1975, *35,* 255–265.

Rock, D. A. The identification and utilization of moderator effects in prediction systems. *Research Bulletin 69-32.* Princeton, N.J.: Educational Testing Service, 1969.

Schmidt, F. L., & Hunter, J. E. Development of a general solution to the problem of validity generalization. *Journal of Applied Psychology,* 1977, *62,* 529–540.

Schmidt, F. L., & Hunter, J. E. The future of criterion-related validity. *Personnel Psychology,* 1980, *33,* 41–60.

Schmidt, F. L., Hunter, J. E., & Caplan, J. R. Validity generalization results for two job groups in the petroleum industry. *Journal of Applied Psychology,* 1981, *66,* 261–273.

Schmidt, F. L., Hunter, J. E., McKenzie, R. S., & Muldrow, T. W. The impact of valid selection procedures on workforce productivity. *Journal of Applied Psychology,* 1979, *64,* 609–626.

Schmidt, F. L., Hunter, J. E., Pearlman, K., & Shane, G. S. Further tests of the Schmidt–Hunter Bayesian validity generalization procedure. *Personnel Psychology,* 1979, *32,* 257–281.

Schmidt, F. L., Hunter, J. E., & Urry, V. W. Statistical power in criterion-related validity studies. *Journal of Applied Psychology,* 1976, *61,* 473–485.

Schmidt, N. Path analysis of multitrait–multimethod matrices. *Applied Psychological Measurements,* 1978, *2,* 157–173.

Schoenfeldt, L. F. Utilization of manpower: Development and evaluation of an assessment– classification model for matching individuals with jobs. *Journal of Applied Psychology,* 1974, *59,* 583–595.

Schoenfeldt, L. F., Schoenfeldt, B. B., Acker, S. R., & Perlson, M. R. Content validity revisited: The development of a content-oriented test of industrial reading. *Journal of Applied Psychology,* 1976, *61,* 581–588.

Smith, P. C. Behavior, results, and organizational effectiveness: The problem of criteria. In M. D. Dunnette (Ed.), *Handbook of industrial and organizational psychology.* Chicago: Rand McNally, 1976. (Copyright © 1976 by John Wiley & Sons.)

Sternberg, R. J. The construct validation of aptitude tests: An information processing assessment. In U.S. Office Personnel Management & Educational Testing Service. *Construct validity in psychological measurement: Proceedings of a colloquium on theory and application in education and employment.* Princeton, N.J.: Education Testing Service, 1980.

Tenopyr, M. L. Content-construct confusion. *Personnel Psychology,* 1977, *30,* 47–54.

Thorndike, R. L. *Personnel selection.* New York: Wiley, 1949.

U.S. Equal Opportunity Commission, U.S. Civil Service Commission, U.S. Department of Justice, U.S. Department of Labor, & U.S. Department of the Treasury. Uniform Guidelines on Employee Selection Procedures. *Federal Register,* 1978, *43*(166), 38295–38309.

U.S. Office of Personnel Management & Educational Testing Service. *Construct validity in psychological measurement: Proceedings of a colloquium on theory and application in education and employment.* Princeton, N.J.: Educational Testing Service, 1980.

Vale, J. R., & Vale, C. A. Individual differences and general laws in psychology. *American Psychologist,* 1969, *24,* 1093–1108.

Wallace, S. R. Criteria for what? *American Psychologist,* 1965, *20,* 411–417.

Werts, C. E., Joreskog, K. G., & Linn, R. E. A multitrait–multimethod model for studying growth. *Educational and Psychological Measurement,* 1972, *32,* 655–678.

Whitely, S. E. Latent trait models in the study of intelligence. *Intelligence,* 1980, *4,* 97–132. (a)

Whitely, S. E. Multicomponent latent trait models for ability tests. *Psychometrika,* 1980, *45,* 479–494. (b)

Zedeck, S. Problems with the use of "moderator" variables. *Psychological Bulletin,* 1971, *71,* 295–310.

5

Social and Legal Influences on Test Development and Usage

Donald N. Bersoff
Ennis, Friedman, Bersoff & Ewing
Washington, D.C.
University of Maryland School of Law and
The John Hopkins University

It was the Chinese over 3000 years ago, not the Americans in this century, who first used large-scale psychological testing (Dubois, 1966). But, as with many other technological developments, it was the United States that enthusiastically adopted the method (Haney, 1981). By now it is highly probable that every person in our country has been affected in some way by the administration of tests. Testing has become the means by which major decisions about people's lives are made in industry, education, hospitals, mental health clinics, and the civil service.

Tests themselves, by and large, are facially neutral. They do not inherently discriminate against those who take them and, undoubtedly, scores derived from tests have been used to admit, advance, and employ. For most people, however, test results have served as exclusionary mechanisms—to segregate, institutionalize, track, and deny access to coveted and increasingly scarce employment opportunities.

At one time, the work of academic and applied psychometricians went virtually unexamined by the law, but as the use of tests increased in the United States, so did their potential for causing legally cognizable injury to test takers. As a result, there is probably no current activity performed by psychologists so closely scrutinized and regulated by the legal system as testing.

SOCIAL INFLUENCES

Although recent ligitation and legislation directly affect the continued administration of psychological testing, most especially in employment and educational settings, it is my contention that what appears to be an antitesting movement in the courts and in Congress is not an antitesting movement at all. It is my thesis that, in the main, the law's concern about testing has been evoked by the following three major social developments.

1. Our society in the last 30 years has made attempts, albeit unevenly, to undo the effects of history of *de jure* segregation and *discrimination against racial and ethnic minorities*. Many of the more familiar cases, such as *Larry P. v. Riles* (1979) affecting individual intelligence scales, *Debra P. v. Turlington* (1981)[1] concerning minimal competency tests, and *Teal v. Connecticut* (1982) litigating nuances of employment selection assessment, flow inexorably from *Brown v. Education* (1954) and are simply renewed claims by minorities for the fulfillment of the meaning of the 14th Amendment's equal protection clause. They reflect the most recent challenges to practices that are perceived as attempts to continue, in a more sophisticated manner, the racial and ethnic separation more blatantly used in the early 1950s and 1960s by educational institutions and public and private employers.

2. The courts have recognized, as a constitutional imperative, the *right against impermissible intrusion by the government* into the private lives of its citizens. Defining the right to privacy has been difficult for the courts, but recently the Supreme Court noted that one aspect of the right "is the individual interest in avoiding disclosure of personal matters [*Whalen v. Roe,* 1977, p. 598]" or as the late Justice Brandeis more esthetically phrased it, "the right to be let alone [*Olmstead v. United States,* 1927, p. 478]." If, as Reubhausen and Brim (1965) assert, the "essence of privacy is . . . the freedom of the individual to pick and choose for himself the time and circumstances under which, and most importantly, the extent to which, his attitudes, beliefs, behavior and opinions are to be shared with or withheld from others [pp. 1189–1190]," one can easily see why the broad spectrum of testing, but particularly personality and attitude testing, would be the object of legal scrutiny.

3. Finally, there has been a third social development that has influenced the law's concern with testing. Unlike judicial declarations concerning discrimination and privacy, this last influence is not of recent vintage. As a social phenomenon it has been part of human culture since its beginning. If you will pardon a highly technical psycholegal term, I would like to call this third aspect *stupidity*. Stupidity may be defined as negligence or, alternatively, the failure to use reasonable care in carrying out one's obligations. Although it does not connote

---

[1]Complete citations for all cases referenced in the text are found in Table 5.1.

intentional or willful desire to harm, negligent harm can be just as damaging as purposefully inflicted injury. It is my thesis that stupidity, more than modern interpretations of equal protection and privacy, has been responsible for the increased legal regulation of psychological testing. On this count, both psychologists and judges must be faulted.

I believe that almost all the important legal decisions concerning psychological testing may be viewed as various combinations of the social phenomena identified as items 1 to 3 just given. I would like to spend some time in developing this thesis by giving several pertinent examples from educational, employment, and forensic settings.

SOCIAL INFLUENCES ON LEGAL DECISIONS: SOME EXAMPLES

Education

The Supreme Court's ringing declarations in *Brown v. Board of Education* (1954) ended state-imposed segregation in the public schools. But in the decade after *Brown,* many southern school systems refused to accept the Court's decision as final. They interpreted the Court's assertion that separation of black children from white "solely because of their race generates a feeling of inferiority . . . that may affect their hearts and minds in a way unlikely ever to be undone [p. 494]" as an empirically testable hypothesis, not a normative legal principle. Thus, in the early 1960s one of Georgia's school systems sought to disprove what it believed to be an erroneous factual premise. It alleged the segregation they were accused of perpetuating was not based on color "but rather upon racial traits of educational significance as to which racial identity was only a convenient index [*Stell v. Savannah–Chatham County Board of Education,* 1963, p. 668]." They attempted to show that differences in learning rates, cognitive ability, behavioral traits, and capacity for education in general were so great that not only was it impossible for black children and white children to be educated effectively in the same room but that to "congregate children of such diverse traits in schools . . . would seriously impair the educational opportunities of both white and Negro and cause them grave psychological harm [p. 668]."

To prove their contentions the defendants called several expert witnesses, among them two psychologists, Travis Osborne and Henry Garrett. Based on such instruments as the California Achievement Test and the California Mental Maturity Tests, they testified that significant differences in test scores were indicative of inherent differences in the races and that only minor changes could be achieved by educational readjustment or other environmental change. Al-

TABLE 5.1
Table of Cases

Albemarle Paper Co. v. Moody, 422 U.S. 405 (1975).
Ballew v. Georgia, 435 U.S. 223 (1978).
Battie v. Estelle, No. 79-1567 (5th Cir. Sept. 11, 1981).
Brown v. Board of Education, 347 U.S. 483 (1954).
Debra P. v. Turlington, 644 F.2d 397 (5th Cir. 1981).
Estelle v. Smith, 451 U.S. 454 (1981).
Firefighters Institute v. City of St. Louis, 616 F.2d 350 (8th Cir. 1980), *cert. denied sub nom.*
    United States v. City of St. Louis, 452 U.S. 938 (1981).
Frye v. United States, 293 F. 1013 (D.C. Cir. 1923).
Griggs v. Duke Power Co., 401 U.S. 424 (1971).
Guardians Association v. New York Civil Service Commission, 630 F.2d 79 (2d Cir. 1980),
    cert. denied, 452 U.S. 939 (1981).
Hobson v. Hansen, 269 F. Supp. 401 (D. D.C. 1967) *aff'd sub nom.* Smuck v. Hobson, 408
    F.2d 175 (D.C. Cir. 1969).
Kirkland v. New York State Dep't. of Correctional Services 520 F.2d 430 (2d Cir. 1975), *cert.
    denied.* 429 U.S. 823 (1976).
Larry P. v. Riles, 495 F. Supp. 926 (N.D. Cal. 1979) *appeal docketed.* No. 80-4027 (9th Cir.,
    Jan. 17, 1980).
Merriken v. Cressman, 364 F. Supp. 913 (E.D. Pa. 1973).
Olmstead v. United States, 227 U.S. 439 (1928).
PASE v. Hannon, 506 F. Supp. 831 (N.D. Ill. 1980).
Stell v. Savannah-Chatham Board of Education, 200 F. Supp. 667 (S.D. Ga. 1963), *rev'd* 333
    F.2d 55 (5th Cir. 1963), *cert. denied,* 379 U.S. 933 (1964).
Teal v. Connecticut, U.S., 102 S. Ct. 2525 (1982).
Washington v. Davis, 426 U.S. 229 (1976).
Whalen v. Roe, 429 U.S. 589 (1977).

---

though these test results and testimonies went unchallenged by attorneys fighting to enforce desegregation, the idea that such devices could measure innate ability found its way into a 1967 decision that, at the time, became the most persuasive and widely quoted legal opinion of its kind. That case is *Hobson v. Hansen.*

At issue in *Hobson* was not psychological testing but rather the constitutionality of disparities in the allocation of financial and educational resources in the Washington, D.C., public school system that, it was claimed, favored white children. Also at issue was the overrepresentation of black children in lower, and white children in upper, ability groups. But, in the course of the trial, it was adduced that the method by which track assignments were made depended almost entirely on such standardized group ability scales as the Metropolitan Readiness and Achievement Test and the Otis Quick-Scoring Mental Ability Test. *Hobson,* when read in its entirety, represents the justified condemnation of rigid, poorly conceived classification practices that negatively affected the educational opportunities of minority children and led to permanent stigmatization of blacks as unteachable. But swept within *Hobson's* condemnation of harmful classification practices were ability tests used as the sole or primary decision-making devices to justify placement. Not only was ability grouping as then practiced in the District of Columbia abolished, but tests were banned unless they could be shown to measure children's innate capacity to learn. No psychologist who has written on the subject, including Jensen (1969, 1980), believes that tests solely measure hereditary endowment (Anastasi, 1976; Cleary, Humphreys, Kendrick, & Wesman, 1975). No test could pass such a criterion.

Left unscathed in *Hobson* were the stately, revered, and venerated devices against which all other tests were measured—the individual intelligence scales. But that was soon to change as the result of actions brought in San Francisco and Chicago. Two diametrically opposed decisions, *Larry P. v. Riles* (1979) (the San Francisco case) and *PASE v. Hannon* (1980) (the Chicago case) are seen by psychologists as attacks on IQ tests. That, however, is a significant misperception. Like *Hobson,* these two pieces of litigation are actually challenges to educational practices deemed to be discriminatory. [Similarly, the recent attack on minimal competency tests, see *Debra P. v. Turlington* (1981), is more appropriately seen as a claim by black children that the use of such tests is merely a subtle but effective effort by states to resegregate the public schools.]

The real issue was the basis for disproportional placement of black children in segregated, self-contained classes for the educably mentally retarded. Throughout his opinion, Judge Peckham in *Larry P. v. Riles* [hereafter *Riles*] labeled the EMR program "dead-end," "isolating," "inferior," and "stigmatizing." Relying on the testimony of state employees or printed material from the state department of education, the court concluded California's EMR classes were "designed to separate out children who are *incapable* of learning in regular classes [*Riles,* 1979, p. 941]" and were not meant to provide remedial instruction so that children could learn the skills necessary for eventual return to regular instruction. Given these characteristics, the court considered "the decision to place children in these classes . . . a crucial one. Children wrongly placed in these classes are unlikely to escape as they inevitably lag farther and farther behind the children in regular classes [p. 942]." And, as in *Hobson,* the primary basis for these decisions were found to be tests—most often the WISC-R and the Stanford–Binet.

Interpreting the nondiscriminatory provisions of the Rehabilitation Act of 1973 and the Education for All Handicapped Children Act of 1975 (Pub. L. 94-142), particularly regulations requiring that assessment instruments be "validated for the specific purpose for which they are used [35 C.F.R. §104.35; 34 C.F.R. §300.532]," Judge Peckham found the challenged tests unable to meet that requirement. The tests, the court ruled, would have to be shown valid for selecting children who belonged in substandard, segregated educational anachronisms (otherwise known as EMR classes). And because that kind of validation had not been done, the court permanently prohibited California "from utilizing, permitting the use of, or approving the use of any standardized tests . . . for the identification of black EMR children or their placement into EMR classes [p.

989]'' without first securing the court's approval. Even Judge Grady, who in *PASE v. Hannon* (1980) upheld the use of individual intelligence tests in a similar challenge concluded that inappropriate placement in an EMR class was an educational tragedy that was likely to be totally harmful.

Employment

Similar phenomena as I have described in public schools occurred in employment settings. *Griggs v. Duke Power Co.* (1971), which introduced the concept of ''job-relatedness'' into the law of employment testing and created a morass not yet fully resolved, would never have been decided if the defendants had not had a history of racial discrimination. Prior to 1965, the Duke Power Co. openly discriminated on the basis of race in the hiring and assigning of employees at its Dan River plant. Blacks were employed only in the lowest level jobs and at the lowest rate of pay. In 1964 Congress passed Title VII of the Civil Rights Act prohibiting discrimination in employment on the basis of race, religion, sex, or national origin. On July 2, 1965, the date on which Title VII took effect, Duke Power decided to no longer restrict blacks to the lowest level positions. However, at the same time, it instituted a policy that, to qualify for placement in higher level positions, employees would have to achieve satisfactory scores on the Wonderlic Personnel Test, purportedly an intelligence measure, and the Bennett Mechanical Comprehension Test. Blacks challenged the tests, claiming that neither instrument was directed or intended to measure the ability to learn to perform a particular job or category of jobs. A unanimous Supreme Court faulted the company for using ''broad and general testing devices [p. 433]'' and reminded the defendants that although the use of tests was permissible under Title VII, they had to ''fairly measure the knowledge or skills required by the particular job [p. 433].''

Similarly, accusations of purposeful discrimination in both the private and public sector has stimulated litigation in such cases as *Albemarle Paper Co. v. Moody* (1975) and *Firefighters Institute v. City of St. Louis* (1980). The result has been increasingly sophisticated challenges to professionally developed tests even in situations where purposeful discrimination is not an issue [e.g., *Guardian Association of New York City v. Civil Service Commission* (1980); *Teal v. Connecticut* (1982)]. Like educational tests, ''employment tests are being subjected to a degree of governmental scrutiny that very few human contrivances could bear [Wigdor, 1982, p. 67].''

Privacy

Although discrimination has evoked judicial scrutiny of ability tests, the concern for the right to privacy has stimulated similar examination of personality tests. If stupidity has ever fostered a judicial decision concerning testing, there is no better example than *Merriken v. Cressman* (1973). The case had its origins in 1970 when a survey, ordered by the Commission of Montgomery County, Pennsylvania and conducted by a company called Scientific Resources, revealed that many children in the county were heavily involved with drugs. Most of the children who used drugs, the study claimed, possessed some common characteristics. For example, one finding indicated that 80% of the identified drug abusers felt estranged from their families. On the basis of such data, Scientific Resources proposed that the County Drug Commission sponsor a drug prevention program, later labeled CPI, for the Critical Period of Intervention. All three of the county school districts agreed to participate in the program.

There were two phases to the study: identification and remediation. In the first phase, tests were given to eighth-grade students and their teachers so that certain students, deemed potential drug abusers, could become part of the remediation program. The teachers were asked to identify pupils who most and least fit eight descriptions of antisocial behavior (e.g., "This pupil makes unusual or inappropriate responses during normal school activity"). The student form was to be somewhat lengthier. First, students would be asked to assess their own behavior, that is, to state which of the following statements was most like themselves: (1) someone who will probably be a success in life; (2) one who gets upset when faced with a difficult school problem; (3) someone who has lots of self-confidence; and (4) a student who has more problems than other students. In the next part of the scale they would be asked questions about their relationships with their parents and the behavior of their parents (e.g., to indicate whether one or both parents "tell me how much they love me" or "make me feel unloved" or "seem to regret that I am growing up and spending more time away from home"). Finally, the students would select from their classmates those who fit certain descriptive statements similar in kind to the ones given the teachers.

The second phase of the study was intervention. When the CPI staff had analyzed all the results, they would compile a list of children who would have significant potential for becoming drug abusers. This list would then be given to the school superintendent who would organize a joint effort among guidance counselors, teachers, school psychologists, and others to provide group therapeutic experiences to which the identified students would be involuntarily assigned.

When the program was first developed the school system did not intend to obtain the affirmative consent of the parents for their children to participate. They did plan to send a letter home to each parent, as follows:

Dear Parent:
    This letter is to inform you that, this fall, we are initiating a Drug Program called "Critical Period of Intervention" (CPI). The aim of this program is to identify children who may be susceptible to drug abuse and to intervene with concrete measures to help these children. Diagnostic testing will be part of this

program and will provide data enabling the prevention program to be specific and positive.

We ask your support and cooperation in this program and assure you of the confidentiality of these studies. If you wish to examine or receive further information regarding the program, please feel free to contact the school. If you do not wish to participate in this program, please notify your principal of this decision. We will assume your cooperation unless otherwise notified by you [*Merriken v. Cressman*, 1973, p. 917].

Also, as originally proposed, the study contained no provision for student consent.

Sylvia Merriken, the mother of one of the intended participants in the study, who happened to be a therapist in a drug and alcoholic rehabilitation center, complained to the principal of the school where her son was enrolled and to the school board. The American Civil Liberties Union (ACLU) then announced it would represent Mrs. Merriken in an attempt to enjoin the school permanently from carrying out its plans. The ACLU began by filing a complaint in federal district court claiming that the program would violate the constitutional rights of both Mrs. Merriken and her son. It quickly obtained a temporary injunction prohibiting the county from implementing its proposal until the litigation was completed. At that point, two of the three schools in Montgomery County decided to discontinue their participation but the Norristown system, where Mrs. Merriken's son attended, persisted, although it honored the temporary injunction.

When the suit itself began, the school system offered to change the format of their letter to include parental consent. In another attempt at compromise, the school modified the test so that students who did not want to be included could return an uncompleted protocol. But the proposal contained no provision for student consent and no data were to be provided whereby students could make an informed choice about participating.

Of the many constitutional challenges Mrs. Merriken made, the court entertained only one of them seriously—the right of privacy. The court found that the highly personal nature of the instrument disrupted family associations and interfered with the right of the mother to rear her child. It said, "There is probably no more private a relationship, excepting marriage, which the Constitution safeguards than that between parent and child. This Court can look upon any invasion of that relationship as a direct violation of one's Constitutional right to privacy [p. 918]." And although there was no precedent to the effect in the Supreme Court, the district court declared that privacy was entitled to as much constitutional protection as free speech.

Although the court failed to analyze the privacy rights of her son (but see Bersoff, 1983), the court found that Mrs. Merriken was unable to give genuinely informed consent to the invasion of her personal life because the parental permission letter was so inadequate. The court deridingly compared the letter to a Book-of-the-Month Club solicitation in which parents' silence would be construed as acquiescence. The letter was also criticized as a selling device in which parents were convinced to allow children to participate. It was not, as it properly should be, an objective document telling parents of the potentially negative feature and dangerous aspects of the program.

There were other problems with the program. The promotional letter promised confidentiality, but the program contemplated the development of a "massive data bank" and the dissemination of data relating to specific, identifiable students to school superintendents, principals, guidance counselors, coaches, social workers, PTA members, and school board members. And even if the school system had been more circumspect and had constructed means by which the data were less widely distributed (or not distributed at all), no promise of confidentiality could take precedence over a subpeona compelling the disclosure of the material to law enforcement officers. As the court warned:

> [T]here is no assurance that should an enterprising district attorney convene a special grand jury to investigate the drug program in Montgomery County, the records of the CPI Program would remain inviolate from subpoenas and that he could not determine the identity of children who have been labeled by the CPI Program as potential drug abusers [p. 916].

Parents were not at all informed of this possibility.

Compounding the other problems was the fact that the identification instruments did not possess enough psychometric soundness to overcome the hazards that may have flowed from their use. Although there could have been considerable harm done to children correctly identified, the court was particularly concerned about those children incorrectly identified. In a statement that should raise the anxiety level of psychologists, it said, "When a program talks about labeling someone as a particular type and such a label could remain with him for the remainder of his life, the margin of error must be almost nil [p. 920]."

Forensics

Ironically, the one use of tests that has remained relatively uncriticized is in forensic assessment. Ability tests used in educational and employment decision making, despite their myriad problems, have been subjected to decades of empirical analysis and validation. Yet, they have undergone the most scathing review by the legal system. On the other hand, based on personality and projective instruments, forensic psychologists since the 1940s have routinely testified in cases involving competency to stand trial, insanity, civil commitment, the causal connection between negligent conduct and emotional and physical injury, child custody, and the eligibility of criminal defendants for the death penalty.

Whereas such determinations are at least as crucial to the interests of the test taker and society, personality and projective instruments have escaped wholesale scrutiny by the courts and remain largely untouched.

As long as psychologists possess the requisite indices of expertise such as proper education, training, experience, scholarly publications, and professional affiliation, they are permitted to offer opinions on the kinds of ultimate issues I have just cataloged based on the administration of tests like the Rorschach, MMPI, and TAT. Although such testimony has subjected individual psychologists to harsh cross-examinations (Ziskin, 1981), the courts have never seriously questioned whether these tests are sufficiently precise to evoke probative expert testimony or to support valid opinions that will be more helpful than testimony of the thoughtful layperson to the jury.

The confused approach to expert testimony by psychologists is, in part, explained by a failure to recognize that it is not a unidimensional concept but, rather, involves three levels of inference. The first level consists of the psychologist's personal observation of the client made during the course of the clinical evaluation, including essentially objective data about the individual's behavior and the uninterpreted results of psychological testing. The second level moves from reporting observations to the synthesis of data to form a diagnosis that will classify, and perhaps account for, the behavior manifested during the course of the evaluation or at the time of the event in question. It is on this level that psychologists make a judgment about whether the person has a mental disorder. Whether the diagnosis is presented in terms of a particular label or a lengthy description of personality, the critical element is that the diagnosis derives its value from the psychometric soundness of the assessment devices used. The third level concerns an opinion about the ultimate issue (i.e., child custody, or insanity) that the jury or judge must resolve. Whereas I have significant reservations about any testimony by experts as to level three (Comment, 1978; Gass & Bersoff, submitted for publication), it is concern about testimony at level two that is most relevant to this chapter.

The test for the admissibility of scientific evidence was developed 60 years ago in *Frye v. United States* (1923), which limited such evidence to that which has gained "general scientific acceptance." Under its modern interpretation by subsequent tribunals, the courts require not only acceptance within the scientific community but also accuracy. Thus, assessment devices used in the forensic arena should not only have gained acceptance within psychology but, more importantly, the accuracy of the technique should be demonstrated to yield information that is more likely to be true than could be gleaned from lay testimony. Results from polygraphs and voice spectrography have been denied admissibility because the error rate is considered to be 10 to 25%. If such a criterion were applied to most clinicians' favorite projective devices, none of the information or diagnostic conclusions derived from them would be admitted in court. Validity coefficients that clinicians might find highly acceptable may not pass legal muster. Tests' vulnerability to situational and experimenter effects and to such phenomena as illusory correlations (Chapman & Chapman, 1969) have been well documented (Comment, 1978; Monahan, 1981).

The scientific literature regarding reliability and validity of tests used by forensic experts suggests that, at best, they are highly suspect and susceptible to a variety of significant sources of psychometric and interpretive error. They have limited psychometric soundness even in the hands of the most skilled clinicians, and there is little basis to assert that expert opinions, based on projective tests, are more accurate than layperson's opinions. But, although forensic psychologists may have little empirically based expertise to offer the legal system, they are uniformly permitted to testify and their judgments often carry great weight with the jury. On the other hand, the work of educational and industrial psychologists undergo close review, even though there is greater reason to believe that the instruments upon which they rely are more demonstrably accurate. Why? The answer is partly rooted in tradition—such issues as insanity have confronted the courts for decades; issues such as proper placement in special education programs or promotion to fire captains have not. But, more importantly, the tests used in forensic settings do not impinge on privacy or disproportionately affect racial or ethnic minorities. It is interesting to note, however, that recently forensic examinations used in criminal settings have raised concerns about the privilege against self-incrimination and right to counsel (see *Estelle v. Smith,* 1981, and *Battie v. Estelle,* 1981).

SOCIAL SCIENCE EVIDENCE AND THE COURTS

All of these conflicting perceptions about psychological tests raise a final issue with which I wish to conclude—that of the relationship between the social sciences and the courts. If that relationship were to be examined by a psychoanalyst, the analyst would no doubt conclude that it is a highly neurotic, conflict-ridden ambivalent affair (I stress "affair" because it is certainly no marriage). Thirty years ago the vitality of data generated by psychologists seemed assured when the Supreme Court in *Brown v. Board of Education* (1954) conspicuously referred to studies by Kenneth and Mamie Clark concerning the effect of segregation on black children. The reference to those studies in a now famous footnote created a controversy that still exists concerning their relevance and validity (Cahn, 1955; Clark, 1980; Kluger, 1975; Levin, 1978). Despite that controversy there is little doubt that *Brown* represents the most dramatic use of social science scholarship.

But if *Brown* produced optimism, subsequent events did not uniformly reinforce those buoyant feelings. In the past 5 years the Supreme Court has rejected empirical data in cases concerning sex discrimination, the death penalty, and corporal punishment. Perhaps most clearly exemplary of the Court's ambivalence is its decision in *Ballew v. Georgia* (1978) where it unanimously agreed that criminal trials before five-member juries unconstitutionally deprived defendants of the right to trial by jury. Justice Blackmun announced the judgment of the Supreme Court and in his decision relied heavily on the work of social psychologists and others to support the conclusion that less than six-person panels substantially and negatively altered the jury process. However, only one other justice joined that opinion. Three justices were particularly critical of his use of social science data. In a concurring opinion (indicating agreement with the outcome but not the reasoning of the primary opinion) Justice Powell, joined by Chief Justice Burger and Justice Rehnquist, acerbically noted his "reservations as to the wisdom . . . of Mr. Justice Blackmun's heavy reliance on numerology derived from statistical studies [p. 246]."

The same love–hate relationship finds its way into lower-court opinions concerning testing. These opinions, regardless of whether one likes the result, are generally devoid of sound psychometric reasoning. Even if the conclusions are correct, the courts often fail to cite the relevant literature in a way that convinces the reader that the conclusion is empirically supportable.

Social Science in Education and Employment Cases

Education. We can once again return to the education and employment testing cases for the most pertinent examples. As you may recall, the court in *Riles* permanently prohibited the state from using any standardized intelligence tests for the identification of black children for placement into EMR classes and held that before the state could use IQ tests, it would have to meet the following standards:

1. Tests would have to yield the same pattern of scores when administered to different groups of students.
2. Tests would have to yield approximately equal means for all subgroups included in the standardization sample.
3. Tests would have to be correlated with relevant criterion measures, that is, IQ scores of black children with classroom performance.

The implication in *Riles* that an unbiased test must yield the same pattern of scores when administered to different groups of people is psychometrically unsound. It is generally, though not uniformly, conceded that tests are fair when they predict with equal accuracy, not with equal results, for all groups. If that position is correct, then the court's definition "eliminates a priori any possibility of real group differences on various psychological traits [Schmidt & Hunter, 1974, p. 1]." The court rejected the possibility of genuine inferiority and social-class differences. Though the court rested its decision on the finding that the tests were culturally biased, it provided little hard data to support such a conclusion and was tentative in discussing it. In fact, the court's empirical support for its conclusions consumed only 1 of 70 printed pages. Moreover, the court's determination that the tests contain questions biased against poor black children is not uniformly accepted, and there are some data to suggest that whatever discrimination there is in tests, lower scores in blacks are not totally the result of content bias.

By definition, achievement and intelligence tests will always fail to meet the demand for assessment devices devoid of environmental influence. Given what they purport to measure, they inevitably reflect the social setting of the test taker: "[All] behavior is . . . affected by the cultural milieu in which the individual is reared and since psychological tests are but samples of behavior, cultural influences will and should be reflected in test performance. It is therefore futile to try to devise a test that is *free* from cultural influences [Anastasi, 1976, p. 345]."

Efforts to produce culture-free tests or to reduce content bias have met with little success. "Nonverbal or performance tests are now generally recognized as falling short of the goal of freedom from cultural influences, and attempts to develop culture fair verbal tests . . . are recognized as failures [Reschly, 1979, p. 231]." More specifically, Anastasi (1976) states: "On the WISC, for instance, black children usually find the Performance Tests as difficult or more difficult than the Verbal Tests; this pattern is also characteristic of children from low socioeconomic levels [p. 348]." Kirp (1973) concludes: "[It] is sobering but instructive to recognize that minority children do poorly even on so-called culture-free tests [p. 758]."

There has been relatively little research on content bias itself, particularly with regard to individual intelligence tests. What has been found with regard to standardized tests generally (Flaugher, 1978; Green, 1978), or individual intelligence tests specifically (Reynolds, 1982; Reschly, 1980; Sandoval, 1979), does not support Judge Peckham's conclusions. For example, contrary to popular thought, such widely criticized questions on the WISC-R comprehension subtest as, "What is the thing to do if a boy (girl) much smaller than yourself starts a fight with you?" (a question that even Judge Grady in *PASE* found biased) may actually be easier for black children than they are for white (Reschly, 1979). Eliminating 13 items perceived to be biased from a widely used 02 item elementary reading test "did not improve the performance of schools with high-minority populations relative to their performance on the original 'biased version' [Flaugher, 1978, p. 675]." Deleting what appear to be idiosyncratic items from group ability tests results only in "making the tests considerably more difficult for everyone, since many of the items [exhibiting] the widest discrepancy between groups [are] moderate to low in overall difficulty [Flaugher, 1978, p. 675]" (but see Oakland & Matuszek, 1977). Most pertinently, Sandoval (1979) found no evidence of items bias on the WISC-R: "The notion that there may be a number of items with radically different difficulties for children from different ethnic groups has not been supported [p. 925]." Moreover, the interjudge agreement concerning cultural bias on the WISC-R appears very low (see Reschly citing Sandoval, 1980).

Although Judge Peckham can be faulted for his analysis of cultural discrimination in intelligence tests and for implying that the issue is more settled than it is, any criticism of his analysis does not imply that his conclusion is incorrect or that there is support for such alternative hypotheses as genetics—rejected by all parties in *Riles* and *PASE*—or socioeconomic explanations. In any event, the court in *Riles* was correct in criticizing test publishers for not adequately standardizing and validating their instruments on discrete minority populations. The court could only rest its holding on the data presented to it by the parties. The state's defense was made difficult by the lack of relevant studies on differential validity, the absence of systematic research concerning content bias, and California's concession that cultural differences affected IQ scores.

If Judge Peckham's analysis of the issue of cultural bias was scanty and faulty, Judge Grady in *PASE v. Hannon* (1980) can best be described as naive. At worst it was unintelligent, and completely devoid of empirical content. Distrustful of the expert testimony in the case, he felt it imperative to examine the tests themselves so he could judge whether the claim of cultural bias could be sustained. Thus, in a startling and extraordinary manner, he proceeded to cite each question on the Wechsler and Binet scales in an attempt to determine which, in his estimation, were culturally biased. The result of this analysis was the judgment that only eight items on the WISC/WISC-R and one item on the Stanford–Binet were suspect or actually biased. At bottom, what it represented was a single person's subjective and personal judgment cloaked in the apparent authority of judicial robes. If submitted as a study to one of psychology's more respected refereed journals, rather than masquerading as a legal opinion, it would have been summarily rejected as an experiment whose sample size and lack of objectivity stamped it as unworthy of publication. The court's opinion in *PASE* amply supports Reschly's (1980) conclusion that with regard to item bias on the individually administered intelligence tests, "subjective judgments appear to be unreliable and invalid in terms of empirical analysis. . . . The only data confirming test bias that exists now is judgmental and speculative [p. 127]."

What makes Judge Grady's opinion interesting, if not precedent setting, is the fact the decision contains the questions and correct answers to every item on the WISC, the WISC-R, and the Stanford–Binet. McClelland (1973) suggested several years ago that tests should be given away. Whether inadvertently or purposely, Judge Grady has done just that. Those who wish to destroy the usefulness of these tests need only inform parents and·antitest advocates of the existence of the decision and its citation to the proper volume in the series of legal reports that publishes verbatim all federal district court opinions. Although Judge Grady eventually upheld the tests as valid, his decision, to a far greater extent than Judge Peckham's decision in *Riles,* may have the effect of invalidating the tests as they are presently used. The Psychological Corporation, publisher of the Wechsler Scales (and the System of Multi-Pluralistic Assessment [SOMPA] that uses these scales), tried unsuccessfully to convince Judge Grady to seal that part of his decision containing the questions and answers to the scales so that their content would not be published and thus made public. It has since issued a statement attempting to protect its copyright in the tests and threatens legal action if it is not protected: "The Psychological Corporation considers unauthorized reproduction of its copyrighted material from any source, including a court's opinion, to be an invasion of its rights, including its copyright, and the right to maintain the necessary security of its tests [Udell, 1980]." As of this writing, there has not been specific legal action against those who have informed general audiences of its existence. But one potential outcome of the decision is that the security of these tests may have, indeed, been seriously compromised, if not destroyed.

Employment. The situation with regard to employment testing does not evoke any greater confidence. There are sharp differences among the federal courts, Equal Employment Opportunity Commission (EEOC), and psychometric experts as to the proper conceptualization of test validation within the industrial setting. Novick (1981) has perceptively summarized the struggle:

Individual federal agencies have responsibilities and goals delegated by the executive and legislative branches of government, monitored by the judicial branch, and ultimately specified by the incumbent agency management. Although these agencies share concern for benefits to society as a whole, they tend to focus attention on their own particular mandates, and for this reason they often view testing and other issues quite differently. In fact, it is not uncommon for government agencies to be on opposite sides in litigation involving tests, for employers to receive conflicting directives from different government agencies, and for employees to find that their test scores are considered in light of widely varying objectives by employers and government agency representatives [p. 1035].

The Supreme Court has been particularly unhelpful in sorting out this confusion. For example, in *Griggs v. Duke Power Co.* (1971) a unanimous court stated that the EEOC Guidelines on Employment Testing were "entitled to great deference" (p. 434). Four years later, Chief Justice Burger, who had written the decision in *Griggs* now complained in a minority opinion in *Albermarle Paper Co. v. Moody* (1975) about the Court's "slavish adherence" (p. 452) to those same Guidelines. Perhaps in a more important example, one I described at some length in a recent *American Psychologist* article (Bersoff, 1981), the Court has badly muddled the whole issue of test validation. In *Washington v. Davis* (1976) in support of its opinion that validation could be accomplished in "any one of several ways," the Court cited the then extant version of the *Standards for Educational and Psychological Tests* (APA, AERA, NCME, 1974) to the effect that there were "three basic methods of validation: 'empirical' or 'criterion' validity . . . 'construct validity' . . . and 'content' validity [*Washington v. Davis*, 1976, p. 247, fn. 13]."

Many industrial and academic psychologists (Guion, 1980; Messick, 1980; Tenopyr, 1977) contend that insofar as the courts have interpreted the test standards and the EEOC Guidelines (superseded now by the Uniform Guidelines on Employee Selection Procedures, see EEOC et al., 1978) and its implementing "Question and Answers" (EEOC et al., 1979) to mean that content, criterion, and construct validity are distinct forms of validation, those interpretations are oversimplified, if not erroneous. The Uniform Guidelines, according to this view, inappropriately treat three aspects of validity as "something of a holy trinity representing three different roads to psychometric salvation [Guion, 1980, p. 386]" rather than viewing them as subsets within the unifying and common framework of construct validity. Most judicial opinions, with one or two conspicuous exceptions (see *Guardians Association of New York City v. Civil Service Commission,* 1980), concerned with the controversy over content versus criterion versus construct validity in employment tests also view the three as separable entities rather than on a continuum and fail to cite or even recognize the work of psychologists who have urged a more sophisticated approach to validation analysis. It has been suggested that the term *construct-referenced* validity (Messick, 1975) would more precisely encompass almost all discrete and specialized validation terms, integrating content relevance and content coverage as well as predictive and diagnostic utility. "The bridge or unifying theme that permits this integration is the meaningfulness of interpretability of the test scores, which is the goal of the construct validation process [Messick, 1980, p. 1015]."

In 1982, the Supreme Court had the opportunity to review the EEOC Guidelines and its implementing Questions and Answers in *Teal v. Connecticut* (1982) but carefully avoided the issue. In that case, the plaintiffs are four black provisional state employees who, when they sought to attain permanent status in their jobs as Welfare Eligibility Supervisors, were obliged to participate in a selection process requiring a passing score on a written test. Those who passed the test became part of an eligibility pool from which the state would select successful applicants. The final determinations were made on the basis of a number of nontest criteria (e.g., past work, recommendation).

All the plaintiffs failed to achieve the cutoff score of 65 on the test which would have made them eligible for further consideration. As a whole, the passing rate for blacks was 68% of that of whites. The unsuccessful plaintiffs then instituted a suit claiming that the state's use of the test violated Title VII. However, a month prior to trial, the state made its final selection, the result of which was that 23% of the eligible blacks and 13.5% of the eligible whites were promoted to supervisor. The actual promotion rate of blacks, therefore, was 169.5% of the actual promotion rate of whites. Thus, whereas the end result of the state's selection process (the so-called "bottom line") was nondiscriminatory to blacks as a class, the threshold testing component did not meet the Uniform Guidelines "four-fifths" rule, which provides that a "selection rate for any race, sex, or ethnic group which is less than [80%] of the rate for the group with the highest rate will generally be regarded . . . as evidence of adverse impact [29 C.F.R. §1607.4(c)]."

The federal district court dismissed the plaintiffs' claims, holding that they failed to prove a *prima facie* case of disparate impact. It asserted that although the ratio of the black *passing* rate to the white passing rate was 68%, the ratio of the black *appointment* rate to the white appointment rate was almost 170%. Thus, under the bottom-line approach found in the EEOC Guidelines, the plaintiffs' Title VII claim has to fail.

The plaintiffs appealed. The Court of Appeals reversed the lower court, holding that "where a plaintiff establishes that a component of a selection process produced disparate results *and* constituted a pass–fail barrier beyond which the complaining candidates were not permitted to proceed, a prima facie case of disparate impact is established, not withstanding that the entire selection procedure did not yield disparate results [*Teal v. Connecticut,* 1981, p. 135]."

In concluding that the district court was wrong in ruling results of the written examination alone were insufficient to support a *prima facie* case of disparate impact, it distinguished an earlier decision by the second circuit court. In *Kirkland v. New York State Dept. of Correctional Services* (1975), the Court of Appeals held that proof concerning disparate impact of certain subtests within a larger examination did not constitute an unlawful discriminatory impact. But, the second circuit said in *Kirkland,* all applicants were subjected to a complete selection process that, when viewed as a whole, did not produce disparate results. In *Teal,* however, the pass–fail barrier denied employment opportunity to a disproportionately large number of minorities and prevented them from proceeding to the next step in the selection process. Thus, the court concluded, affirmative action policies that may benefit minority groups as a class do not excuse employers' discriminatory conduct affecting specific and readily identifiable individuals. It held that "Title VII was designed to protect the rights of individuals" and that it "matters very little to the victimized individuals that their group as a whole is well represented in the group of hirees [pp. 139–140]."

The trial court, finding no evidence of *prima facie* discrimination, never reached the question of the test's validity (i.e., its "job-relatedness"), even though it had been fully tried before the court. However, in addition to reversing the trial court's decision, the Court of Appeals remanded the case with instructions that the lower court evaluate the test itself in light of the EEOC Guidelines.

The state of Connecticut, in June of 1981, asked the Supreme Court to review the second circuit's opinion, arguing that their decision was antagonistic to that of other circuits who had adopted the bottom-line concept in Title VII cases. The state also asserted that scrutiny of testing practices in those instances where hiring or promotion practices revealed no disparate impact would redirect employers' concerns from "the overall hiring process to the testing process, and in that sense [the federal courts would] be restructuring business practices."

The Supreme Court agreed to review the case and in June 1982 it rendered its opinion. The Court held, in a 5–4 decision, that "the 'bottom line' does not preclude . . . employees from establishing a prima facie case [of employment discrimination] nor does it provide [an] employer with a defense to such a case [*Teal v. Connecticut,* 1982, p. 2529]." The Court reminded employers that Section 703(a)(2) spoke not in terms of jobs and promotions but of limitations and classifications that would deprive individuals of employment opportunities. Thus, "when an employer uses a non-job-related barrier to deny a minority or woman applicant employment or promotion, and that barrier has a significant adverse effect on minorities or women, then the applicant has been deprived of an employment *opportunity* 'because of . . . race, color, religion, sex, or national origin' [p. 2532]." Therefore, Title VII protects individuals, not groups prohibiting victims of a facially discriminatory policy to be told that they have not been wronged simply because other persons of their race or sex were hired: "Every *individual* employee is protected against both discriminatory treatment and against practices that are fair in form, but discriminatory in operation. . ." [p. 2535] [emphasis added]."

As a result, the Court refused to permit employers to claim as a defense in disparate impact cases that discriminatory, non-job-related tests that serve as a pass–fail barrier to employment opportunities are permissible because the tests did not actually deprive disproportionate numbers of blacks of promotions. "It is clear," the Court asserted, "that Congress never intended to give an employer license to discriminate against some employees on the bias of race or sex merely because he favorably treats other members of the employees' groups [p. 2535]."

The dissenters, led by Justice Powell, speaking for the Chief Justice and Justices Rehnquist and O'Connor, agreed that the aim of Title VII was to protect individuals, not groups. But, they interpreted disparate impact claims to require proof of discrimination to groups. The dissenting opinion argued that prior cases had made it clear that discriminatory impact claims cannot be based on how an individual is treated because those claims are necessarily based on whether the group fares less well than other groups under a policy, practice, or test. The dissent warned that the majority's holding could "force employers either to eliminate tests or rely on expensive, job-related, testing procedures, the validity of which may or may not be sustained if challenged. For state and local governmental employers with limited funds, the practical effect of today's decision may well be the adoption of simple quota hiring [p. 2540]." Moreover, it cautioned, substantially fewer minority candidates ultimately could be hired simply by employers integrating consideration of test results into one overall hiring decision because, by so doing, "they will be free to select *only* the number of minority candidates proportional to their representation in the workforce [p. 2540 n.8].''

All these decisions reveal that the issue of test bias is complex and controversial and that opinions concerning its existence are contradictory. Several models of test bias, particularly with regard to its effect on prediction and selection, have been offered (Jensen, 1980; Peterson & Novick, 1976), none of which seem to have gained favor over others. As Ysseldyke (1978) recently commented:

> Several investigators have reviewed the models of test fairness and have concluded that there is little agreement among the several models. It is readily apparent that major measurement experts have been essentially *unable* to agree on a definition of a fair test, let alone identify a test that is fair for members of different groups. There is little agreement on the *concept* of nondiscriminatory assessment [p. 150].

Definitions of test bias may not only be "widely disparate," stemming "from entirely different universes of discourse [Schmidt & Hunter, 1974, p. 1]" but ethical positions regarding test bias may be "irreconcilable [Hunter & Schmidt, 1976, p. 1069]." Finally, and perhaps more importantly, reliance on psychometric models for test bias without consideration of the social and ethical consequences of test use ignores the concerns of significant segments of society. Although the American Psychological Association Ad Hoc Committee Report on the Educational Uses of Tests with Disadvantaged Students (Cleary et al., 1975) defended the technical adequacy of tests for prediction and selection, it failed to consider what minority groups charge was the egregious misuse of tests having a negative impact on the lives of minorities (Bernal, 1975; Jackson, 1975). As Reschly (1979) points out: "to defend tests on the basis of evidence of common regression systems or to attempt to separate the issues of technical adequacy from the social consequences is insufficient [p. 235]." In that light, recent attempts to examine the ethical, legal, and social implications of various models of test bias are valuable additions to the literature (Cole, 1981; Hunter & Schmidt, 1976; Messick, 1980; Novick & Ellis, 1977; Reynolds, 1982). In essence, even the selection of a model to measure and ameliorate test bias is ultimately a value judgment (Kaplan, 1982).

PSYCHOLOGISTS AND PUBLIC POLICY

My complaints about the Supreme Court should not deflect responsibility from psychologists. I think it may be legitimate to place at least part of the fault for the current and continuing confusion concerning tests on psychologists themselves. One of the more intriguing aspects of Judge Grady's decision in *PASE v. Hannon*

(1980) was his almost utter rejection of the testimony of expert psychologists who testified either for the black children challenging the IQ tests or for the school system seeking to defend them. In a quote that I think deserves some thought he said:

> None of the witnesses in this case has so impressed me with his or her credibility or expertise that I would feel secure in basing a decision simply on his or her opinion. In some instances, I am satisfied that the opinions expressed are more the result of doctrinaire commitment to a preconceived idea than they are the result of scientific inquiry. I need something more than the conclusions of witnesses in order to arrive at my own conclusion [p. 836].

Several years ago Cronbach (1975) warned psychologists involved in testing issues not to be advocates. But, far too often they have testified *for* one side or the other. Although psychologists perform a valuable service when they testify as expert witnesses, they should be aware that their data, interpretations, and opinions will be tested in the crucible of courtroom cross-examination whose very purpose is to destroy credibility and evoke evidence of bias on the part of the expert. Whereas the distillation of that process may yield testimony of great consequence and weight to the court, it can be highly anxiety provoking for the psychologist who acts as an injudicious advocate pleading for a position rather than as a cautious, neutral scientist presenting data in an even-handed manner.

Recently, concerned psychologists have indicated the many ways social scientists can influence public policy effectively (Bersoff, 1983; DeLeon, O'Keefe, Vandenbos, & Kraut, 1982; Horowitz & Katz, 1975; Loftus & Monahan, 1980; Saks, 1978). Within the bounds of scientific and professional ethics, that is an important, if not crucial, role. But, if psychologists are to be respected by the courts and treated as more than mere numerologists attempting to convince the judiciary of doctrinaire positions, they must offer more situation-specific, ecologically valid, objective data that serve science, not a particular adversary. In that way, perhaps, courts may finally arrive at not only judically sound but psychometrically justified decisions that will withstand both appellate and scientific scrutiny.

ACKNOWLEDGMENTS

One receives invitations to prestigious conferences like this only after one has written a great deal on a particular topic. Unfortunately, by the time the invitation arrives, the writer has said almost everything he or she has to say. I am afraid this is true about this chapter. Although I have tried to be original, much of the material is based on prior publications, most especially Bersoff (1979, 1981, 1982a, 1982b).

REFERENCES

American Psychological Association, American Educational Research Association, & National Council on Measurement in Education. *Standards for educational and psychological tests.* Washington, D.C.: American Psychological Association, 1974.

Anastasi, A. *Psychological testing* (4th ed.). N.Y.: Macmillan, 1976.

Bernal, E. A response to "Educational uses of tests with disadvantaged students." *American Psychologist,* 1975, *30,* 93–95.

Bersoff, D. Regarding psychologists testily: Legal regulation of psychological assessment in the public schools. *Maryland Law Review,* 1979, *39,* 27–120.

Bersoff, D. Testing and the law. *American Psychologist,* 1981, *36,* 1047–1056.

Bersoff, D. *Larry P.* and *PASE:* Judicial report cards on the validity of individual intelligence tests. In T. Kratochwill (ed.), *Advances in school psychology* (vol. 2). Hillsdale, N.J.: Lawrence Erlbaum Associates, 1982. (a)

Bersoff, D. The legal regulation of school psychology. In C. Reynolds & T. Gutkin (Eds.), *The handbook of school psychology.* New York: Wiley, 1982. (b)

Bersoff, D. Children as participants in psychoeducational assessment. In G. Melton, G. Koocher, & M. Saks (Eds.), *Children's competence to consent.* New York: Plenum, 1983.

Cahn, E. Jurisprudence. *New York University Law Review,* 1955, *30,* 150–169.

Chapman, L., & Chapman, J. Illusory correlations as a obstacle to the use of valid psychodiagnostic signs. *Journal of Abnormal Psychology,* 1969, *74,* 271–280.

Clark, K. Racial justice in education: Continuing struggle in a new era. *Howard Law Journal,* 1980, *23,* 93–106.

Cleary, A., Humphreys, L., Kendrick, S., & Wesman, A. Educational uses of tests with disadvantaged students. *American Psychologist,* 1975, *30,* 15–41.

Cole, N. Bias in testing. *American Psychologist,* 1981, *36,* 1067–1077.

Comment. Psychologist as expert witness: Science in the courtroom? *Maryland Law Review,* 1978, *38,* 539–621.

Cronbach, L. Five decades of public controversy over mental testing. *American Psychologist,* 1975, *30,* 1–14.

DeLeon, P., O'Keefe, A., Vandenbos, G., & Kraut, A. How to influence public policy: A blueprint for activism. *American Psychologist,* 1982, *37,* 476–485.

Dubois, B. A test-dominated society: China, 1115 B.C.–1905 A.D. In A. Anastasi (Ed.), *Testing problems in perspective.* Washington, D.C.: American Council on Education, 1966.

Equal Employment Opportunity Commission, Civil Service Commission, Department of Labor, & Department of Justice. Adoption by four agencies of Uniform Guidelines on Employee Selection Procedures. *Federal Register,* 1978, *43,* 38920–39315.

Equal Employment Opportunity Commission, Office of Personnel Management, Department of Justice, Department of Labor, & Department of the Teasury. Adoption of questions and answers to clarify and provide a common interpretation of the Uniform Guidelines on Employee Section Procedures. *Federal Register,* 1979, *44,* 11996–12009.

Flaugher, R. The many definitions of test bias. *American Psychologist,* 1978, *33,* 671–679.

Gass, R., & Bersoff, D. *Psychologist as expert witness: Taking a stand.* (Manuscript submitted for publication).

Green, B. In defense of measurement. *American Psychologist,* 1978, *33,* 664–670.

Guion, R. On trinitarian doctrines of validity. *Professional Psychology,* 1980, *11,* 385–398.

Haney, W. Validity, vaudeville, and values. *American Psychologist,* 1981, *36,* 1021–1034.

Horowitz, J., & Katz, J. *Social science and public policy in the United States.* New York: Praeger, 1975.

Hunter, J., & Schmidt, F. Critical analysis of the statistical and ethical implications of various definitions of test bias. *Psychological Bulletin,* 1976, *83,* 1053–1071.

Jackson, G. On the report of the Ad Hoc Committee on Educational Tests with Disadvantaged Students: Another psychological view from the Association of Black Psychologists. *American Psychologist,* 1975, *30,* 88–92.

Jensen, A. How much can we boost IQ and scholastic achievement? *Harvard Educational Review,* 1969, *39,* 1–123.

Jensen, A. *Bias in mental testing.* New York: Free Press, 1980.

Kaplan, R. Nader's raid on the testing industry. *American Psychologist,* 1982, *37,* 15–23.

Kirp, D. Schools as sorters: The constitutional and policy implications of student classification. *University of Pennsylvania Law Review,* 1973, *121,* 705–797.

Kluger, R. *Simple justice: The history of Brown v. Board of Education and black America's struggle for equality.* New York: Knopf, 1976.

Levin, B. School desegregation remedies and the role of social science research. *Law and Contemporary Problems,* 1978, *42,* 1–36.

Loftus, E., & Monahan, J. Trial by data: Psychological research as legal evidence. *American Psychologist.* 1980, *35,* 270–283.

McClelland, D. Testing for competence rather than for intelligence. *American Psychologist,* 1973, *28,* 1–14.

Messick, S. The standard problem: Meaning and values in measurement and evaluation. *American Psychologist,* 1975, *30,* 955–966.

Messick, S. Test validity and the ethics of assessment. *American Psychologist,* 1980, *35,* 1012–1027.

Monahan, J. *The clinical prediction of violent behavior.* Washington, D.C.: NIMH, 1981.

Novick, M. Federal guidelines and professional standards. *American Psychologist,* 1981, *36,* 1035–1046.

Novick, M., & Ellis, D. Equal opportunity in educational employment selection. *American Psychologist,* 1977, *32,* 306–320.

Oakland, T., & Matuszek, P. Using tests in nondiscriminatory assessment. In T. Oakland (Ed.), *Psychological and educational assessment of minority children.* New York: Brunner/Mazel, 1977.

Peterson, N., & Novick, M. An evaluation of some models for culture-fair selection. *Journal of Education Measurement,* 1976, *13,* 3–29.

Reschly, D. Nonbiased assessment. In G. Phye & D. Reschly (Eds.), *School psychology: Perspective and issues.* New York: Academic Press, 1979.

Reschly, D. Psychological evidence in the Larry P. opinion: A case of right problem—wrong solution? *School Psychology Review,* 1980, *9,* 123–135.

Reubhausen, D., & Brim, O. Privacy and behavioral research. *Columbia Law Review,* 1965, *65,* 1184–1215.

Reynolds, C. The problem of bias in psychological assessment. In C. Reynolds & T. Gutkin (Eds.), *The handbook of school psychology.* New York: Wiley, 1982.

Saks, M. Social psychological contributions to a legislative subcommittee on organ and tissue transplants. *American Psychologist,* 1978, *33,* 690–690.

Sandoval, J. The WISC-R and internal evidence of test bias and minority groups. *Journal of Consulting and Clinical Psychology,* 1979, *47,* 919–927.

Schmidt, F., & Hunter, J. Racial and ethnic bias in psychological tests: Divergent implications of two definitions of test bias. *American Psychologist,* 1974, *29,* 1–8.

Tenopyr, M. Content-construct confusion. *Personnel Psychologist,* 1977, *30,* 47–54.

Udell, R. Personal communication with *APA Monitor,* Nov. 1, 1980.

Wigdor, A. Psychological testing and the law of employment discrimination. In A. Wigdor & W. Garner (Eds.), *Ability testing: Uses, consequences, and controversies.* Washington, D.C.: National Academy of Sciences, 1982.

Ysseldyke, J. Implementing the "Protection in Evaluation Procedures" provisions of Public Law 94–142. In L. Morra (Ed.), *Developing criteria for the evaluation of protection in evaluation procedures provisions.* Washington, D.C.: Bureau of Education of the Handicapped, 1978.

Ziskin, J. *Coping with psychiatric and psychological testimony.* (3d ed.). Beverly Hills, Calif.: Law and Psychology Press, 1981.

6 Testing and the Oscar Buros Lament: From Knowledge to Implementation to Use

James V. Mitchell, Jr., Director
Buros Institute of Mental Measurements

The field of measurement can be conceptualized as having three different but interrelated aspects. First of all, it is a science or a body of knowledge concerned with the development of theory and methodology and with the identification and confirmation of generalizations governing interrelationships among variables appropriate to its content. Measurement theory and its application to measurement problems are important contributors here. Second, it is an applied science or technology concerned with the development of products that represent a useful application of such a science or body of knowledge. For the field of measurement, test development and validation are important exemplars. Third, it is a body of information concerned with why, when, and how these products are used, and the results of such use, in the practical measurement setting for which they were typically intended. This sequence of interrelated aspects of measurement, from knowledge to implementation to use, is the conceptual foundation for much of what follows.

Within such a context as that just described, the Buros Institute of Mental Measurements has always played a unique role. The science of measurement or measurement theory has not been one of the Institute's chief concerns, although the Institute is often an indirect beneficiary of such contributions. However, the Institute has had major involvement with the evaluation of test products, the products of an applied science, and with the education of test users in the more effective selection and use of those products. Because of the nature of this involvement, the Institute has had a perspective on the three separate aspects of the field of measurement that is not typical of those representing only the singular aspects of the continuum. It is this unique perspective of the Institute that will serve as the distinguishing feature of the discussion to follow.

The purpose of this discussion is to evaluate critically the contributions and progress made in these separate, but interrelated, aspects of measurement: knowledge, implementation, and use. The theme of this discussion is that the greatest progress has been made in our knowledge, lesser progress in implementation, and the very least progress in selection and effective use. The implication of the discussion is that there is a pressing need to redress the imbalance that has developed.

MEASUREMENT THEORY AND KNOWLEDGE

No one can accuse the field of measurement of being static. Ferment seems to be the rule. With this ferment has come new theories and models, controversy that sometimes yields as much light as heat, new understanding, and some fresh perspectives. Although it typically seems that activity has been greater than results, the results themselves show evidence of progress. Two of the more recent reviews of test theory (Subkoviak & Baker, 1978; Weiss & Davison, 1981) both devoted considerable attention to criterion-referenced testing, latent-trait theory, and issues of test bias. Another recent review devoted entirely to latent-trait theories (Traub & Wolfe, 1981) described the promise of latent-trait theories in their application to educational measurement but also issued a caveat about work to date and needed precautions. The overall impression obtained from these reviews is that criterion-referenced testing, latent-trait theory, and test bias have received the attention deserved from an able group of professionals and that some relevant problems have been addressed, development has occurred, and progress has been and will continue to be made. A similar reassurance is felt with the more central role accorded to construct validity evidence in all areas of testing, the attention given to problems with minimum competency testing and the setting of standards, and the development of adaptive testing in relation to its needed theoretical underpinnings. The influence of cognitive psychology on testing has also been beneficial and holds important promise for the future. All in all, psychometric theory and knowledge seem to be active, developing, productive enterprises that will continue to furnish strong and supportive bases for the technology of testing and the wise selection and effective use of tests. The foundation is promising; whether its promise will be paralleled by equal promise in the technology or applied science it supports, or in the intelligent utilization of that technology by its consumers, is the critical question to which we now turn.

TEST TECHNOLOGY AND THE CHALLENGE OF
IMPLEMENTATION

In comparison with the relatively strong showing of psychometric theory and knowledge, the application of that theory and knowledge to the development and validation of commercially published tests has produced mixed results at best. In

The Seventh Mental Measurements Yearbook (1972) and again in *The Eighth Mental Measurements Yearbook* (1978), Oscar Buros, after describing the "crusading" or "missionary" objectives of the *Yearbooks*, complained that:

> Our success in attaining the last five missionary objectives has been disappointingly modest. Test publishers continue to market tests which do not begin to meet the standards of the rank and file of MMY and journal reviewers. At least half of the tests currently on the market should never have been published [Buros, 1972, p. XXVII; 1978, p. XXXI].

These are harsh words; yet as one who has followed Oscar Buros as Institute director and editor of the *Yearbooks*, it is difficult to find fault with his statement even now. The situation is a curious mixture of positives and negatives. On the one hand, there is little doubt that some of the major test publishers employ extremely able measurement specialists who have had much impact, for example, on translating new developments like latent-trait theory into practice in the construction of new tests. On the other hand, there is much of the cottage industry ambience to the test publishing business, and there are many test publishers who are simply test authors distributing their own tests or very small test publishers with single or extremely limited test offerings or book or instructional materials publishers who have acquired a few tests and publish them in a manner almost incidental to their major interest and thrust. Of the 496 test publishers that are listed in *Tests in Print II* (Buros, 1974), it is startling to discover that over one-half, or 58%, have only a single test listed; 75% have three or fewer tests listed; and 85% have five or fewer tests listed. The 58% who have but one test listed account for only 11% of the tests published. The 85% who have one to five tests listed account for only 16% of the tests published. Although Buros may have missed tests published by some companies, the Buros reputation for accuracy cannot be denied, and the overall impression is doubtlessly correct. On the other end of the continuum, where the large test companies predominate, a mere 1.4% of the publishers are responsible for publishing 26% of the tests! Teachers of measurement looking for strikingly skewed distributions need look no further. With a publishing field as skewed and fragmented as this, there is little wonder that Oscar Buros often despaired about the likelihood of improved quality control.

Quality Issues in Test Publishing

Limitations of size and resources are quite likely to influence quality control despite the efforts of a small test entrepreneur to meet or exceed minimal standards and produce a professional product. One president of a small operation lamented that:

> We are a very small cooperative venture with quite limited resources. For this reason we have as yet not been able to move to a professional finish on the

_____ , _____ , and _____ manuals. However, in spite of typos and home-grown typing each of the rough drafts gives ample information to permit an assessment of the instruments. They have continued to prove themselves in actual use. For this reason I am forwarding additional copies of the forms and manuals (rough or otherwise). None of the manuals are "finished." We will revise them as information and funds permit.

This is an instance where the spirit is willing but the funds are weak. There are other instances where the markedly skewed distribution of sizes and resources of test publishers reported earlier seem to be accompanied by a parallel marked skewness in the demonstration of psychometric savvy. The president of one test publishing company, after expressing considerable resistance to our request for complimentary test materials for review, stated that the company:

> was highly critical about present methods used for determining the reliability and validity of a psychometric tool. For example, often the concept of concurrent validity is used to determine if a particular test is a valuable tool. Actually what this means is that one or the other tool is unnecessary because they are virtually measuring the same thing. If the correlation is not significant, we know that we are measuring some aspect of behavior not currently being tapped. Buros, however, chose to use this lack of correlation as a reason to reject or criticize a test.

Aside from the fact that Buros let the reviews and reviewers speak for themselves, the statement contains much that would cause concern if not apoplexy among contemporary measurement specialists. Another company divides its tests into those that have validity evidence and those that do not. One wonders what kind of reassurance this provides to its clients!

Some Evidence on Test Quality

If we move from the level of specific examples to the more generic, it is regrettably true that there are still a surprising number of tests that are published without reliability evidence, validity evidence, or norms. When this occurs, it has been and will continue to be the practice of the Buros Institute to point out this critical lack in the descriptive entry accompanying the reviews in the *Mental Measurements Yearbook*. A small descriptive study was recently conducted by Institute personnel to determine how often these critical data were lacking. The results are not encouraging. They showed that 22% of the tests listed in *The Eighth Mental Measurements Yearbook* (1978) were without any reliability data whatever; 8½% had no validity data whatever; 7% had neither reliability nor validity data; and an additional 1% had neither reliability nor validity data for certain parts, levels, or editions. Another 5% had no reliability data for certain scores, and 9% had no reliability data for certain grades, subtests, or forms. All together, some 41% of the tests listed in *The Eighth Mental Measurements Yearbook* were lacking reliability and/or validity data in some important respect.

Tests in the areas of reading, vocations, and speech and hearing were the worst offenders.

The data for norms were somewhat better but still not encouraging. Of the tests listed in *The Eighth Mental Measurement Yearbook,* 11% had no norms whatever. Another 3% had no norms for certain scores, and 8% had norms only for certain subtests, forms, or parts of the standardization population. One percent had no description of the normative population, and for 4 percent the norms consisted only of means and standard deviations. All told, some 28% of the tests listed in *The Eighth Mental Measurements Yearbook* were inadequately normed in some important respect.

It should not be concluded that the 41% of tests lacking in validity and/or reliability data or the 28% lacking in normative data were the result of very rigorous criteria applied by the Buros Institute. As a matter of fact, any kind of correlation coefficient would usually serve to remove the accusing statement for either reliability or validity, and the situation for normative data was equally charitable. The standards for declaring such inadequacies in the descriptive entries were minimal at best, and still many of the tests listed in the *8th MMY* made an unhappy showing. If 41% of the tests listed in the *8th MMY* were lacking in validity and/or reliability data and 28% were lacking in normative data, was Oscar Buros far wrong in asserting that at least half of the tests currently on the market should never have been published?

Some Affirmations

To consider the implementation of test theory and knowledge in actual test products is a frustrating exercise in the reconciliation of opposites. On the one hand, one observes the amazing rapidity with which a complex development like latent-trait theory has been seized by the test constructor and incorporated into instruments like the British Ability Scales; on the other hand, one observes 41% of the tests in the *8th MMY* lacking in the simplest kinds of reliability and validity data. Test manuals seem to be improving and more technical manuals are being offered, many of them well conceived and executed; yet there are still commercially published tests that have no manual, an inadequate manual, or instructions for administration masquerading as a manual. *American Psychologist* (Glaser & Bond, 1981) issued a special edition on testing that provides abundant evidence of continuing progress and sophistication in the field of measurement and its application; yet there are some reading and personality tests and diagnostic inventories whose authors appear never to have seen the inside of an elementary measurement text. Because of the makeup of the testing industry, such contradictions are likely to exist for the foreseeable future.

In the face of such contradictions one could argue a good case for applying some minimum competency criteria to the testing industry itself! In any event, it seems clear that the number of poor or marginal tests could be substantially reduced if a climate of opinion could be created for both test developers and users that would ensure a severe fiscal disadvantage for the test author or publisher who did not meet certain minimal criteria. Specific problem areas are summarized below.

1. Proliferation of Tests.   There is a finite amount of money that will be spent on tests, especially with current economic conditions and current attitudes toward testing. Under these circumstances we must do whatever we can in the future to ensure that it will be in the best interests of test authors and publishers, reputationally and fiscally, to publish far fewer tests but much better tests. This was the rallying cry of Oscar Buros for over 40 years, and the years have not diminished its truth or urgency. The proliferation of tests continues unabated, however, and the best defense seems to be that of educating people to be more discriminating test users. Obviously the Institute of Mental Measurements has a critical role here and so do the teachers of measurement. But the amount of money still spent on poor and marginal tests, and the startling amounts of money acquired from the sale of such tests, suggest that we are probably losing ground rather than gaining.

2. Missing Reliability Information.   The fact that 22% of the tests in the *8th MMY* were without reliability data is alarming and absolutely without justification. We have to find better ways to prevent or discourage a test author or publisher from publishing and accepting payment for an instrument that suffers from such a basic deficiency. Consumer protection for a gullible testing public is far behind consumer protection in other areas.

3. Inadequate Validity Evidence.   It was reported earlier that some tests are published without any validity evidence. More often, however, validity evidence is insufficient and flimsy and offered more as a ritual than to make a firm case. We have reached a point in measurement where many measurement specialists feel that all or most validity evidence is properly subsumed under the concept of construct validity. The determination of construct validity requires the marshalling of a comprehensive and integrated set of evidence that is no less demanding than the scientific method itself. We should increasingly insist that test authors and publishers meet these more comprehensive criteria of validity evidence. There is a long way to go from flimsy, halfhearted evidence offered as ritual to construct validity evidence meeting the basic tenets of construct definition and validation in scientific method. This further requirement, however, could be very beneficial in encouraging improvement in the quality of commercially published tests and further reducing the number of poor and marginal tests.

4. Publishers' Claims vis-à-vis Validity Evidence.   Measurement professionals should increasingly insist that test authors and publishers bring test validity and putative test benefits into a more reasonable relationship with one another. Often it seems that modest to weak validity evidence is offered but is somehow shunted aside into insignificance by an attitude and aura that implies far more benefits emanating from the test than is justified by the evidence. Many examples could be offered, but a case in point is the Common Examinations of the National Teacher Examinations (NTE). A review of seven studies relating the Weighted Common Examination score with ratings given by principals and supervisors during the first year of teaching revealed a median correlation of .11. Although attenuation could be a factor here, particularly with respect to the criterion, the evidence is hardly encouraging. But the publisher can and does maintain that the NTE is a measure of academic preparation only, and thus the validity issue can be at least partially sidestepped. The public most likely assumes that effective teaching is a simple function of knowledge attained, cares and understands little about the technical aspects of validity issues, and thus uncritically accepts the NTE into its belief system as a guardian of teaching standards. The practical result is that 50% of U.S. teachers college graduates took the NTE in 1980–1981 and nine states now use the NTE as part of the teacher certification process. An overstatement of test benefits, either explicit or implicit, in the face of weak evidence and a public inclination to believe, will not serve us well at a time when test critics are mounting new and more knowledgeable attacks on the industry and the profession. The tendency to promote test utility despite weak validity evidence is surely an obstacle to better understanding and another potential source of public backlash as well.

THE BOTTOM LINE: THE SELECTION AND EFFECTIVE USE OF TESTS

If the application of test theory and knowledge to the development and validation of commercially published tests has produced some mixed results, the actual use of tests in practical settings has departed even further from the ideal. In the Introduction to *The Eighth Mental Measurements Yearbook,* Oscar Buros (1978) defined five objectives of the *Yearbook,* in his own inimitable manner, as his "crusading" objectives. The three crusading objectives that related to users of tests were as follows:

1. To foster in test users a greater awareness of both the values and limitations involved in the use of standardized tests.
2. To suggest more discerning methods to test users of arriving at their own appraisals of tests in light of their particular values and needs.
3. To make test users aware of the importance of being suspicious of all tests—even those produced by well-known authors and publishers—which are not accompanied by detailed data on their construction, validation, uses, and limitations [p. XXXI].

As reported earlier, Buros felt that his success in attaining all his crusading objectives, including these three, was "disappointingly modest." It could be of some use now to take each of these objectives and see what they highlight with respect to current standards and practices of test usage.

In relation to the first objective, what can be said about the level of awareness of the rank-and-file test user about the values and limitations of current standardized tests? Buros felt that we have gone through too many periods of "unwarranted optimism" about standardized tests (Buros, 1978, p. 1973). Although some segments of the public may have unwarranted optimism and a lack of appreciation about the limitations of standardized tests, there is some recent evidence that this is not true of teachers and administrators in the public schools. In a study reported by Salmon-Cox (1981), it was found that teachers, when questioned about how they assessed the progress of their students, most frequently mentioned "observation" as their principal tool. Test scores served a merely confirmatory role to observation; a child's classroom performance, as observed, was given more credence than a test score. In another report in the same series, Resnick (1981) summarized the Salmon-Cox results by suggesting that: "Tests are, quite simply, a natural feature of the U.S. educational environment; it appears that teachers and administrators have adjusted to their presence, neither desiring much benefit from them nor suffering much distress as a result of them [p. 624]."

This certainly seems to suggest rather strongly that teachers are not overly impressed with standardized tests or ignorant of their limitations. They may even be hard pressed to appreciate their values. Unwarranted optimism about tests surely exists, but it is not likely to be found in the rank and file of teachers who must administer the tests and interpret the scores.

In relation to the second Buros objective, what can we say about the methods test users employ in their appraisals of tests? It is difficult to find helpful or trustworthy data on this question, but it seems safe to say that there has been little improvement in the sophistication of methods used to select tests. Perhaps there is a more general understanding of how achievement test objectives and content should match curriculum objectives and content, and perhaps some large school districts with testing offices use the more "discerning methods" referred to by Buros. But despite all the efforts of teachers of measurement and the Buros Institute, test appraisal and selection in the field has still far to go before it becomes the cautious, systematic, methodologically sound process that measurement specialists want it to be.

In relation to the third Buros objective, concerned with the "suspicious" attitudes test users should have in the absence of data on test construction, validation, uses, and limitations, the best available evidence seems to indicate that many test users may not be interested enough to *be* suspicious. This conclusion, obviously, is quite congruent with the Resnick (1981) quotation reported earlier. If they are interested enough to exercise some careful judgment or show some suspicion, that judgment or suspicion seems quickly allayed by the cosmetic assurance of face validity evidence that seems compelling to many who have the strong will to believe in the absence of substantive evidence. "If it looks good, use it," is not a consciously palatable slogan to most people, but it must be an unconscious determinant for many people in the selection of tests or we wouldn't observe so many poor tests being purchased. At the Buros Institute we are continually amazed at how much money a poor test can make. For example, we received word some months ago that one such test, with little to commend it, was responsible for sales amounting to 5 million dollars in 2 years.

Perhaps part of the problem here is that the criteria for determining whether a test is useful or not are all bound up with that esoteric body of thought called *psychometric theory,* which is available and valued by the specialist but seems downright forbidding and scary for those uninitiated or of uncertain understanding. If a person looks for a new car, the criteria for what constitutes a good car are reasonably within reach and understandable. For tests those criteria are enmeshed in a scientism that for some people might as well be mysticism, with a jargon that seems sufficiently repelling to some to justify ignoring it. Is it any wonder, then, that it is the face validity features of a test that can so often commend the test's use to a potential purchaser and just as often mislead that purchaser after use to believe that the test did in fact yield the results desired?

Perceptions of the General Public about Tests

It is probably in that vast body called the *general public* where the threat of misunderstanding about tests is greatest and where a little suspicion, or at least a questioning attitude, might be a good thing. Resnick (1981) reports on a 1979 Gallup Poll that indicated that 81% of those polled thought that standardized tests were "useful" or "somewhat useful," with only 17% thinking they were "not too useful." Yet it is this same general public that is likely to be least informed and most confused about testing. Such confusion, lack of information, or evident misinformation has become a critical factor with such issues as bias in testing, minimum competency testing, and evaluation of the public schools. A vague conviction that something is useful combined with a lack of specific understanding about its most appropriate uses and interpretations and no conception of its limitations is a recipe for social disaster. Testing in the public domain has become such a social disaster. One feels it keenly when called upon, as I have been, to participate in briefings to the public about the proper uses and the limitations of tests and testing. One feels it keenly again when two federal district judges in California and Illinois reach diametrically different judgments about whether standardized intelligence tests discriminate against black children, with little evidence that either one of them had an adequate understanding, or cared to obtain such an understanding, of the psychometric issues involved (*Larry P. v. Riles,* 1979; *PASE v. Hannon,* 1980).

It is clear that the opportunity for the general public to raise its level of understanding about testing is even more limited than it is for public school personnel or people in business and industry. As professional people with both a moral as well as professional responsibility for our field, I do not believe we can ignore the public's need for greater understanding of testing without even graver social consequences in the future. If continuing education and lifelong learning are to be as important as some higher education specialists think, I suggest that we do our part to ensure that increased understanding about tests and testing is promoted as a critical component of such lifelong learning. How that is to be done is an issue that deserves the very careful consideration of every person in measurement.

Vocational Tests for Business and Industry

An area of special concern about test usage is the area of vocational tests for business and industry. Recently the Buros Institute conducted a study on who purchased the *Mental Measurement Yearbooks,* and we were surprised to find that the group that purchased the most yearbooks was not education but business and industry, which accounted for almost half of the yearbooks sold. We are grateful for that, because it has often appeared to us that it is tests for business and industry, among all others, that are most likely to be promoted with very strong promises in the face of little or no evidence that the tests can deliver on those promises. Such ambitious and poorly substantiated claims sorely need the antidote that critical reviews from the *Yearbooks* can provide. Many tests in business, particularly those in the management area, involve elaborate conceptual schemes, sometimes associated with training programs, that are magnificent in their aspirations and complexity and attractiveness to would-be true believers. Such conceptual schemes would constitute ideal settings for obtaining construct validity evidence, but you can bet your entrepreneurial dollar that there is little effort to do that in the great majority of cases. It would likely prove too embarrassing. What happens instead is that these tests for business and industry are among the most serious offenders when it comes to the simplest kinds of validity evidence, let alone construct validity evidence, and we have found that 57% of the "Vocations" tests listed in *The Eighth Mental Measurements Yearbook* were lacking reliability and/or validity data in some way that was important for test use.

Test use in business and industry, of course, is coming under the increasingly heavy fire directed toward tests in general. As a result of this double vulnerability stemming from inadequate psychometric evidence and potential criticism or even litigation, some test publishers show resistance to providing the Buros Institute with the complimentary copies of tests needed for review purposes. Fortunately, they remain a distinct minority. One test publisher, for example, was reluctant to provide complimentary copies of his tests for fear that the reviews of these tests "might be used as 'authoritative' evidence in a discrimination suit." He then went on to say that:

> No test's technical report is so comprehensive or so perfect that it cannot be adversely criticized.
>   It seems to me that we have an obligation to our test users to avoid providing plaintiffs with ready-made attack weapons which appear to have the prestige of the Buros Institute behind them.

What interesting questions this raises, especially in relation to the concerns with "obligation" raised in this letter. In a recent article on professional standards in testing Novick (1981) pointed out that "There are generally three participants in the ability testing process: the institution, or *test user*, which requires the test for some decision-making purpose; the *test producer*, which develops, markets, and/or administers and scores the test; and the *test taker*, who takes the test by choice, direction, or necessity [p. 1035]." Any reasonable set of professional standards would have to take into consideration issues of obligation to all three of these parties, but particularly to the *test taker*, who is still the least powerful of the three. The Buros Institute has an obligation to be fair to all three parties involved while providing consumer protection to the test user and the test taker. Although no test is so perfect that it cannot be criticized, it is only the nonexistence or glaring inadequacy of reliability or validity data that can furnish the ready-made attack weapons referred to in this letter, and under such circumstances it is the test producer, not the Buros Institute, that has fashioned the weapons and handed them over to the attacker. The best defense for the test user is to select tests that are well-constructed and validated and that can stand the light of day and not to rely on test companies that have an understandable but misplaced motivation to protect the user from test inadequacies that would be avoided altogether by not using the test.

Test Advertising

A very great influence on test selection and usage is test advertising, and it is test advertising that constitutes one of the greatest current concerns of the Buros Institute. It was reported earlier that Oscar Buros was concerned about "unwarranted optimism" about tests; it is in test advertising that "unwarranted optimism" reaches its peak. Good and poor tests alike are subjected to advertising claims that cannot be substantiated. The influence of such advertising is considerable, and the situation now is no different than it was in 1968 when Oscar Buros, in a presentation to the Association for Measurement and Evaluation in Guidance, reported the following:

> At present, no matter how poor a test may be, if it is nicely packaged and if it promises to do all sorts of things which no test can do, the test will find many

gullible buyers. When we initiated critical test reviewing in *The 1938 Yearbook,* we had no idea how difficult it would be to discourage the use of poorly constructed tests of unknown validity. Even the better informed test users who finally become convinced that a widely used test had no validity after all are likely to rush to use a new instrument which promises far more than any good test can possibly deliver [p. 94].

The appeals to gullible buyers still ring loud and clear. A diagnostic–prescriptive reading program is described as "so effective a system that it's been known to actually improve reading level by one year in only 11 to 12 one hour lessons!" A personality inventory is described as "the quintessential assessment tool for the 80s and beyond—the wave of the future among diagnostic instruments." The same kind of extravagant advertising mania also affects scoring and interpretive services. A reviewer of several of the scoring and interpretive services for the Minnesota Multiphasic Personality Inventory expressed his strong concern about the advertising for these services in the following excerpted comments from *The Eighth Mental Measurements Yearbook* (Adair, 1978):

In reviewing the several scoring services for this yearbook, the writer was impressed with a curious dichotomy that appears to exist between the professional psychologist who is obliged to uphold the ethics of the profession and the entrepreneurial psychologist who is obliged to make a profit in order to maintain a position in the market. . . . The dilemma of whether to uphold professional ethics or to make a profit is seen most vividly in the promotional literature of the several services. . . . The literature of promotion takes on a Madison Avenue-like quality where caveats are included in the fine print [p. 940].

Examples could be multiplied endlessly. The sins of advertising claims are so numerous that the Institute may well consider sending out test advertising to be reviewed critically right along with the tests themselves. The issue of extravagant and unfounded test advertising claims must receive much greater attention in the next revision of the *Standards for Educational and Psychological Tests.* In the face of such claims the major agents for consumer education and protection are the *Standards,* Buros Institute publications, and a few beleaguered measurement teachers. In terms of current standards of test selection and use and the continued gullibility of the test-buying public in relation to extravagant test advertising claims, even the best efforts of all of these are apparently not enough to change the situation as much as it desperately needs to be changed.

CONCLUSIONS AND RECOMMENDATIONS

This chapter has been quite different from the others with which it appears because of its concern with the interrelationships and current status and development of the entire measurement continuum as it encompasses knowledge, implementation, and use. The latter two elements are the historic concerns of the

Buros Institute. The conclusion that seems apparent from the evidence discussed is that the theory and knowledge base of measurement is strong and evolving, the implementation of that knowledge base in developed products has brought tremendous variety and very mixed results, but that the selection, use, and interpretation of tests has been fraught with major difficulties and some unfortunate social consequences. It is my strong conviction that although professionals in measurement are usually most identified with the first or possibly second element of this measurement continuum, they have a strong professional obligation to be alert to and to join with others to take action against the continuing serious offenses and mistakes that take place through ignorance at the level of test usage. Professional support for the *Standards for Educational and Psychological Tests,* especially as those *Standards* relate to test use, is one example of responsible professional concern and action in this area. But in view of the extent of the abuses and the strength of the need, it is not enough. The Buros Institute and the *Standards* cannot do it alone.

A Call to Action

What, then, can be done to stimulate substantial improvement in the selection, use, and interpretation of tests (and perhaps, as a consequence, make it unprofitable to publish poor tests)? I submit that it will require nothing less than an organized campaign, launched and sponsored by NCME or the same consortium that produced the *Standards,* that would increase substantially the public understanding about testing concepts; the values and limitations of tests; and the selection, use, and interpretation of tests. Perhaps some funds could be obtained, most likely from private philanthropies in this day and age, that could help support such a campaign. Of what would such a campaign consist? The following are illustrative:

1. Convention Programing. In our professional conventions (NCME, AERA, APA, etc.) there should be more discussion of what practical steps could be taken to improve the selection, use, and interpretation of tests. Symposia could be organized on the topic. Although the 1980 NCME meeting featured some useful examples of this kind of programing (Beck & Stetz, 1980; Crocker, 1980; Yeh & Herman, 1980), generally there is far too little of this done at the present time. Practitioners often feel isolated at professional conventions. What a fine opportunity this might provide for greater dialogue among the theory and knowledge oriented and the practitioners. Benefits could be twofold: the development of ideas for improved test usage and the increased recognition by participants of their responsibility for what happens in testing at the grass-roots level.

2. Education of the Public.   There is much talk these days about how the U.S. population is changing, how people are developing new careers and interests, and how there is more need than ever before for the implementation of a philosophy of ''lifelong learning.'' Continuing education has become an important topic and need. Why shouldn't increased understanding of measurement concepts, tests, and testing be considered an important component of continuing education or a lifelong learning program—or indeed—for citizenship education itself? As a part of such continuing education the following kinds of projects might be implemented:

a. Public television could sponsor a series of TV programs on measurement concepts and contemporary testing practices. To stimulate interest some dispassionate discussion of contemporary testing issues and controversies could be intermixed with the foundational learning of concepts. The success of the program, ''Who's Keeping Score?'', which included parts of NIE's Minimum Competency Clarification Hearing, suggests that much more could be done with the media to promote greater understanding of testing in the general public. Further prospects should be actively explored.

b. Many continuing education programs offer ''minicourses,'' typically with continuing education credit, that are designed to accomplish short-term objectives focused on the development of basic understandings, skills, or interests. Why shouldn't measurement people develop and offer such short courses not only to principals and teachers but also to the general public? When a local or national testing controversy develops, why shouldn't minicourses be developed to help the public better understand the real issues involved and the knowledge bases for intelligent decision making?

c. Perhaps the Buros Institute should develop a short pamphlet describing useful procedures and criteria for selecting a test and using and interpreting it properly. Such a pamphlet could be sold to the public at minimal cost and could also be included in the introduction to *The Mental Measurements Yearbook*. This might also be a useful project for NCME. A pamphlet of this kind would have to be much shorter and more readable than the *Standards for Educational and Psychological Testing,* which is tedious and forbidding reading at best.

d. As suggested earlier, it may well be appropriate for the Buros Institute to send out advertising as well as the test itself for review. Some bad press in response to extravagant claims might at least temper those claims and motivate those involved toward more recognition of their responsibility for their advertising as well as for their product. ''Truth-in-packaging'' is a desperate need in testing.

e. More ways should be found to reward and reinforce those test authors and publishers whose products represent high standards of construction and validation. The professional organizations provide this kind of recognition for researchers; why shouldn't test authors and publishers receive a parallel form of professional recognition? The development of a good test is a very difficult and painstaking process, and its achievement should be professionally acknowledged. The Buros Institute would like to participate in a program with such an emphasis on the positive. Perhaps our reviewers could nominate tests that they judged to be exceptional exemplars of test construction and validation, and members of our National Advisory Committee could select one or two tests from each area deserving of special commendation. Or perhaps the professional organizations would wish to provide such recognition. There are possible pitfalls in such an undertaking, of course, but a few minor risks may have to be accepted in order to accomplish what is considered just and motivating for test authors and publishers and beneficial for the field and for test users.

f. There are strong professionals in the test publishing organizations, and they are doubtlessly professionally and personally interested in being part of an organization that subscribes to the highest standards of test authorship and publication. Individuals who join professional associations are often subject to a collective code of ethics promulgated by the association. Perhaps an association like NCME should have institutional as well as individual memberships, and both individuals and organizations should be subject to such a code of ethics. Part of that code could cover professional responsibilities relevant to test development, validation, and advertising. A test publishing company that joined the professional association would have to make a written and signed commitment to the code of ethics and could indicate in its advertising that it had done so. But if any members of the professional association, or a duly constituted professional ethics committee, uncovered evidence of code violation by a test publishing organization, constitutionally defined steps could be taken to conduct a hearing in accordance with rules of evidence and ultimately, if necessary, to take action ranging from mild reprimand to ouster from the professional association. This too is a rather radical suggestion, but the epidemiology of the disease seems to require radical cures.

Scientists of any kind, whether they be natural, physical, or social scientists, are increasingly being called upon to recognize the moral and ethical implications of their work. Yet there is a tendency for many professionals in measurement to focus on the theoretical and knowledge bases of their field and to lose sight of what is going on at the levels of implementation and use. It is our business at the Buros Institute to be aware—and sometimes painfully aware—of what is going on at these levels. We recommend that other measurement professionals and social scientists direct more attention to such grassroots issues, encourage their wider discussion, and join with the Buros Institute of Mental Measurements in seeking more effective solutions to these problems than we have ever had in the past. The social utility and reputation of a professional field may hang in the balance.

REFERENCES

Adair, F. L. Review of the computerized scoring and interpretive services for the MMPI. In O. K. Buros (Ed.), *The eighth mental measurements yearbook*. Highland Park, N.J.: Gryphon Press, 1978. Pp. 940–942.

Beck, M., & Stetz, F. *Standardized tests as viewed by test specialists and test users.* Paper presented at the meeting of the National Council on Measurement in Education, Boston, April 1980.

Buros, O. K. The story behind *The mental measurements yearbooks. Measurement and Evaluation in Guidance,* 1968, *1,* 86–95.

Buros, O. K. *The seventh mental measurements yearbook.* Highland Park, N.J.: Gryphon Press, 1972.

Buros, O. K. *Tests in print II.* Highland Park, N.J.: Gryphon Press, 1974.

Buros, O. K. *The eighth mental measurements yearbook.* Highland Park, N.J.: Gryphon Press, 1978.

Crocker, L. *Choosing the right test: The user's dilemma.* Paper presented at the meeting of the National Council on Measurement in Education, Boston, April 1980.

Glaser, R., & Bond, L. (Eds.). Testing: Concepts, policy, practice, and research. *American Psychologist,* 1981, *36,* No. 10.

Larry P. v. Riles, 495 F. Supp. 926 (N.D. Cal. 1979) appeal docketed, No. 80-4027 (9th Cir., Jan. 17, 1980).

Novick, M. R. Federal guidelines and professional standards. *American Psychologist,* 1981, *36,* 1035–1046.

PASE v. Hannon, 506 F. Supp. 831 (N.D. Ill. 1980).

Resnick, L. B. Introduction: Research to inform a debate. *Phi Delta Kappan,* 1981, *62,* 623–624.

Salmon-Cox, L. Teachers and standardized achievement tests: What's really happening? *Phi Delta Kappan, 62,* 1981, 631–634.

Subkoviak, M. J., & Baker, F. B. Test theory. In L. S. Shulman (Ed.), *Review of research in education* (Vol. 5). Washington, D.C.: American Educational Research Association, 1978.

Traub, R. E., & Wolfe, R. G. Latent trait theories and the assessment of educational achievement. In D. C. Berliner (Ed.), *Review of research in education* (Vol. 9). Washington, D.C.: American Educational Research Association, 1981.

Weiss, D. J., & Davison, M. L. Test theory and methods. In M. R. Rosenzweig & L. W. Porter (Eds.), *Annual review of psychology* (Vol. 32). Palo Alto, Calif.: Annual Reviews Inc., 1981.

Yeh, J. P., & Herman, J. L. *Test use in the schools.* Paper presented at the meeting of the National Council on Measurement in Education, Boston, April 1980.

INFLUENCES ON APTITUDE AND ACHIEVEMENT TEST DEVELOPMENT AND USAGE

7 Aptitude and Achievement Tests: The Curious Case of the Indestructible Strawperson[1]

Anne Anastasi
Fordham University

In a talk I gave at the 1979 ETS Invitational Conference, I remarked that, if I were suddenly endowed with the appropriate occult powers, I should choose to eliminate certain words from the psychometric vocabulary. Among them were the words *aptitude* and *achievement* (Anastasi, 1980). These terms have led to nearly as much confusion, misinterpretation, and misuse of tests as has the more notorious term *intelligence*. Having been asked once more to discuss the same general topic in 1982, it occurred to me that I might consider *why* the myths that surround these terms are so persistent—and persistent they certainly are.

Let us examine specifically the traditional distinction between aptitude and achievement tests. Aptitudes are typically defined more precisely than intelligence, to designate more narrowly limited cognitive domains. Nevertheless, like intelligence, they have traditionally been contrasted with achievement in testing terminology. This contrast dates from the early days of testing, when it was widely assumed that achievement tests measured the effects of learning, whereas intelligence and aptitude tests measured so-called innate capacity, or potentiality, independently of learning. This approach to testing in turn reflected a simplistic conception of the operation of heredity and environment that prevailed in the 1920s and 1930s. The relevant historical background has been thoroughly examined in a recent book by a science historian, Hamilton Cravens,

[1]Paper presented in Invited Symposia: State of the Art Series—Achievement Testing, at the meeting of the American Psychological Association, Washington, D.C., August 1982.

which covers the heredity–environment controversy among American scientists between the two World Wars (Cravens, 1978; see also Anastasi, 1979).

HISTORICAL ANTECEDENTS

Common misconceptions about the relation between aptitude and achievement tests are highlighted by an index introduced in the 1920s and variously named an achievement quotient or an accomplishment quotient. Both terms having the same initials, this index soon came to be known as the AQ. Its origin is generally attributed to Raymond Franzen (1920, 1922). The AQ could be found by dividing the individual's educational quotient (EQ) by his or her intelligence quotient (IQ). The EQ was the ratio of educational age (EA) to chronological age (CA). The AQ could also be computed more directly by dividing educational age by mental age. The educational age was found by referring the score on an achievement battery to the age norms for that battery. Still another procedure was to use age norms for tests in particular academic subjects, like reading or arithmetic, to find ''subject ages'' for the individual, and then to average these subject ages to obtain the educational age.

Early textbooks on testing regularly included a discussion of the AQ as a means of evaluating a student's educational performance in relation to that student's intellectual potential—a means of comparing achievement with capacity to learn (Freeman, 1926, 1939; Garrett & Schneck, 1933; Greene, 1941; Lincoln & Workman, 1935; Mursell, 1947). It is interesting to trace the statements about the AQ in texts appearing from the 1920s to the 1940s and early 1950s. Even the earliest discussions called attention to the technical and statistical weaknesses of the AQ as a ratio. The major criticisms fell into two categories: The first category was similar to the now familiar criticisms of the traditional ratio IQ; the second was similar to the equally familiar criticism of grade norms—educational age norms were certainly no better than educational grade norms.

These and other technical criticisms, however, were usually mentioned as limitations, which might be avoided under proper conditions or which should be kept in mind in interpreting results. By the 1940s and early 1950s, the criticisms had become more vigorous. The reader was now told that the AQ *as a technique,* ''cannot be recommended'' (Mursell, 1947, p. 373), that it has ''nearly gone out of use'' (Greene, 1941, p. 251), ''is in growing disrepute'' (Cronbach, 1949, p. 282), and ''is now practically extinct'' (Anastasi, 1954, p. 463).

Psychological criticisms of the use of AQs, as contrasted to statistical criticisms, are found in some textbooks from the outset. Frank N. Freeman's 1926 book, *Mental Tests,* a widely used text of the period, referred to two unwarranted assumptions: first, that intelligence tests provide a measure of innate capacity independent of training; second, that all educational achievement depends on the same unitary intellectual capacity (Freeman, 1926, pp. 287–288). These concerns were expressed more mildly and less clearly in other early books. Nevertheless, the same authors who criticized the AQ on either statistical or psychological grounds accepted and even recommended a more general, qualitative, informal procedure for using intelligence test scores in interpreting measures of educational achievement. By midcentury, the AQ itself had in fact disappeared, at least from the major textbooks—but its ghost lingered on.

Closely linked to the AQ is the concept of underachievement and overachievement, which was first introduced in attempts to interpret deviant AQs. If children were performing up to capacity, it was expected that their AQs would be close to 100. Those with AQs under 100 were designated underachievers; those with AQs above 100 were the overachievers. Several writers did express some discomfort with the finding of overachievement as thus measured, because it implied that certain persons were performing above their capacity, which seemed a logical impossibility (e.g., Lincoln & Workman, 1935). Nevertheless, they tried to defend the AQ by attributing values over 100 largely to unreliability of both intelligence tests and educational tests and to inaccuracy of educational age norms. They also suggested that unusually strong interest and motivation might account for a few remaining AQs above 100.

Actually, the question of underachievement and overachievement can be more properly formulated as overprediction and underprediction from the first to the second test (Thorndike, 1963). Such intraindividual differences from one test to another simply reflect the well-known fact that no two tests are perfectly correlated. Of course, this statement is also true of other performance indicators, such as course grades. Among the reasons for the prediction errors in individual cases are not only the unreliability of the measuring instruments but also differences in content coverage, the varied effects of attitudinal and motivational factors on the two measures, and the impact of such intervening experiences as remedial instruction.

It should be noted that underprediction or overprediction will occur regardless of the type of test used. It occurs not only when an intelligence test is used to predict subsequent achievement test performance but also if an achievement test is used to predict subsequent intelligence test performance. Furthermore, the same prediction errors are likely to occur in either direction, whether we estimate scores on the later test from scores on the earlier test, or vice versa. From a practical standpoint, the administration of alternate forms or different levels of an achievement test before and after a course of instruction permits a more accurate analysis of individual accomplishment than does the use of two different tests. To take an extreme example, if achievement in reading comprehension is predicted from a nonverbal intelligence test that is heavily loaded with spatial aptitude, the children with higher spatial than verbal aptitude will look like underachievers, whereas those with higher verbal than spatial aptitude will look like overachievers.

DEBUNKING VENTURES

Psychology has come a long way since World War I. And some psychometricians have made repeated efforts to exorcise the AQ ghost. That intelligence and aptitude tests are not fundamentally different from achievement tests was illustrated as early as 1927 by Truman L. Kelley. In this connection, Kelley coined the expression "jangle fallacy" to designate the opposite of the "jingle fallacy" whereby things called by the same name are assumed to be the same. Kelley (1927, p. 64) defined the jangle fallacy as "the use of two separate words or expressions covering in fact the same basic situation, but sounding different, as though they were in truth different." Through an analysis of correlational data, Kelley demonstrated that widely used intelligence tests and achievement batteries overlapped by about 90% (Kelley, 1927, pp. 193–209).

Since that time, other investigators have again reported extensive overlap between these two types of tests (e.g., Coleman & Cureton, 1954; Cronbach, 1970, pp. 284–285). In fact, in some instances, the correlation between intelligence tests and achievement batteries is about as high as the reliability coefficients of each. Over the intervening decades, there have been repeated attempts to dispel the myths and clarify the relation between aptitude and achievement tests. Relevant discussions can be found in the successive editions of widely used textbooks (e.g., Anastasi, 1982; Cronbach, 1970; Thorndike & Hagen, 1977). They can likewise be found in the published reports of conferences devoted wholly or largely to this topic (e.g., DuBois, 1969; D. R. Green, 1974; Schrader, 1980).

In major addresses and papers by psychologists, the terms *aptitude* and *achievement* have been used time and again with precision and with sensitivity to their possible misapprehensions. For example, in his presidential address to the APA Division of Evaluation and Measurement, Bert Green observed that "tests of general verbal and numerical skills are usually called aptitude tests, which is unfortunate since the term *aptitude* seems to suggest an inborn, unchangeable trait. Actually the tests assess developed abilities—skills acquired through years of training and practice with verbal and numerical material [B. F. Green, 1978, p. 669]." Further on, he referred to "the long-range achievement tests we call 'aptitude tests' [p. 669]."

It is also enlightening to read what the College Board writes about its Scholastic Aptitude Test (SAT) and its series of achievement tests. In various current publications regularly distributed to students, counselors, and other persons concerned with these tests, the College Board consistently describes the SAT as a measure of developed verbal and mathematical reasoning abilities that are related to successful performance in college (e.g., College Entrance Examination Board, 1981a, 1981e). In a fuller statement, the Board (1981d) adds that the SAT "is not a test of some inborn and unchanging capacity. Scores on the SAT are subject to improvement as educational experience, both in and out of school, causes these verbal and mathematical abilities to develop.'' In the same sources, the achievement tests are described as measuring the student's ''knowledge and ability to apply that knowledge in specific subject areas.'' The distinction that emerges is primarily one of breadth versus specificity of test content and of antecedent learning experience.

Following the same trend, Snow (1980) described the SAT as ''a test of *extended* or *generalized* achievement designed to be indicative of aptitude for college work, that is, for work requiring broader, deeper, higher, and more elaborate organizations and reorganizations of scholastic learning than that represented *directly* in prior public schooling, or in conventional school achievement tests [pp. 43–44].'' At the 1981 ETS Invitational Conference, Christopher Jencks presented a paper in which he discussed the SAT and argued quite convincingly that what the SAT measures is not fundamentally different from what the College Board's achievement tests measure. For many in the audience, these arguments came as no surprise. Jencks went on to suggest, however, that because of widespread misconceptions about the meaning of ''aptitude,'' college-bound high school students do not study the subject matter taught in their high school courses as thoroughly and as earnestly as they otherwise might (Jencks & Crouse, 1982).

Even more recently, the GRE Board has taken decisive action to help dispel the false aptitude–achievement distinctions. In a recent GRE Board Newsletter (1982), it was announced that ''effective with October 1982 administrations of the Graduate Record Examinations, the Aptitude Test will become the General Test and the Advanced Tests will be called Subject Tests. The GRE Board approved the name changes to avoid any potential misunderstanding about the purpose of the tests [p. 3].'' Viewing the question from a broader perspective, the National Academy of Sciences Committee on Ability Testing, in its recently issued formal report, clearly asserts that both aptitude and achievement tests measure developed abilities, and both serve as indicators of the ability to learn (Wigdor & Garner, 1982, pp. 27, 163).

And so it goes on and on. Still the popular misconceptions persist. These viable misconceptions are especially evident in some of the current popular attacks on testing, particularly on tests such as the SAT and other measures of academic aptitudes. The criticisms follow a monotonously uniform pattern. First comes the false attribution. For example, aptitude tests are supposed to assess innate potential. Second comes disproof, which should be quite easy for such an outrageously irrational and naive statement. Third comes the conclusion: Tests are wrong, bad, and should be abandoned.

This brings me to my subtitle, ''The Curious Case of the Indestructible Strawperson.'' First, the critics set up what in folk language is known as a strawman; but in deference to editorial policies to avoid sexist language, I have renamed it a strawperson. After the many decades of persistent efforts by psychometricians to dispel these misconceptions, anyone who accepts them as the major premise is certainly building a strawperson. Once the strawperson is up, it is easily demolished, and the demolition carries the tests along with the straw. But the question still remains: *Why* do the misconceptions survive in the first place? *Who* keeps them alive?—certainly not the psychometricians and test constructors.

Actually, the misconceptions survive among the general public and among those test users who are not knowledgeable about either testing or psychology. I would not be so bold as to claim that I have the answer to the indestructibility of my strawperson. But I suggest that one explanation may be found in the desire for magic—the desire for easy answers, quick solutions, and shortcuts. It is the desire to which charlatans have catered across the centuries and which accounts for the popularity of astrology, phrenology, palmistry, and all the other fanciful shortcuts for understanding ourselves and our associates. It is these pseudo-sciences that the first applied psychologists had to compete with. Now that psychology has expanded into the public arena, it is the psychologists themselves who are expected to produce the magic. And, of course, they will be damned if they do and damned if they don't.

THE CONTINUUM OF DEVELOPED ABILITIES

So much for misconceptions. What do we actually know about the relation between aptitude and achievement tests? We may begin by recalling that *any* psychological test is essentially an objective and standardized measure of a sample of behavior. With regard to cognitive behavior, test scores tell us what the individual is able to do at the time. They do not tell us why individuals perform as they do. To answer that question, we need to know something about each person's experiential background. Both aptitude and achievement tests can be best characterized as tests of developed ability. I first heard this term used in the 1950s by Henry Dyer,[2] in a College Board committee meeting. It was probably an idea ahead of its time and did not then have wide impact. It seems we are now beginning to catch up with it. The term *developed abilities* is appearing with increasing frequency in publications on testing. It will be recalled, too, that the College Board now regularly uses this term to describe the SAT.

---

[2]I am differentiating here between the concept of developed abilities and an experimental battery, the Tests of Developed Abilities, produced by ETS for the College Board in the late 1950s (Anastasi, 1961, pp. 442–443; Dyer, 1954; Dyer & Coffman, 1957). Those tests were eventually abandoned because they proved no more predictive of college success than a combination of the SAT and existing achievement tests in specific fields, while being more costly to prepare, administer, and score and less flexible in their use.

What of the differences between instruments traditionally designated aptitude tests and those designated achievement tests? First, tests of developed abilities do not fall into sharply differentiated categories but rather along a continuum. Both aptitude and achievement tests vary widely among themselves; and those near the center of the continuum overlap to such a degree as to be nearly indistinguishable. Nevertheless, if we arrange the instruments that have traditionally been called aptitude tests and achievement tests in this continuum and strip them of unwarranted assumptions about their nature, we can discern some meaningful and useful differences. A number of such differences have been identified with considerable clarity by several psychometricians, including Lee Cronbach (1970, pp. 281–285), Robert Ebel (1974, p. 316), and Lloyd Humphreys (1974, p. 263), among others. Each formulated the distinction somewhat differently and focused on different aspects of the comparison; but their approaches to the question have much in common. I should like to sum up the distinction between instruments at opposite ends of the continuum under two headings: one pertains to antecedent experience, the other to the use of test scores. From the standpoint of any particular test, we might say that one distinction concerns its past and the other its future.

Antecedent Experience

The tests traditionally designated *aptitude* tests, at one end of the continuum, differ from those designated *achievement* tests, at the other end, in the degree of precision with which relevant antecedent experience is defined. This does *not* necessarily mean generality or specificity of test content, nor does it imply breadth of transfer effect or of applicability of the instrument. Intelligence tests and educational achievement batteries can be equally broad in content coverage and in the situational scope of their predictive validity. A spatial aptitude test and an achievement test in typewriting can be equally specific and limited in content coverage and in applicability. What I am referring to instead is essentially the *experiential pool* upon which the test constructor draws in formulating test items. This experiential pool is defined with considerable clarity and precision in constructing, let us say, an achievement test in solid geometry, or medieval history, or motor vehicle operation. At the other extreme is a test like the Stanford–Binet, in which the definition specifies little beyond growing up in America in the twentieth century. Broadly oriented educational achievement batteries, which endeavor to dissociate themselves from specific course content, add little to this definition. Their domain of antecedent experience could be defined as growing up and going to school in America in the twentieth century.

I am reminded in this connection of the difference between a learning curve and a growth curve plotted with test scores. The growth curve is a learning curve covering a longer period of time and obtained in the absence of precise knowledge about the independent variables that bring about the observed behavioral changes.

To sum up the first difference, tests of developed ability differ in the degree of precision versus vagueness with which tbe relevant domain of antecedent experience is defined.

Use of Test Scores

The second difference concerns the way in which test scores are utilized. It is generally recognized that traditional achievement tests are designed and used primarily to assess current status, whereas traditional aptitude tests are designed and used to predict future performance following a specified learning experience. Typical tests of current status, at one end of this continuum, can be illustrated by a licensing examination (as in obtaining a driver's license), a typing test (as in hiring a secretary), a French test (as in selecting an interpreter), a test to assess the effects of self-study or life experiences (as in credit by examination), and a competency test in so-called basic skills (presumably chosen because they are prerequisite to a wide variety of roles in our contemporary culture).

At the other end of the continuum, we find typical "intelligence" and "aptitude" tests designed particularly for predictive purposes. What can the individual learn—how much and how fast can he or she learn—when put through a particular course of study, educational program, industrial apprenticeship, or other systematic learning experience? I'm sure that at this point many of you are thinking that traditional achievement tests can often serve as effective predictors of future learning. That is certainly true. An achievement test in arithmetic is a good predictor of students' subsequent performance in an algebra class.

We must remember that all tests actually assess current status, whether their purpose is terminal assessment or prediction. Hence it is not surprising that some aptitude tests look very much like achievement tests and vice versa. In fact, some writers (Carroll, 1974; Snow, 1980) have argued for aptitude as a concept or construct, defined as all the characteristics of an individual that predispose him or her to success or failure in new learning or in the performance of some future activity. An aptitude *test,* according to this view, is only one indicant of aptitude; other indicants would include achievement tests, data on prior performance, and information regarding relevant personality and physical characteristics. This definition of aptitude obviously focuses on the predictive use of information about the individual, including current test scores of all sorts.

MORE ABOUT APTITUDES

Let us take a closer look at the concept of aptitude itself. This, after all, is where myths and excess meanings have accumulated. In discussions of aptitude and achievement tests, it is generally the misconceptions about aptitude that have led to false distinctions and to misuse of scores. Aptitude, as we have seen, has been identified with the predictive use of tests. Prediction, in turn, has traditionally been linked with the process of selection: Some students are admitted (to college, medical school, or whatever) and others are not; some job applicants are hired and others are not. As a result of several emerging societal changes, selection is beginning to give way to classification. Tests are being used increasingly for such purposes as assisting individuals to choose among courses of study, careers, or other alternative action plans; placing applicants in different jobs for maximal utilization of their individual qualifications; and assessing the prerequisite skills and knowledge of individual students in order to fit instructional programs to specific needs.

In all these contexts, the concept of *diagnostic testing* is coming to replace that of testing for prediction. But the role of tests in diagnosis and prediction is not fundamentally different. In all these situations, appropriate tests should be chosen or constructed in the light of a task analysis of the desired behavior domain—whether identified through an academic curriculum, a career, a particular job, or whatever. To be effective, a predictive or diagnostic test should assess the development of those prerequisite skills and knowledge that the individual needs before taking the next step. Although test content may be drawn from a common pool of experiences shared by the examinee population, the selection of relevant items from that pool should be oriented toward the requirements of the subsequent performance pool. Every test has both this backward and forward reference. The forward reference, however, is especially relevant for tests used to assess one's readiness to advance from where one is to where one wants to go—for instance, into a particular job or educational program.

The concept of aptitude as prerequisite skills and knowledge is exemplified in what Ben Bloom (1976, 1980) calls cognitive entry behaviors and affective entry characteristics. The cognitive entry behaviors include such general skills as reading comprehension, basic quantitative skills, writing competence, logical reasoning processes, and possibly still broader skills such as attention skills and study skills. These are the skills tapped in most scholastic aptitude and academic intelligence tests. Bloom maintains, however, that the more specific cognitive entry behaviors identified as prerequisites for a particular set of learning tasks provide more accurate assessment and are more readily alterable by appropriate instruction. Affective entry characteristics also influence the individual's subsequent learning performance. They include relevant emotional, motivational, and self-concept variables. To some extent, they too can be altered by subsequent instruction adapted to individual needs. Effective instruction requires full information regarding the individual's status upon entry into the instructional program (initial aptitude), as well as clear specification of what is to be learned (achievement goals).

School readiness is another condition associated with the concept of aptitude. It refers essentially to the attainment of prerequisite skills, knowledge, attitudes, motivations, and other behavioral traits that enable the learner to profit max-imally from school instruction. These prerequisites are what Hunt and Kirk (1974) have called the "entry skills" that the child needs to cope with the teaching–learning situation encountered in the first grade. At one time, such readiness was conceived largely in terms of maturation. To be sure, the development of certain minimum physical qualifications facilitates some kinds of learning. Unless children can make the necessary auditory discriminations, they cannot learn to speak by the usual procedures; without the ability for fine motor coordination, they are unable to manipulate a pencil in writing. Most school learning, however, is not so closely linked to sensorimotor development. In the mastery of educational tasks, the importance of prior learning is being increasingly recognized. More and more emphasis is now placed on the hierarchical development of knowledges and skills, whereby the acquisition of simple concepts equips the child for the learning of more complex concepts at any age.

Still another way to conceptualize aptitude and achievement in an educational context is presented by Robert Ebel (1969, 1974). In an incisive analysis of the goals of education, Ebel (1969) concluded that the essence of educational achievement is "command of useful verbal knowledge [p. 66]" and that this objective should be reflected in the construction of educational tests. In order to be meaningful to the individual learner and retrievable when relevant, each new acquisition must be integrated into a coherent structure of knowledge. According to this view, "aptitude for learning consists mainly and essentially of relevant knowledge. . . . What the student has achieved in learning becomes, if it is relevant, his aptitude for further learning" (Ebel, 1974, p. 316). This process cannot occur independently of the subject matter to which it is applied. We do not think content-free thoughts nor develop content-free abilities. The availability of a large, well-organized, and easily retrievable content store is also emerging as a major difference between the performance of expert and novice in such activities as playing chess and solving difficult problems in physics (Glaser, 1981).

The increasing recognition of the importance of the knowledge context of developed abilities is reflected in a recent statement prepared under College Board auspices. The statement concerns the basic academic competencies that college-bound high school students should develop (College Entrance Examination Board, 1981b, 1981c). Following an initial year of intensive discussions by representative groups of educators, a plan was formulated covering both broad developed abilities (called academic competencies) and recommended curricular fields. The list of academic competencies, although defined at a higher academic level, sounds very much like the cognitive entry behaviors described by Bloom. They include developed abilities in reading, writing, listening and speaking, mathematics, reasoning, and studying. A major conclusion was "that acquisition of the competencies and achievement in the curriculum are interdependent—that is, subject matter cannot be mastered without the necessary competencies, and the competencies cannot be developed in a vacuum without reference to subject-matter content [College Entrance Examination Board, 1981c, p. 10]."

Despite the indestructible strawperson, we have indeed been making steady progress in expanding, clarifying, and refining our understanding of what aptitude and achievement tests measure. Our main problem is still how to communicate this growth in understanding to test users, test takers, and the general public.

REFERENCES

Anastasi, A. *Psychological testing* (1st ed.). New York: Macmillan, 1954.

Anastasi, A. *Psychological testing* (2nd ed.). New York: Macmillan, 1961.

Anastasi, A. A historian's view of the nature-nurture controversy: Review of H. Cravens, The triumph of evolution—American scientists and the heredity-environment controversy, 1900–1941. *Contemporary Psychology*, 1979, *24*, 622–623.

Anastasi, A. Abilities and the measurement of achievement. In W. B. Schrader (Ed.), *Measuring achievement: Progress over a decade*. San Francisco: Jossey-Bass, 1980.

Anastasi, A. *Psychological testing* (5th ed.). New York: Macmillan, 1982.

Bloom, B. S. *Human characteristics and school learning*. New York: McGraw-Hill, 1976.

Bloom, B. S. New directions in educational research: Alterable variables. In W. B. Schrader (Ed.), *Measuring achievement: Progress over a decade*. San Francisco: Jossey-Bass, 1980.

Carroll, J. B. The aptitude-achievement distinction: The case of foreign language aptitude and proficiency. In D. R. Green (Ed.), *The aptitude-achievement distinction*. Monterey, Calif: CTB/McGraw-Hill, 1974.

Coleman, W., & Cureton, E. E. Intelligence and achievement: The "jangle fallacy" again. *Educational and Psychological Measurement*, 1954, *14*, 347–351.

College Entrance Examination Board. *ATP guide for high schools and colleges, 1981–82*. New York: Author, 1981. (a)

College Entrance Examination Board. *Preparation for college in the 1980s*. New York: Author, 1981. (b)

College Entrance Examination Board. *Project EQuality*. New York: Author, 1981. (c)

College Entrance Examination Board. *Taking the SAT: A guide to the Scholastic Aptitude Test and the Test of Standard Written English*. New York: Author, 1981. (d)

College Entrance Examination Board. *Your student report, 1981–82*. New York: Author, 1981. (e)

Cravens, H. *The triumph of evolution: American scientists and the heredity-environment controversy, 1900–1941*. Philadelphia: University of Pennsylvania Press, 1978.

Cronbach, L. J. *Essentials of psychological testing*. (1st ed.). New York: Harper, 1949.

Cronbach, L. J. *Essentials of psychological testing* (3rd ed.) New York: Harper & Row, 1970.

DuBois, P. H. *Toward a theory of achievement measurement: Proceedings of the 1969 Invitational Conference on Testing Problems*. Princeton, N.J.: Educational Testing Service, 1969.

Dyer, H. S. *A common philosophy for the Tests of Developed Ability*. Unpublished Memorandum, January 5, 1954.

Dyer, H. S., & Coffman, W. E. The Tests of Developed Ability. *College Board Review*, 1957, No. 31, 5–10.

Ebel, R. Knowledge vs. ability in achievement testing. In P. H. DuBois (Ed.), *Toward a theory of achievement measurement*. Princeton, N.J.: Educational Testing Service, 1969.

Ebel, R. L. The relation of aptitude for learning to achievement in learning. In D. R. Green (Ed.), *The aptitude-achievement distinction*. Monterey, Calif.: CTB/McGraw-Hill, 1974.

Franzen, R. H. The accomplishment quotient, a school mark in terms of individual capacity. *Teachers College Record*, 1920, *21*, 432–440.

Franzen, R. H. The accomplishment ratio: A treatment of the inherited determinants of disparity in school product. *Teachers College Contributions to Education,* 1922, No. 125.

Freeman, F. N. *Mental tests: Their history, principles and applications.* Boston: Houghton Mifflin, 1926.

Freeman, F. N. *Mental tests: Their history, principles, and applications* (rev. ed.). Boston: Houghton Mifflin, 1939.

Garrett, H. E., & Schneck, M. R. *Psychological tests, methods, and results.* New York: Harper, 1933.

Glaser, R. The future of testing: A research agenda for cognitive psychology and psychometrics. *American Psychologist,* 1981, *36,* 923–936.

GRE Board Newsletter. No. 36, February 1982. Graduate Record Examination Board, Princeton, N.J. 08541.

Green, B. F., Jr. In defense of measurement. *American Psychologist,* 1978, *33,* 664–670.

Green, D. R. (Ed.). *The aptitude-achievement distinction: Proceedings of the Second CTB/McGraw-Hill Conference on Issues in Educational Measurement.* Monterey, Calif.: CTB/McGraw-Hill, 1974.

Greene, E. B. *Measurements of human behavior.* New York: Odyssey, 1941.

Humphreys, L. G. The misleading distinction between aptitude and achievement tests. In D. R. Green (Ed.), *The aptitude-achievement distinction.* Monterey, Calif.: CTB/McGraw-Hill, 1974.

Hunt, J. McV., & Kirk, G. E. Criterion-referenced tests of school readiness. A paradigm with illustrations. *Genetic Psychology Monographs,* 1974, *90,* 143–182.

Jencks, C., & Crouse, J. Should we relabel the SAT—Or replace it? In W. B. Schrader (Ed.), *Measurement, guidance, and program improvement: Proceedings of the 1981 ETS Invitational Conference.* San Francisco: Jossey-Bass, 1982.

Kelley, T. L. *Interpretation of educational measurements.* Yonkers, N.Y.: World Book Co., 1927.

Lincoln, E. A., & Workman, L. L. *Testing and the use of test results.* New York: Macmillan, 1935.

Mursell, J. L. *Psychological testing.* New York: Longmans, Green, 1947.

Schrader, W. B. (Ed.). *Measuring achievement: Progress over a decade (Proceedings of the 1979 ETS Invitational Conference).* San Francisco: Jossey-Bass, 1980.

Snow, R. E. Aptitude and achievement. In W. B. Schrader (Ed.), *Measuring achievement: Progress over a decade.* San Francisco: Jossey-Bass, 1980.

Thorndike, R. L. *The concepts of over- and under-achievement.* New York: Teachers College Press, 1963.

Thorndike, R. L., & Hagen, E. *Measurement and evaluation in psychology and education* (4th ed.). New York: Wiley, 1977.

Wigdor, A. K., & Garner, W. E. (Eds.). *Ability testing: Uses, consequences, and controversies. Part I. Report of the Committee.* Washington, D.C.: National Academy Press, 1982.

8 Achievement Test Items: Current issues

Robert L. Ebel
Michigan State University

The writer of achievement test items is confronted with two major problems, as Lindquist pointed out nearly half a century ago (Lindquist, 1936, p. 17). The first of these is the problem of what to measure. The second is how to measure it. The solution proposed for the first problem is to focus primarily on testing for knowledge and only secondarily on testing for abilities. Cognitive abilities, it is reasonable to believe, depend entirely on knowledge. Although the term *knowledge,* as commonly used, includes both information and understanding, the most useful kind of knowledge, the kind that will occupy our attention almost exclusively, is that which involves understanding. Understood knowledge is a structure of relations among concepts. To understand is to be aware of relationships. Each of these relationships can be expressed in words as a proposition.

The solution proposed for the second problem is to present the examinee with a series of incomplete propositions, accompanied by two or more alternative completions, only one of which makes the proposition true. Many of the current issues in the writing of achievement test items are related to these two proposed solutions.

A CONCEPTION OF KNOWLEDGE

Knowledge originates in information that can be received directly from observations or indirectly from reports of observations. These observations may be external (objects or events) or internal (thoughts and feelings) (Scheffler, 1965, p. 137). Information feeds the mind and, like food for the body, it must be digested and assimilated. Thinking is the process by which these things can be accomplished (Newman, 1852, p. 134). Information that is simply stored in memory remains only information, the lowest, least useful form of knowledge.

But if the information becomes the subject of reflective thought, if those who received it ask themselves, "What does it mean?" "How do we know?" "Why is it so?", the information may come to be understood. It may be integrated into a system of relations among concepts and ideas that constitutes a structure of knowledge. This has been referred to as "semantic encoding" (Anderson, 1972, p. 146). Information that is understood, that is incorporated into a structure of knowledge, tends to be more powerful, more useful, and more satisfying. It is likely to be a more permanent possession than information that is simply remembered (Boulding, 1967, pp. 7–8).

The basis for verbal knowledge exists in the mind in a form that Polanyi (1958) has called "tacit knowledge." In that form, it is a purely private possession. But if concepts can be abstracted from these images and expressed in words, and if the relations among the concepts can be expressed in sentences, then tacit knowledge is converted into verbal knowledge. This can be communicated and thus made public. It can also be recorded and stored for future reference. It can be manipulated in the processes of reflective thinking. It is thus a very powerful form of knowledge. The peculiar excellence of human beings among all other creatures on earth is their ability to produce and to use verbal knowledge. Thinkers produce it. Teachers and students, planners, and managers use it. Classrooms and libraries and study rooms are full of it. So are conference rooms, memoranda, and reports. It would be difficult to overstate the importance of structures of verbal knowledge in human affairs (Hayakawa, 1941, pp. 15–25; Langer, 1957, pp. 200–204).

If a structure of verbal knowledge consists entirely of a system of articulated relations among concepts and ideas, can it be described *completely* by listing the elements (propositions) that compose it? Might not a complex structure involve relations or dimensions that are not expressed by the constituent elements of the structure? Indeed it is possible that a listing of the elements of a structure might omit some that *have not been* perceived or expressed in words. But it is unreasonable to believe that there might be important elements of the structure that *could not be* perceived and expressed; to cite an example of such an unperceived and unexpressed element, one would have to perceive and express it. Once it had been expressed, it could be added to the list. The conclusion that a structure of verbal knowledge can be described completely by listing the elements that compose it appears to be logically necessary. Where structures of knowledge are concerned, the whole seems to be precisely equal to the sum of *all* the parts.

THE RELATION OF KNOWLEDGE TO ABILITY

The contribution of knowledge to effective human behavior is sometimes questioned. Knowledge alone is not enough, says the businessman. It does not guarantee financial success. Knowledge alone is not enough, says the college president. It does not guarantee scholarly achievement. Knowledge alone is not enough, says the religious leader. It does not guarantee virtue. Knowledge alone is not enough, says the philosopher. It does not guarantee wisdom.

They are all right, of course. Knowledge alone is not enough. But in this complex world of chance and change, no one thing nor any combination of things ever will be enough to guarantee financial success or scholarly achievement or virtue or wisdom. Although this is true, few would deny that the command of knowledge does contribute greatly to the attainment of these other, more ultimate goals.

The term *knowledge,* as it is used in this chapter, means considerably more than the same term means in the Bloom Taxonomy (Bloom, 1956, pp. 201–297). There, knowing something means simply being able to recall it. Having knowledge is nothing more than having information. Here, the term *knowledge* refers not only to information but also and, far more importantly, to understanding, which requires a structure of relations among concepts. In addition, the emphasis here is on useful knowledge. If knowledge is not available to be used, it is not fully possessed. Thus the possession of knowledge, as the term is used here, should enable a person to demonstrate all the other abilities and skills identified in the other categories of Bloom's Taxonomy: comprehension, application, analysis, synthesis, and evaluation. If one *knows* how to do these things, one ought to be *able* to do them.

THE MEASURABILITY OF HUMAN CHARACTERISTICS

Any important human characteristic is necessarily measurable. To be important, a personal characteristic must make an observable difference, that is, at some time, under some circumstances, a person who has more of it must behave differently from a person who has less of it. If different degrees or amounts of a personal characteristic never make any observable difference, what evidence can be found to show that it is, in fact, important?

But if such differences can be observed, then the characteristic is measurable, for all measurement requires is verifiable observation of a more–less relationship. Can integrity be measured? It can if verifiable differences in integrity can be observed among men. Can mother love be measured? If observers can agree that a hen shows more mother love than a female trout or that Mrs. A. shows more love for her children than Mrs. B, then mother love can be measured. The gist of the argument is this. To be important, a personal characteristic must make a difference. If it makes a difference, the basis for measurement exists.

In principle, then, any important human characteristic is measurable. In practice, however, many characteristics said to be important seem to be very difficult to measure. Where can one find a reliable test of ability to see relations, to formulate hypotheses, to interpret data, to organize ideas, to draw conclusions, to solve problems, or to think?

Perhaps the difficulty may lie in the characteristics themselves. Perhaps they simply do not exist as separate, unified, measurable abilities. Perhaps what we call abilities are simply categories of tasks that have some superficial characteristics in common but which cannot be dealt with effectively by the application of a single general task-related ability. Perhaps what they may require mainly is knowledge of the special context in which the tasks arise. Take problem solving for example. The problems a physician must solve are likely to be quite different from those a chess player or a football coach or a highway engineer or a theoretical physicist must solve. No test of general ability to solve problems is likely to predict very accurately how successful a practitioner of each of these arts or crafts is likely to be. Too little of what makes a physician successful in problem solving is also likely to make the chess player, the coach, the engineer, or the physicist successful.

Many of the alleged abilities that are said to be important human characteristics have never been defined operationally, which must be the first step in developing valid measures of them. If an operational definition of one of these very general abilities could be developed, it might lead to a test composed of such a heterogeneity of tasks, with very low intertask correlations, that the test scores would be very low in reliability. When this is the case, differences among individuals in the amount of this general ability are likely to be difficult to discern. It will probably be equally difficult to show that such differences matter very much. If they make little difference on a test designed to measure them, they are unlikely to make much difference in other contexts. If this is the case, they cannot be of great importance.

It may be a waste of time and energy to try to measure "hard to measure" human characteristics. Their measurability is directly related to their importance. For the same reason it may be a waste of time and energy to try to develop these "hard to measure" characteristics through instruction. A teacher who claims to be doing so without being able to produce evidence of success in doing it (because, you see, they are "hard to measure") may be simply throwing dust in our eyes. Those who argue that "what can be easily assessed should not dictate what is taught" are mistaken. If it cannot be easily assessed it cannot be surely taught. It is not likely to be worth trying to teach.

An instructor who wishes to develop in pupils some important characteristic must first devise a method for measuring reliably how much of that characteristic each pupil has acquired. Then the instructor must devise a method for developing that characteristic. Finally the instructor ought to measure the effectiveness of his efforts. Most teachers can find a sufficient challenge to their abilities and commitments in teaching things that are not "hard to measure." They should not add unnecessarily to the difficulties and frustrations of their work by undertaking to teach and to test "hard to measure" achievements. Teachers would teach more effectively and talk more sensibly if they would ban references to "hard to measure" qualities from their discourses.

THE RELATIVE MERITS OF ESSAY AND OBJECTIVE TESTS

Specialists in testing tend to recommend the use of objective tests in general and multiple-choice items in particular. They claim not only that objective tests are more objective and convenient but that they provide more extensive samples of the ability to be tested and yield scores of higher reliability. Critics of multiple-choice tests claim that essay tests, despite their limitations and the difficulties of using them, provide more valid measures of ability and encourage more wholesome educational practices.

In considering the relative merits of essay and objective tests, it is important to make this point at the outset. If the purpose of the test is, as it is usually, to determine how much useful knowledge a person has on some subject, then that purpose can be achieved by using either an essay or an objective test. The point is important because some believe that essay tests call for a different, and higher, level of mental ability than is required by an objective test. The fact, however, is otherwise. There is no empirical evidence to support belief in such a difference and no rational basis for expecting it.

It is reasonable to believe that any cognitive ability consists entirely of knowledge of how to do something. That knowledge is made up of a structure of elements of knowledge, a structure of relations between concepts and ideas. By testing examinees for possession of a sample of those elements, one can determine the extent and strength of their structures of knowledge relevant to the ability and, thus, the degree to which they possess the ability.

If person A knows more about a subject than person B, then A is likely to write a better answer than B to an essay question on the subject. A is also likely to give more correct answers than B to an objective test on the subject. The correctness of the answers either person gives to either type of test question depends largely on the extent and firmness of that person's structure of knowledge.

It is true that essay tests present tasks to the examinees that are distinctly different from the tasks presented in objective tests. The difference, however, is more one of form than of substance. In both cases the information used in giving the answer comes from the examinee's structure of knowledge. In both cases an examinee must choose information relevant to the question being asked. Then, with an essay test answer, the examinee must choose how to express in words the relevant items of information and the conclusions to which they lead. With an objective test, the examinee must choose how to relate the relevant items of information to the questions posed by the item and then choose which of the answer options is best supported by the relevant information. In both cases the foundation for an answer is the examinee's structure of knowledge. In both cases the process of arriving at an answer involves making repeated choices. In both cases the examinee must apply the knowledge possessed, must relate and infer as well as remember.

The advantage that essay tests have in not suggesting the correct answer to a question, or providing clues to it, is more apparent than real. Those who are most successful in selecting correct answers to a multiple-choice question tend to be also more successful in producing good answers to essay test questions (Cook, 1955). The cues to the correct answer that multiple-choice items provide seldom give away the correct answer to one who lacks knowledge of it or ability to infer it. Multiple-choice items often prove to be too difficult to discriminate well despite the cues they may provide. If the multiple-choice items are well written, cues to the correct answer will be offset to some degree by other cues that suggest incorrect answers to poorly informed examinees. The items in which cues are likely to be most helpful are the less desirable kinds in which a previously learned answer simply must be recognized. If the item requires application of what has been learned to answer a question or solve a problem that has never been encountered before, cues will be less helpful. Presenting a good test question in multiple-choice form seldom if ever makes the question too easy to do its job well. Seldom if ever does presentation of correct answers keep objective tests from clearly distinguishing those who know more from those who know less about a subject.

Whatever theoretical advantages there might be to having the examinee produce an answer are likely to be offset by the tedious, subjective process of evaluating the answer and the unreliable scores that often result. Errors in scoring objective tests are quite rare and usually very small. Differences of opinion in judging the quality of essay test answers are often substantial. This is not to say that there are no occasions on which an essay test should be used in preference to an objective test. It is to say that a general preference for essay tests is unwarranted. The ability tested by an item is determined mainly by the content of the question, not by the form of the response.

THE MERITS OF ITEMS BASED ON REALISTIC PROBLEM SITUATIONS

For over 40 years some test specialists have recommended the use of test items based on verbal descriptions of realistic problem situations. Items of this kind are suitable for inclusion in paper and pencil tests. They are more realistic than items that test directly for possession of knowledge or for understanding of principles and procedures. They are less realistic than performance tests presented in simulations of "real-life" situations. A discussion of the possibilities and problems of applied performance testing can be found in Fitzpatrick and Morrison (1971).

The inclusion in paper and pencil tests of items that present verbal descriptions of realistic problem situations has several attractions to test constructors. It demonstrates that objective tests are not limited to testing for recall of isolated, trivial factual details. Situation-based items cannot be answered correctly by simple recognition of the right answer. They force the examinee to think. They obviously require the application of knowledge to real-life problems. Realism in the test encourages faith in the validity of the test scores. These are valuable assets. But situation-based items also have disadvantages. They tend to be complex and wordy. Complexity may obscure the crucial element in the situation, complicate the task of the examinee, and thus lower the discriminating power of the items. It is true that the real problems we face in living are complex. Unfortunately, complex, real problems seldom have single demonstrably correct right answers. Giving a person a complex problem to solve may not be the best way to estimate that person's capability of solving such problems.

Ordinarily a complex test question contributes only a single unit to the total test score. It is answered correctly (1) or incorrectly (0). But to arrive at the final answer to a complex question, the only answer that counts, the examinee must provide himself with a multitude of intermediate or contributory answers that do not count. To reach a correct answer, each of a number of contributory steps must be taken correctly. A single error in any one of them may lead to a final answer that is wrong. The value of nine correct decisions can be offset by the penalty for one that is incorrect. Should not right and wrong decisions carry more nearly equal weight in judging an examinee's capabilities? Would it not be more reasonable, would it not be more informative, would it not lead to more accurate measurement of the mental ability being tested to assess the correctness of each step independently?

Some would say not, arguing that the whole is more than and more significant than the sum of its component parts; that ability to avoid even a single error during a complex process is the essence of competence. The argument is not without merit. Surely it is true that in the ordinary affairs of living, single errors can be very costly. One thing done wrong can cancel the rewards for doing many things right. But is our purpose in measuring mental abilities to imitate life? Or is it mainly to assess a person's cognitive resources, that is, the person's knowledge and mental abilities? For that purpose it may be appropriate and advantageous to take each decision into account and to assess them independently. It may be inappropriate and disadvantageous to consider only a single outcome from a sequence or cluster of related, contributory decisions.

Wordiness should make the items more time-consuming so that fewer could be included in a test of given duration. Obviously a test composed of simple items will yield more independent scorable responses per hour of testing time and hence will tend to yield more reliable scores than a test composed of complex items. Simple test items should also be easier to comprehend and present fewer ambiguities or occasions for misinterpretation by the examinees. Because of these differences one would expect scores of higher reliability from simple than from complex items in tests of similar duration. Experimental studies by Howard (1943) and by Ebel (1953) have confirmed these expectations. It seems difficult to obtain scores of reasonable reliability in tests of reasonable duration if the test items are situation based. This has been true of patient–management problems in medicine (Skakun, 1979), of air crew problems derived from critical incidents in military aviation, and of simulations in legal education (Alderman, Evans, & Wilder, 1981). There seems to be an inverse relation between the realism of the problem situations in the test and the reliability of the scores yielded by the test.

Recognizing these disadvantages, the test constructor may still favor the use of situation-based items. For they do test examinee understanding, abilities to apply knowledge, and ability to think. Is there any better alternative? There may be. Whereas items involving complex, realistic problem situations are often inefficient, ambiguous, and indeterminate, items testing elements of knowledge tend to be efficient and can be less ambiguous and more determinate. There are reasons for believing that most cognitive abilities that can be measured by situation-based test items can also be measured, perhaps with greater efficiency and reliability, by proposition-based items. In many situations, tests composed of simple items may provide more efficient and accurate measures of mental abilities than can be provided by complex test items. In item writing as in many other arts, simplicity can be a virtue.

THE MERITS OF ALTERNATE-CHOICE ITEMS

A simple approach to assessing knowledge is available to those who can accept the idea that knowledge is a structure of relations among concepts. Each of the relations that makes up the structure can be expressed as a proposition. A proposition is simply a sentence that can be said to be true or false (Cohen & Nagle, 1934, pp. 27–30). Propositions similar in appearance to those that are part of the structure but expressing relations that are not part of the structure can also be written. The person whose knowledge is being assessed is asked to distinguish between the correct and the incorrect propositions.

This sounds suspiciously like a true–false test, as indeed it is. True–false tests, however, have been condemned by many specialists in testing, often with considerable vehemence (Adkins, 1947, p. 41; Travers, 1950, p. 42). Other authorities have suggested a different view, which I share. The faults found in true–false items are not inherent in the form but sometimes result from careless or incompetent use of it (Bergmann, 1981, p. 92; Popham, 1981, p. 243).

Both the amount of guessing pupils do in taking true–false tests (Ebel, 1968) and the amount of error that the guessing contributes to their scores (Hills & Gladney, 1968) tend to be exaggerated. Classroom true–false tests of approximately 100 items have yielded coefficients of reliability in the .80s and .90s. These results would be most unlikely if the scores were distorted seriously by guessing.

Each true–false item tests only one element in a structure of knowledge, but there can be many such items in a test. No single essential element in an important structure can be regarded as trivial. If the item is seriously ambiguous, or if it encourages rote learning, much of the fault must be with the one who wrote it. Elements in a structure of knowledge *can* be expressed clearly. They do not need to reward rote learning by being expressed in the exact words or sentences of the textbook or lecturer. The fear that incorrect propositions in a true–false test will lead to wrong learning has proved to be unjustified (Ross, 1947, p. 349; Ruch, 1929, p. 368).

Despite their intrinsic relevance to the assessment of achievement in learning, true–false test items can be ambiguous. They call for absolute judgments of truth or falsity. They do not offer different answers among which the examinee can choose. Because few statements are complete and accurate enough to be perfectly true, the examinee must decide how far the statement can deviate from perfect truth and still be called true. This is one source of ambiguity. Another is lack of clarity in the focus of the item. The element in the statement that is crucial to its truth or falsity is not identified clearly to the examinee.

An alternative to the true–false item, designed to remove some of the ambiguity, is the alternate-choice item. It consists of an incomplete statement of a proposition along with two or more alternative completions, only one of which makes the statement true. For example:

> An eclipse of the sun can only occur when the moon is:
> (1)full (2) new.

Items of this kind do not call for absolute judgments of truth or falsity. The critical element in the statement they make should be quite clear. Their indices of discrimination should be higher on the average than the indices of comparable true–false items given to the same examinees. The test scores therefore should be more reliable. A recent study has verified this expectation. Students ($N = 28$) enrolled in a class in educational measurement took parallel 25-item true–false and alternate-choice tests on each of eight units of instruction in the course. The Kuder–Richardson 20 reliability coefficients for the true–false tests ranged from .13 to .71, with a mean of .47. Those for the alternate-choice tests ranged from .56 to .76, with a mean of .66 (Ebel, 1982).

Alternate-choice items are distinctively different from the familiar four-alternative multiple-choice items in ways other than the number of response options offered. Because they tend to be simpler and use fewer words, they take less time per item (Ebel, 1953). This could lead to higher reliability for tests of a given duration. The response options tend to be shorter, often one or two words, which focuses the attention of the examinee more clearly on the element of knowledge being tested.

One objection likely to be raised to the use of the alternate-choice items is that they deal with isolated factual details. Their brevity and specificity may be taken as indications of triviality (Highet, 1950, p. 120). But if the conception of knowledge presented in this chapter is correct, if verbal knowledge can be expressed completely as a structure of relations, if each of these relations (the elements of the structure) can be expressed as a proposition, and if each proposition is used as the basis for an alternate-choice item, then one can assess the extent and firmness of the whole structure by examining the parts that compose it (Thorndike, 1935; Wood & Beers, 1936, p. 162). The choice of a response to an alternate-choice item is simple to indicate, but the process of making it rationally may be quite complex. If a problem like the following has not been encountered before, it is likely to test understanding and application as well as recall.

> The buoyant force on a ping-pong ball immersed in water is:
> (1) greater than (2) the same as (3) less than   that
> on an iron ball of the same size.   (Answer 2)

Even if the problem has been encountered before, it is reasonable to suppose that the person who understands the basis for the answer is more likely than the one who does not to give the correct answer.

When using the alternate-choice item form, the item writer is free to pose questions that admit only two good alternative responses. Here are some examples:

1. The density of ice is (1) greater (2) less than that of water.

2. A point on the surface of the Earth moves toward the (1) east (2) west as the Earth turns.

3. The average size of farms in the United States has (1) increased (2) decreased during this century.

Often, as in these examples, there is only one plausible alternative to the key word or phrase in the proposition.

When item writers are obliged to produce four-alternative multiple-choice items, they sometimes do so by combining several alternate-choice items. They may present four propositions and ask which one is true or not true. They may ask if a statement is true or false, and why. The responses might be: (1) true, because A; (2) true, because B; (3) false, because C; (4) false, because D. They may ask if something is true of both X and Y. The responses might be: (1) yes, both; (2) no, only X; (3) no, only Y; (4) no, neither. They may ask the speed and direction of a change, so that the responses might be: (1) rapid increase; (2) slow increase; (3) slow decrease; (4) rapid decrease. Presented separately the two or more alternate-choice items would yield two or more independent indications of achievement. Combined, they yield only one. The result is likely to be a loss of reliability (Ebel, 1978).

Three other characteristics of alternate-choice items give them some advantage over conventional multiple-choice items. When the response options are brief, as they usually are, they can be included as parts of a continuous sentence and need not be listed below an item stem. This makes the typing simpler and the resulting pages more compact. When it is awkward to arrange the wording of the sentence so that the response options come at the end, they can be put in the middle or at the beginning. This sometimes simplifies the wording of the item. Finally, because alternate-response items are simple in structure, they are easier to write. There are fewer opportunities for errors in item writing that might spoil the effectiveness of the item.

One other point ought to be mentioned before concluding this case for alternate-choice items. There are items like the following in which more than two good response options are readily available. For example:

1. The gas given off in photosynthesis is (1) carbon dioxide (2) hydrogen (3) oxygen (4) nitrogen.   (Answer 3)

2. Most of the territorial possessions of the United States were gained as a result of the   (1) War of 1812 (2) Civil War (3) Spanish-American War (4) World War I.   (Answer 3)

When more than two good response options are available, the item writer should probably offer more than two.

PROSPECTS FOR A TECHNOLOGY OF ITEM WRITING

Cronbach (1970) expressed the opinion that "The design and construction of achievement test items has been given almost no scholarly attention. The leading works of the generation—even the Lindquist *Educational Measurement* and the Bloom *Taxonomy*—are distillations of experience more than scholarly analysis [p. 509]." The contrast implied here between "distillation of experience" and "scholarly analysis" is interesting. Did not Lindquist and Bloom rely on scholars to aid in the distillations? Did not these scholars analyze the experiences of which they were aware? Is it obvious that a theory of item writing has much to add to the "distillation of experience" in the development of a technology of item writing?

Roid and Haladyna (1980) have reviewed recent research on item writing, with special attention to the more or less mechanistic or semiautomatic methods of item generation. Their article contains descriptions and discussions of six classes of methods for producing test items:

1. Those in which the item writer is guided by statements of the objectives of instruction.

2. Those whose items must meet specifications of the domain of content to be covered and the forms of items to be used.

3. Those in which items are produced by linguistic transformations of segments of prose instruction.

4. Those in which mapping sentences derived from facet theory are used to define a content domain.

5. Those whose items are designed to test understandings of concepts.

6. Those in which items are stored in or actually produced by computers.

The limitations of these methods is acknowledged clearly in the review. Each method appears to have a particular application. They cannot be applied to any content level and at any cognitive level. They require ingenuity and the exercise of judgment. At present they are in the infancy of their development. Cronbach believes that they will mature into useful tools for the test constructor. Others, including this writer, are more skeptical. Roid and Haladyna endorsed Berk's (1978) observation that the rigor and precision of item-writing specifications are inversely related to their practicability.

In a sense, the item development procedures outlined in earlier sections of this chapter constitute a technology for item writing. The form and derivation of the items is specified quite precisely. The content of the items depends on the item writers' knowledge and skills. Propositions that are important and defensible must be selected. They must be expressed clearly, accurately, and concisely. Incorrect answer options that have commonsense plausibility must be provided. The judgment involved in these choices is crucial, and no algorithm or computer program is likely to provide it.

CONCLUDING STATEMENT

This chapter has attempted to make 15 points.

1. Information is the source but not the substance of knowledge.
2. Useful knowledge is a structure of relations among concepts and principles.
3. The peculiar excellence of human beings is their ability to produce and to use verbal knowledge.
4. Cognitive abilities are entirely dependent on the possession of relevant knowledge.
5. The assumption that each kind of cognitive task requires a separate special cognitive ability is unnecessary and probably unwarranted.
6. Special tasks are more likely to require special knowledge than special abilities.

7. Any important human characteristic is necessarily measurable.
8. Human characteristics that are hard to measure are likely to be of limited importance.
9. Either an essay test or an objective test can be used to measure any important cognitive achievement.
10. Multiple-choice items that *present* correct answers among the response options can indicate quite accurately an examinee's ability to *produce* correct answers.
11. Items based on realistic problem situations tend to yield unreliable test scores.
12. Items that consist of incomplete propositions each of which is accompanied by one correct and one or more incorrect completions can yield valid measures of achievement.
13. Items that provide only two response options can measure achievement satisfactorily.
14. Technologies for the mechanical or semiautomatic generation of test items are likely to be of limited value.
15. Simplicity in the conception of what to test and in the means used to test it is commendable.

Paraphrasing Plato's assessment of the ideas he attempted to illustrate in the *Allegory of the Cave*, "Heaven knows if these things are true, but this, at any rate, is how they appear to me."

REFERENCES

Adkins, D. C. *Construction and analysis of achievement tests.* Washington, D.C.: U.S. Government Printing Office, 1947.

Alderman, D. L., Evans, F. R., & Wilder, G. The validity of written simulation exercises for assessing clinical skills in legal education, *Educational and Psychological Measurement* 1981, *41*, 1115–1126.

Anderson, R. C. How to construct achievement tests to assess comprehension. *Review of Educational Research*, 1972, *42*, 145–170.

Bergmann, J. *Understanding educational measurement and evaluation.* Boston: Houghton Mifflin Co., 1981.

Berk, R. A. The application of structural facet theory to achievement test construction. *Educational Research Quarterly*, 1978, *3*, 62–72.

Bloom, B. S. *Taxonomy of educational objectives: Cognitive domain.* New York: Longmans, Green, 1956.

Boulding, K. E. The uncertain future of knowledge and technology. *The Education Digest*, November 1967, *33*, No. 3, pp. 7–11.

Cohen, M. R. & Nagle, E. *An introduction to logic and the scientific method.* New York: Harcourt Brace, 1934.

Cook, D. L. An investigation of three aspects of free-response and choice-type tests at the college level. *Dissertation Abstracts* 1955, *15*, 1351.

Cronbach, L. J. Review of *On the theory of achievement test items. Psychometrika*, 1970, *35*, 509–511.

Ebel, R. L. The use of item response time measurements in the construction of educational achievement tests. *Educational and Psychological Measurement*, 1953, *13*, 391–401.

Ebel, R. L. Blind guessing on objective achievement tests. *Journal of Educational Measurement*, 1968, *5*, 321–325.

Ebel, R. L. Proposed solutions to two problems of test construction. *Journal of Educational Measurement*, 1982, *194*, 267–278.

Ebel, R. L. The ineffectiveness of multiple true-false items. *Educational and Psychological Measurement*, 1978, *38*, 37–44.

Fitzpatrick, R. S., & Morrison, E. J. Performance and product evaluation. In R. F. Thorndike (Ed.), *Educational Measurement* (2nd ed.). Washington, D.C.: American Council on Education, 1971.

Hayakawa, S. I. The importance of language. *Language in Action*. New York: Harcourt Brace, 1941.

Highet, G. *The art of teaching*. New York: Vintage Books, 1950.

Hills, J. R., & Gladney, M. B. Predicting grades from below chance test scores. *Journal of Educational Measurement*, 1968, *5*, 45–53.

Howard, F. T. *Complexity of mental processes in science testing*. Contributions to Education No. 879, New York: Teachers College, Columbia University, 1943.

Langer, S. K. Language and thought. In L. G. Locke, W. M. Gibson, and G. W. Arms (Eds.), *Toward liberal education*. New York: Rinehart, 1957.

Lindquist, E. F. The theory of test construction. In H. E. Hawkes, E. F. Lindquist, & C. Mann (Eds.), *The construction and use of achievement examinations*. Boston: Houghton Mifflin Co., 1936.

Newman, J. H. C. *The idea of a university*. London: Longmans, Green, 1925. (originally published, 1852.)

Polanyi, M. *Personal knowledge*. Chicago: University of Chicago Press, 1958.

Popham, W. V. *Modern educational measurement*. Englewood Cliffs, N.J.: Prentice-Hall, 1981.

Roid, G., & Haladyna, T. The emergence of an item-writing technology. *Review of Educational Research*, 1980, *50*, 293–314.

Ross, C. C. *Measurement in today's schools* (2nd ed.). Englewood Cliffs, N.J.: Prentice-Hall, 1947.

Ruch, G. M. *The objectives or new-type examination*. Chicago: Scott, Foresman, 1929.

Scheffler, I. Philosophical models of teaching, *Harvard Educational Review*, 1965, *35*, 131–143.

Skakun, E. N., Taylor, W. C., Wilson, D. R., Taylor, T. R., Grace, M., & Fincham, S. M. A preliminary investigation of computerized patient management problems in relation to other examinations. *Educational and Psychological Measurement*, 1979, *39*, 303–310.

Thorndike, E. L. In defense of facts. *Journal of Adult Education*, 1935, *7*, 381–388.

Travers, R. M. W. *How to make achievement tests*. New York: Odssey Press, 1950.

Wood, B. D., & Beers, F. S. Knowledge versus thinking. *Teachers College Record*, 1936, *37*, 487–499.

9

Abilities and Knowledge in Educational Achievement Testing: The Assessment of Dynamic Cognitive Structures[1]

Samuel Messick
Educational Testing Service

This chapter confronts the question of what role cognitive abilities play or ought to play in educational achievement testing, which raises the prior question of what educational achievement tests are or ought to be. I begin by considering the nature of educational achievement as a construct in an attempt to circumscribe what achievement tests ought to be rather than by examining extant achievement tests that may be variously off target. Similar consideration is accorded cognitive ability as a construct. This distinction between constructs and the imperfect, variously contaminated tests that are purported to measure them is a critical recurrent theme in these deliberations. Other questions to be briefly addressed concern the role of cognitive abilities in the processes of school learning and the role of schooling in the development of cognitive abilities.

STRUCTURES OF KNOWLEDGE AND ABILITY

Educational achievement refers to what an individual *knows* and *can do* in a specified subject area. At issue is not merely the amount of knowledge accumulated but its organization or structure as a functional system for productive

---

[1]This chapter was presented as part of a Division 15 (Educational Psychology) invited symposium on *Achievement Testing* at the annual meeting of the American Psychological Association, Washington, D.C., August 1982.

This chapter is dedicated to the memory of Robert L. Ebel. His enduring commitment to the improvement of educational measurement as a means of improving education is a worthy legacy for the field.

thinking, problem solving, and creative invention in the subject area as well as for further learning. The individual's structure of knowledge is a critical aspect of educational achievement because it facilitates or hinders what he or she can do in the subject area. What a person can do in an area includes a variety of area-specific skills, such as extracting a square root or parsing a sentence or balancing a chemical equation, but also broader cognitive abilities that cut across subject areas, such as comprehension, memory retention and retrieval, reasoning, analysis and restructuring, evaluation or judgment, and fluency.

These broader cognitive abilities contribute to the assembly and structuring of knowledge, to the continual reassembly and restructuring of cumulating knowledge, to the accessing and retrieval of knowledge, and to its use in problem representation and solution. "Thus achievement," in Snow's (1980a) words, "is as much an organization function as it is an acquisition function. And new achievement depends as much on transfer of such organization as it does on transfer of specific prior facts and skills [p. 43]." Because cognitive abilities play a central role in both the acquisition and organization functions of educational achievement, their influence can hardly be suppressed or ignored in educational achievement testing that assesses knowledge structures. However, their role may be reduced in low-level achievement testing that stresses amount of information alone. Let us next consider the nature of developed knowledge structures in more detail and then the nature of developed abilities, before attempting to relate this formulation to other conceptions of educational achievement.

Knowledge Structure as Relational Understanding

A person's structure of knowledge in a subject area includes not only declarative knowledge about substance (or information about *what*) but also procedural knowledge about methods (or information about *how*) and strategic knowledge about alternatives for goal setting and planning (or information about *which, when,* and possibly *why*). Although the acquisition of declarative and procedural knowledge is an explicit goal of typical instruction in most subject areas, strategic knowledge is rarely so and must often be acquired by induction, if at all (Greeno, 1980). Despite enormous variability in the effort, the principles and generalizations and first-order relations among concepts that provide coherent though rudimentary structure to newly acquired knowledge are also often taught explicitly. Possible exceptions are likely to occur at the beginning or elementary levels of learning in a field, where emphasis may be placed on the accumulation of a critical mass of information prior to organizing it. But the more idiosyncratic structures that relate newly acquired knowledge to existent knowledge structures (which sometimes entails qualitative reorganizations) and the more complex structures that evolve as expertise develops (which frequently entails qualitative reorganizations) are rarely under instructional control.

Knowledge structure basically refers to the structure of relationships among concepts. But as knowledge develops, these structures quickly go beyond classifications of concepts as well as first-order relations among concepts and classes to include organized systems of relationships, or schemas. As organizations of present knowledge, these schemas provide a context for the comprehension and interpretation of objects and events; hence, they profoundly influence the acquisition of new knowledge. Schemas guide the storage and retrieval of knowledge, the generalization and interpretation of ideas, and the initiation and regulation of action (Anderson, Spiro, & Montague, 1977). Thus, educational achievement is not just data driven by the bottom–up processing of incoming information but also conceptually driven by top–down assimilation to mental schemas or relational structures. Furthermore, as expertise develops, these schemas or relational systems themselves become organized in complex patterns, hierarchies, and dynamic networks. These networks are called dynamic because the knowledge structures of experts permit and even facilitate flexible reorganizations for the application of multiple perspectives to problem representation and solution. I have more to discuss later about the implications for educational achievement testing of the differences between novices and experts and between beginning learners and experienced learners in a field.

In the context of school learning, the development of students' knowledge structures may be viewed as an explicit educational objective in its own right. In this connection, Scriven (1974) points out that knowledge structures comprise "organized relational knowledge," which is what we ordinarily mean by *understanding,* and that implicit in the use of this latter term are a number of affective educational goals bearing on the development of attitudes, values, sensitivity, and appreciation. As Scriven (1974) put it, "there are *deep* reasons from cognitive psychology why understanding almost has to have an affective component, reasons which emerge in the verstehen theory of the philosophy of history, in the notion of empathy, and in concepts of modelling and role playing [p. 334]." Furthermore, affect and personality are intrinsically implicated in knowledge structure as a consequence of the individual's psychology of knowledge (Tomkins, 1965); that is, what people know and are interested in knowing is a function of the kinds of persons they are and especially of their ideologies. Moreover, the degree of differentiation and hierarchic integration of the knowledge structure, the permeability of its boundaries, and the flexibility or rigidity of its dimensions or compartments are reflective of the individual's personality and cognitive style (Messick, 1976, in press).

This view of educational achievement stresses the assessment of developed knowledge structure because it is both a product of earlier learning and at the same time is instrumental to, or a vehicle for, subsequent learning. Thus, knowledge structure is central whether the aim of achievement testing is the certification of past accomplishment, the diagnosis of present functioning, or the forecasting of future attainment. By emphasizing the role of knowledge structure as the representation each learner constructs of a subject area to comprehend tasks and events, make sense of new experiences, and plan appropriate actions, this view is inherently constructivist in character. It is consistent with a variety of constructivist psychologies but does not derive from any one of them. For example, this view of learning and achievement is closely allied to what Bruner has called "instrumental conceptualism" (Bruner, Olver, & Greenfield, 1966). It is also quite congenial with Piaget's overall stance on developmental process without committing to his position on developmental stages; that is, learning and the development of cognitive structure are seen as the active assimilation of experience to conceptual schemas, in balance with the restructuring of schemas in accommodation to reality-based or theoretically-correct structures.

Cognitive Abilities as Process Structures

Turning now to cognitive ability as a construct, let me stress at the outset that I am speaking of multiple abilities and not a unitary force or power, about developed abilities and not fixed abilities or capacities (Humphreys, 1962). Indeed, these abilities are clearly still developing well into adulthood (Cattell, 1971). They may develop more slowly later in learning than earlier and more rapidly for some individuals than others. Some may decline with advancing age, sometimes being compensated for by increasing facility in the utilization of other abilities. But, in general, cognitive abilities appear to respond over the long term to education and experience throughout the school years and beyond—even such broad intellective abilities as verbal comprehension and quantitative reasoning that are relatively well crystallized by adolescence (Cattell, 1971; Messick, 1980, 1982b).

Nor is there any implication of innateness of these cognitive abilities inherent either in the way they are measured or in the way they are theoretically conceptualized. At the level of measurement, the drawing of inferences about innate ability from an individual's test performance has long been discredited. Such inferences drawn by early intelligence testers were based on two unsupportable assumptions about equality of motivation to learn and equality of opportunity to learn. These early testers reasoned that by selecting skills that all individuals are expected to develop as a matter of course in their culture, gross differences in motivation to learn were avoided; selecting skills that can be mastered on the basis of universally available experiences within the culture avoided gross differences in opportunity to learn. Hence, performance differences on tests of those skills, they would have it, reflect individual differences in innate ability to learn.

The crucial flaw in this reasoning lies in the premises—skills that all examinees have equal motivation and opportunity to acquire probably do not exist (Schwarz, 1971). Efforts to satisfy these assumptions continue, however, in the guise of so-called "culture-free" or "culture-fair" tests. Here, the usual approach is to select novel tasks where the opportunity (or rather, the lack of opportunity) for mastering them is more nearly equivalent in different cultural settings. This may better satisfy the opportunity assumption but at the expense of the motivation assumption, because tasks that are not emphasized in a culture depend for their salience or stimulus value on their intrinsic interest and the presumed importance of the testing to each examinee.

In contrast, the concept of *developed abilities* stresses the individual's current level of consistent proficiency however derived. Individual differences in developed abilities frankly reflect all sources of ability differences, including individual differences in prior motivation and opportunity to learn. Nonetheless, direct measures of the student's current functioning level, whatever its multiple determinants, are important in their own right for a variety of educational purposes. In much instructional planning, for example, it is critical to know what the student can do now. Some instructional strategies may differ, to be sure, depending on whether current ability levels are thought to reflect deficiencies or difficulties deriving from problems of motivation or of opportunity. In these instances, and perhaps as a general rule, measures of developed abilities should be interpreted in the context of independent information about motivation and opportunity, the latter being conceived broadly enough to include the quality of prior and current instruction (Heller, Holtzman, & Messick, 1982; Messick, 1983).

At the level of theory, most modern conceptions of ability development are basically interactionist in character; that is, they accord a causal role to interaction with the environment and hence are counter to earlier traditions of fixed intelligence and of genetically predetermined development (Hunt, 1961; Messick, 1972). Although many theorists hold that the primitive or rudimentary processes that initially interact with the environment are innate, these processes are *not* the abilities that develop out of the interaction. Even in those instances where a basic innate ability is postulated to start the interactive process, such as Cattell's (1971) fluid intelligence, this ability itself develops as a consequence of environmental interaction while it simultaneously facilitates the formation and development of specific abilities in response to differentiated environmental structure.

Many of these theories also stress a central role for positive transfer in learning and development. In the theory of ability development elaborated by Ferguson (1954, 1956), for example, abilities are viewed as learned proficiencies that attain relative stability through overlearning. They develop through repeated performance across similar tasks and gradually attain relative stability through exercise, challenge, and practice. Note that the reference is to relative stability, not fixity—that is, proficiency has developed to that part of the learning curve where additional effort yields small though nonzero increments. Learning that leads to the development of a particular ability, however, is influenced by prior learnings and previously established abilities through mechanisms of transfer. Indeed, one should expect that the most critical variables exerting transfer effects on subsequent learning would be abilities—that is, those earlier acquisitions that have attained stability in performance.

The operative transfer function in this regard relates performance on a particular task, or set of similar tasks, both to training on those tasks and to proficiency levels on relevant abilities. If the learning period is sufficiently prolonged that significant changes in the abilities accumulate as a function of training and experience, those changes would also be taken into account. Ferguson (1954) maintains that "as the learning of a particular task continues, the ability to perform it becomes gradually differentiated from, although not necessarily independent of, other abilities which facilitate its differentiation [p. 110]." Because existing abilities, once developed, thus serve to facilitate the differentiation of other specific abilities, the operation of positive transfer produces positive correlations not only among tasks but among abilities. Thus, positive transfer furnishes a simple rationale for the emergence of broader and broader higher-order abilities organizing the primary abilities. This suggests that individuals not only develop multiple abilities but organized ability structures as well. It also suggests that major gains in intellectual power may not come so much from the further honing of already well-developed specific abilities as from their organization into more general and widely applicable assemblies of integrated ability complexes.

Furthermore, an important implication of Ferguson's (1954, 1956) line of argument is that consistent differential exposure to various task domains leads to differential learning and hence to the emergence of different ability patterns in different learning environments or different cultures (Irvine, 1969; Lesser, Fifer, & Clark, 1965; Stodolsky & Lesser, 1967). One might expect, however, that higher-order abilities, if they indeed reflect general transfer components underlying the mutual facilitation of several primary abilities, would tend to apply across a variety of task requirements. Hence, higher-order abilities should appear more similar from one cultural group to another than do the more specialized primary abilities (MacArthur, 1968; Vernon, 1969).

Given different learning histories and different learning styles, it seems likely that—although the same basic ability processes may be involved in many different tasks—they may be strategically used more or less frequently in different tasks by different persons. Ability processes may also be organized and deployed in different ways for performing the same task, with attendant variation in effectiveness. This has led some investigators, such as Simon (1976) and Snow (1980b), to emphasize the assembly and control functions of abilities and ability structures.

For Guilford as for Ferguson, transfer also plays a critical role in ability development. Guilford (1967) claims that "the brain is apparently predesigned to perform in five major ways [p. 417]" corresponding to the five information-processing operations of cognition or comprehension, memory, convergent production, divergent production, and evaluation that comprise the heart of his factorial model of the structure of intellect. Specific intellectual abilities develop through the repeated use of these five operations to process information in the individual's environment, which Guilford's extensive empirical investigations suggest is so structured as to contain 24 types of information generated by the cross-classification of four types of content (figural, symbolic, semantic, behavioral) and six types of form or product (units, classes, relations, systems, transformations, implications).

In Guilford's (1967) view, these specific abilities are generalized skills or habits that develop through transfer effects occurring by virtue of similarities in the task-to-task activities of a particular operation–content–product type. How well any specific ability develops depends on how much and how effectively the individual exercises the requisite operation in relation to the particular content–product combination. This in turn depends on the opportunities the person's environment offers to operate on such combinations and the individual's needs to cope with those offerings. Because tasks within the same operation–content–product category are more similar in shared activities than those in different categories, a specific ability should eventually develop via transfer for every cell of the operation by content by product cross-classification. This would yield the 120 abilities in Guilford's structure of intellect. Moreover, because similarities in shared activities may cut across content–product differences for a given operation such as memory or across operation–product differences for a given content such as figural, higher-order abilities such as general memory facility or general figural facility may also emerge (Guilford, 1981; Messick, 1973).

Cattell's (1971) theory of ability development is especially pertinent to issues of educational achievement because he explicitly stresses not only the role of transfer processes in development but the transfer power of developed abilities in task performance. Originating in the investment of innate fluid intelligence in the learning of particular tasks or task domains, specific task skills become integrated into primary abilities that cut across similar or related tasks. That is, because of an inherent similarity in the required activities in a particular domain, a unity of functioning develops—or in Cattell's (1971) words, "a coherent set of habit skills, knowledge, conceptual developments, and tactical and strategic 'know how' [p. 319]." These primary abilities, which Cattell calls "agencies," become organized through their mutually facilitative transfer effects and shared investments of fluid intelligence into higher-order abilities.

Cattell (1971) gives major emphasis to those primary abilities derived from the learning of judgmental skills associated with the more abstract parts of school curricula and nonschool experiences, such as verbal ability and numerical ability. In the course of education and experience, these judgmental skills become organized into a broad higher-order ability complex, which Cattell calls crystallized intelligence. Other higher-order abilities include general memory, general visualization, and general retrieval or fluency. In underscoring the increasing transfer power of primary abilities and higher-order abilities, Cattell (1971) likens a specific transferable skill to a "tool," by which he means "some insightful device in thinking and acting which, once picked up, enables the user to handle a whole group of further performances [p. 316]." He conceives of an agency or primary ability as a "whole tool box of cognitively consistent habits [p. 321]," which would make crystallized intelligence a veritable workshop of transferable structures of ability processes. For Cattell, crystallized intelligence comprises highly general abstractions that possess wider transfer effects than those of any of the agencies and hence displays a broad generality of useful application.

From Cattell's (1971) description of abilities as organized complexes of transferable concepts and skills and from Guilford's (1967) formulation of abilities in terms of information-processing operations, it seems clear that abilities in this factor-analytic tradition may be conceptualized as *process structures,* to use Carroll's (1974) term, or as stable constellations of psychological processes. This usage is consistent with information-processing formulations in cognitive psychology, as exemplified by Snow's (1980b) conception of abilities as structures of assembly and control processes as well as performance processes and by Sternberg's (1977) treatment of intellective abilities in terms of both structure and process. On the one hand, Sternberg characterizes abilities as task proficiencies—specifically, as particular constellations of information-processing components that satisfy the requirements of a given task or type of task. On the other hand, he also views abilities as dimensions of individual differences—specifically, as generalized constellations of information-processing components that form stable patterns of individual differences across multiple tasks or types of tasks.

The critical concept bridging these two notions is that abilities are stable consistencies *within* individuals (across variations in setting, time, and task) that reliably differentiate *among* individuals (Messick, 1982a). The *intraindividual* pattern of abilities for a particular student is the ability structure of concern in educational achievement. This may or may not include all the ability dimensions, or interrelate them in the same way, as in *interindividual* structures of between-person differences. Nevertheless, research on the structure of individual differences does provide many of the dimensions and associated ability measures for characterizing and assessing individual structures (Burt, 1949; Cattell, 1971; Ekstrom, French, & Harman, 1976, 1979; Guilford, 1967; Hakstian & Cattell, 1974).

Moreover, because abilities in this view are constellations of information-processing components operative either in a particular task or stably across multiple tasks, they in turn may serve as components or organizers of still more complex or temporally extended sequential processes, such as problem solving or creative production (Guilford, 1967; Messick, 1972, 1973). Thus, functioning much like subroutines or prior assemblies in computer terms, abilities not only facilitate performance on specific tasks and enhance the learning of new tasks but may also serve as operational modules in higher-order psychological processes. Overall, then, a person's developed ability structure is conceptualized here as a multidimensional organization of stable assemblies of information-processing components that are combined functionally in task performance, learning, problem solving, and creative production (Messick, 1972, 1973, 1982a).

In educational achievement, abilities and ability structure are engaged with knowledge structure in the performance of subject-area tasks. Abilities and knowledge combine in ways guided by and consistent with knowledge structure to form patterned complexes that may differ by subject area, so that problem solving in physics, for example, appears different from problem solving in biology or in political science. Furthermore, as expertise develops these ability–knowledge complexes may become markedly, even qualitatively, different by area. Thus, abilities are not revealed directly in educational achievment testing but rather are entailed in ability–knowledge combinations. Yet they do operate in achievement conjointly with knowledge, and hence ability tests and achievement tests will overlap considerably and correlate substantially—except possibly, as indicated earlier, in low-level achievement testing that primarily stresses information retrieval and first-order relations. Moreover, because the engagement of abilities is extensive and complex in high-level achievement, it would not be surprising to find quite high correlations at advanced achievement levels. For example, in a Graduate Record Examinations rescaling study, when 19 advanced subject-matter tests were correlated with a combination of verbal and quantitative abilities, six coefficients were between .71 and .81, whereas nine were between .60 and .70 (Wallmark, 1969).

Still, cognitive abilities are not the same as subject-matter achievement, even those representing generalized school-related learnings such as crystallized intelligence. Indeed, for many educational purposes it is important to assess them separately. That is, a person may fail in subject-area task performance because of inadequate knowledge (especially strategic knowledge), dysfunctional knowledge structure, ineffective mobilization or organization of a complex of relevant abilities, or deficiencies in any one of these abilities. Achievement tests tap all of these in concert and although they may often effectively separate knowledge retrieval from knowledge use, they do not provide independent assessments of cognitive abilities. Thus, the coordinate measurement of cognitive abilities as well as subject-matter achievement may contribute to the comprehensive diagnosis of academic difficulties.

Cognitive abilities are independent of subject matter but they are by no means content-free; rather, they cut across content areas. In some instances, they may be specialized by type of content such as verbal, numerical, or figural, but at higher orders they represent more general functions such as memory or fluency. The route taken to arrive at this point may have appeared to be circuitous, but it was a deliberate attempt to forge an explicit link between concern over the role of cognitive abilities in achievement testing and 50 years of factor-analytic work on the delineation and measurement of abilities.

Contrasting Views of Knowledge Versus Ability in Achievement Testing

This view of educational achievement as a compound of developed ability and knowledge structures shares some important features with other conceptions of achievement but also entails some critical differences in substance and emphasis. As an instance, Ebel (1969, this volume) maintains that "the essence of achievement is command of useful verbal knowledge [1969, p. 66]." Ebel (1974, 1982) makes it clear that he is speaking not merely about amount of knowledge or information but about knowledge structure—that is, about the "structure of relationships among concepts, a structure built out of information by processes of thought [1974, p. 317]." But he limits this structure specifically to verbal knowledge, whereas the present formulation admits any form of knowledge, whether verbal or visuospatial or whatever. Ebel (1969, 1982) also stresses the usefulness of the knowledge, with the implication that useful knowledge is what gets built into the knowledge structure whereas useless knowledge is soon forgotten. In contrast, the present formulation stresses the usefulness of the knowledge structure as a functional system in thinking. However, the critical difference between Ebel's view and the present one is his explicit exclusion of general cognitive abilities except for knowledge-dependent, area-specific skills such as adding fractions or formulating sentences (Ebel, 1969, 1974). This is puzzling in light of Ebel's insistence that achievement is the *command* of knowledge because, as Snow (1980a) has underscored, " 'command' implies organization, generalization, facile adaptation and application of knowledge in new contexts; that is what, I contend, general mental abilities are! [p. 43]."

In contrast to Ebel's exclusion of developed cognitive abilities from achievement, Anastasi (1976, 1980, this volume) subsumes achievement under the rubric of developed abilities. She refers to a continuum of tests of developed abilities that vary in their degree of experiential specificity. Included along with "culture-fair" tests, tests of verbal and nonverbal intelligence, and tests of differentiated cognitive abilities are course-oriented achievement tests of technical skills and factual knowledge as well as broadly oriented achievement tests of major long-term educational goals such as the interpretation of literature or the understanding and application of scientific principles (Anastasi, 1976).

The differentiation among educational and psychological tests in terms of experiential specificity is a helpful one, and the implication that these tests "fuse imperceptibly" with one another is an important caveat against misuse. For example, some tests designed to assess subject-matter achievement so stress the application of learned skills to the solution of new problems in the area that they appear to measure general reasoning and other cognitive abilities fairly independent of factual content; whereas some other tests designed to assess general scholastic ability draw freely on varieties of specific word knowledge and arithmetic principles learned in school. However, the subtle implication that because existing tests overlap markedly or are misaligned with their constructs, therefore the construct distinctions are unimportant—that "the terms *intelligence, aptitudes, abilities,* and *achievements* are indeed different words for essentially the same human characteristics [Ebel, 1980, p. 11]"—does not follow at all and is insidious in its impact on new measurement efforts. What is needed is not a downplaying and blurring of the construct distinctions but, rather, attempts to illuminate these distinctions in refined measures of knowledge structures, of cognitive abilities as process structures, and of ability–knowledge complexes in problem representation and solution.

EXPERTISE AND APTITUDE

It should be noted that the present conception of educational achievement is not tied to program or course objectives. Educational achievment in this view refers to what a person knows and can do in a subject area, not just the degree to which the person knows and can do what was taught. Such a narrowing of purview can of course be imposed and for some uses of achievement tests, such as the certification of curriculum mastery or the evaluation of program or course effectiveness, probably should be imposed. Even here, however, one should not automatically preclude the assessment of generalization and transfer in the former instance or of potential side effects in the latter. The point is that for other uses of achievement tests—such as the diagnosis of academic strengths and weaknesses as a basis for remediation or for adaptive instruction and the prediction of future attainment as a basis for selection, placement, or assignment to alternative treatments—the broader view may offer added value. Some examples of this added value come from a consideration of the differences between beginning and experienced learners in a field and between novices and experts.

Assessing What Is Learned, Not Only What Is Taught

As we have seen, when students learn something specific, they usually also learn something general, that is, they tend to educe general attributes from specific instances and evolve general structures for representing and understanding new specifics. For beginning students in a field, these rudimentary knowledge structures tend to be idiosyncratic, because new information is assimilated to the student's intuitions about the subject derived from everyday experiences. These structures or informal theories are also frequently fragmented or overextended or misaligned with reality. In some instances, these informal theories are simply vague and poorly articulated versions of acceptable structures, requiring the progressive differentiation and reintegration of already existing ideas with new knowledge (Ausubel, 1968). In other instances, however, the student's informal notions may be seriously at variance with formal theories or accepted structures, in which case they constitute what Driver has called "alternative frameworks" (Driver, 1981, 1982; Driver & Easley, 1978). These alternative frameworks, being based on student's intuitions, tend to be quite persistently embraced and are frequently resistant to change through instruction.

A number of common alternative frameworks have been uncovered in science education in particular. For example, some beginning biology students evince a persistent tendency to think in Lamarckian terms (Deadman & Kelly, 1978) and some believe, despite instruction on photosynthesis to the contrary, that plant "food" comes exclusively from the ground (Driver, 1982). Some beginning physics students have been found adhering to non-Newtonian ideas about motion and to notions of impetus reminiscent of pre-Galilean dynamics (Viennot, 1979). It appears that intuitions are not readily abandoned and, in particular, that scientific principles that are counter-intuitive are not easily assimilated. If conceptual learning entails such radical restructurings of ideas, it is not enough to assess for diagnostic purposes whether or not the student knows what was taught—one must also assess what else the student "knows" or believes about the subject.

A similar point holds for the assessment of expert-level achievement but for a different reason: namely, much of what is learned in the development of expertise, we do not know how to teach. However, from a convergence of recent studies we have begun to characterize, albeit tentatively, some of the complexities of developed knowledge and ability structures that constitute the power of expertise (Chi, Feltovitch, & Glaser, 1981; Chiesi, Spilich, & Voss, 1979; Glaser, 1981; Hunter, 1982; Larkin, McDermott, Simon, & Simon, 1980a, 1980b; Rigney, 1980; Simon, 1976). Hence, we may be able to approach the assessment of expertise in terms of these outcomes of learning and development, which are beginning to become clear, rather than in terms of the objectives of teaching, which in the case of expertise continue to be vague and ill-defined.

It appears from this recent work that not only do experts know more than novices or have a vastly richer store of relevant knowledge in long-term memory, they also structure and continually restructure knowledge in more complex ways. In particular, experts construct complex schemas that combine some of the dimensions and simpler schemas used by novices into integrated functional patterns, while at the same time discarding as redundant or irrelevant some other dimensions that novices attend to. Experts also develop new patterns of perceiving, thinking, and acting or what Ian Hunter (1982) calls "adroitly usable patterned complexes." These complex abilities to perceive and apply both patterned relational schemas and the attendant action sequences strongly influence the nature of problem representations, the avoidance of irrelevancies, and the organization of performance and solution processes. Experts also develop greater speed and fluency of performance, implying in addition to the restructuring already mentioned a continual tuning of processes, the automatization of routines and control processes, and the shedding of redundant processes (Rumelhart & Norman, 1976). Furthermore, in contrast to novices, experts appear more capable of flexible restructuring for the application of multiple perspectives to problem representation and solution as well as for the adjustment or replacement of dysfunctional initial schemas as hypotheses change.

In addition to providing possible guidelines for the assessment of expertise, these findings suggest that not only do abilities facilitate the development of more complex abilities but so do rich and extensive knowledge structures. Thus, developed abilities influence the structuring and restructuring of knowledge whereas developed knowledge structures influence the organization and application of abilities, leading to increasingly more complex structures of each. Although the "adroitly usable patterned complexes" of ability developed by experts are inherently knowledge-dependent, some of their structural and functional aspects may be generalizable to the learning of other fields. For example, when an expert in one field attempts to learn a different subject matter, he or she may be more able than the ordinary novice to discern the deep structure of the new field, to ignore irrelevancies, and to perceive the patterned relationships entailed in constructing complex schemas, even though a massive store of knowledge in the field has not yet been acquired. If this is possible, then what we should mean by a generalist is not a jack-of-all trades and a master of none, but a jack-of-all-trades and a master of one or, preferably, two. Thus, expertise in one field may be aptitude for the functional mastery of another.

Aptitudes as Facilitators and Forecasters of Performance

This brings us to the construct of aptitude which, according to Snow (1980a), refers to "psychological characteristics that predispose and thus predict differences in later learning under specified instructional conditions [p. 41]." Again, at the outset I want to make clear that there is no necessary implication of innateness in this use of the term. This conception comprises two distinct but closely related notions of aptitude—namely, aptitude as a forecaster of learning or performance and aptitude as a facilitator of learning or performance (Cronbach & Snow, 1977). Although the applied emphasis may be on predictiveness per se, the scientific emphasis—in such psychoeducational research as the study of aptitude-treatment interactions—is mainly on illuminating the facilitating processes that underlie the prediction (Snow, 1980a). This may lead not only to better prediction but to better and more responsible use of the predictive findings. A compatible conception of aptitude as learning rate is also current (Carroll, 1963; Green, 1974), but again the primary concern is with the process structures that underlie differences in rate (Carroll, 1974).

Considerable confusion arises when aptitude tests as *predictors* are contrasted with achievement tests as *measures,* because achievement in a subject-matter area happens frequently to be quite predictive of subsequent performance in the same field. Subject-matter achievement is also often predictive of performance in related fields, although somewhat less so, whereas measures of general ability complexes such as tests of scholastic ability or of crystallized intelligence tend to be more widely predictive across disparate fields. Furthermore, the distinction between developed abilities and developed knowledge structures cuts across this aptitude–achievement contrast, as does Anastasi's (1976) continuum of experiential specificity and Snow's (1980a) pyramid of referent generality. The latter, consistent with the present formulation, illustrates why ability and achievement constructs are more readily distinguishable both conceptually and empirically at more specific than more general levels.

Aptitudes may be specific or general and so may achievements, developed abilities, or knowledge structures. Developed abilities and knowledge structures, being evolved through education and experience, are both achievements, to be sure. Yet they are also predictive of subsequent learning and performance, more broadly in the case of abilities and in more focused fashion in the case of knowledge structures, thereby qualifying as aptitudes as well. But the predictive developed ability is not the same as the subsequent performance, nor is it a *measure* of that performance. Similarly, current achievement that predicts future achievement is not a *measure* of that later achievement.

This confusion between prediction and measurement has led some investigators to argue that aptitudes, abilities, and achievements are "essentially the same human characteristics [Ebel, 1980, p. 11]" and that aptitude, ability, and achievement tests are "fundamentally similar" in what they measure (Anastasi, 1980). The point may be well taken in regard to many existing tests. But as Carroll (1974) has pointed out, "with a definition of aptitude that identifies it with the *present* state of the individual as symptomatic of *future* performance, it is difficult to see why there should be any great difficulty in distinguishing between aptitude and achievement *as concepts* [p. 287]." Similarly, in spite of high correlations between tests of educational achievement and tests of developed cognitive abilities but in light of their differential responsiveness to direct instruction, their differential involvement in aptitude-treatment interactions, their different courses of development, and differences in their process and content components, it is difficult to see why there should be any great problem in distinguishing between educational achievement and cognitive abilities as constructs.

THE FAILINGS OF FALLACIES

We have been alerted to the *jingle* fallacy, whereby tests purported to measure the same construct are naively taken to measure the same thing, and, to the *jangle* fallacy, whereby tests purported to measure different constructs are naively taken to measure different things (Kelley, 1927). We now find that if tests purported to measure different constructs correlate highly with each other, the constructs are taken to be the same thing. This might be called the *jingle–jangle* fallacy, because convergent correlational evidence, which would support jingles, is taken as tantamount to the absence of discriminant experimental evidence, which would support jangles. However, I prefer to call it the *jungle* fallacy because, by failing to maintain the distinction between constructs and their indicants or measures, we are in danger of reverting to the jungle of operationism whereby test meaning resides in each investigator's measurement operations rather than in validated relational or nomological networks.

What is needed now is what has always been needed—namely, not just the empirical buttressing of constructs inferred from existing measures but the development and validation of measures attuned to constructs, especially as constructs evolve or change with conceptualizations of new evidence. In educational theory and practice today, we must recognize, to use Glaser's (1980) words, that "the study of learning appears to be taking on the characteristics of a developmental psychology of performance changes—the study of changes that occur as different knowledge structures and complex cognitive strategies are acquired, and the study of conditions that affect these transitions in competence [p. 322]." Accordingly, in educational measurement today, we must recognize, to use Snow's (1980a) words, that "achievement constructs refer to complex dynamic cognitive structures [p. 44]." Hence, to better serve both theory and practice, new approaches to achievement measurement should be more complex, dynamic, and cognitive.

REFERENCES

Anastasi, A. *Psychological testing* (4th ed.). New York: Macmillan, 1976.

Anastasi, A. Abilities and the measurement of achievement. In W. B. Schrader (Ed.), *New directions for measurement: Measuring achievement: Progress over a decade—Proceedings of the 1979 ETS Invitational Conference.* San Francisco: Jossey-Bass, 1980.

Anderson, R. C., Spiro, R. J., & Montague, W. E. (Eds.). *Schooling and the acquisition of knowledge.* Hillsdale, N.J.: Lawrence Erlbaum Associates, 1977.

Ausubel, D. P. *Educational psychology: A cognitive view.* New York: Holt, Rinehart & Winston, 1968.

Bruner, J. S., Olver, R. R., & Greenfield, P. M. *Studies in cognitive growth.* New York: Wiley, 1966.

Burt, C. The structure of the mind: A review of the results of factor analysis. *British Journal of Educational Psychology,* 1949, *19,* 100–111; 176–199.

Carroll, J. B. A model of school learning. *Teachers College Record,* 1963, *64,* 723–733.

Carroll, J. B. The aptitude–achievement distinction: The case of foreign language aptitude and proficiency. In D. R. Green (Ed.), *The aptitude–achievement distinction.* Monterey, Calif.: CTB/McGraw-Hill, 1974.

Cattell, R. B. *Abilities: Their structure, growth, and action.* New York: Houghton Mifflin, 1971.

Chi, M. T. H., Feltovitch, P. J., & Glaser, R. Representation of physics knowledge by experts and novices. *Cognitive Science,* 1981, *5,* 121–152.

Chiesi, H. L., Spilich, G. J., & Voss, J. F. Acquisition of domain-related information in relation to high and low domain knowledge. *Journal of Verbal Learning and Verbal Behavior*, 1979, *18*, 257–273.

Cronbach, L. J., & Snow, R. E. *Aptitudes and instructional methods.* New York: Wiley, 1977.

Deadman, J. A., & Kelly, P. J. What do secondary school boys understand about evolution and heredity before they are taught the topics? *Journal of Biological Education*, 1978, *12*, 7–15.

Driver, R. Pupils' alternative frameworks in science. *European Journal of Science Education*, 1981, *3*, 221–230.

Driver, R. Children's learning in science. *Educational Analysis*, 1982, *4*, 69–79.

Driver, R., & Easley, J. Pupils and paradigms: A review of literature related to concept development in adolescent science students. *Studies in Science Education*, 1978, *5*, 61–84.

Ebel, R. L. Knowledge vs. ability in achievement testing. *Proceedings of the 1969 Invitational Conference on Testing Problems: Toward a theory of achievement measurement.* Princeton, N.J.: Educational Testing Service, 1969.

Ebel, R. L. The relation of aptitude for learning to achievement in learning. In D. R. Green (Ed.), *The aptitude–achievement distinction.* Monterey, Calif.: CTB/McGraw-Hill, 1974.

Ebel, R. L. Achievement tests as measures of developed abilities. In W. B. Schrader (Ed.), *New directions for testing and measurement: Measuring achievement: Progress over a decade— Proceedings of the 1979 ETS Invitational Conference.* San Francisco: Jossey-Bass, 1980.

Ekstrom, R. B., French, J. W., & Harman, H. H. *Kit of factor-referenced cognitive tests.* Princeton, N.J.: Educational Testing Service, 1976.

Ekstrom, R. B., French, J. W., & Harman, H. H. Cognitive factors: Their identification and replication. *Multivariate Behavioral Research Monographs*, No. 79–2, 1979.

Ferguson, G. A. On learning and human ability. *Canadian Journal of Psychology*, 1954, *8*, 95–111.

Ferguson, G. A. On transfer and the abilities of man. *Canadian Journal of Psychology*, 1956, *10*, 121–131.

Glaser, R. General discussion: Relationships between aptitude, learning, and instruction. In R. E. Snow, P-A. Federico, & W. E. Montague (Eds.), *Aptitude, learning, and instruction.* Hillsdale, N.J.: Lawrence Erlbaum Associates, 1980.

Glaser, R. The future of testing: A research agenda for cognitive psychology and psychometrics. *American Psychologist*, 1981, *36*, 923–936.

Green, D. R. *The aptitude–achievement distinction.* Monterey, Calif.: CTB/McGraw-Hill, 1974.

Greeno, J. G. Some examples of cognitive task analysis with instructional implications. In R. E. Snow, P-A. Federico, & W. E. Montague (Eds.), *Aptitude, learning, and instruction* (Vol. 2). Hillsdale, N.J.: Lawrence Erlbaum Associates, 1980.

Guilford, J. P. *The nature of human intelligence.* New York: McGraw-Hill, 1967.

Guilford, J. P. Higher-order structure-of-intellect abilities. *Multivariate Behavioral Research*, 1981, *16*, 411–435.

Hakstian, A. R., & Cattell, R. B. The checking of primary ability structure on a broader basis of performances. *British Journal of Educational Psychology*, 1974, *44*, 140–154.

Heller, K., Holtzman, W. H., & Messick, S. *Placing children in special education: A strategy for equity.* Washington, D.C.: National Academy Press, 1982.

Humphreys, L. G. The nature and organization of human abilities. *19th Yearbook of the National Council on Measurement in Education,* 1962.

Hunt, J. McV. *Intelligence and experience.* New York: Ronald Press, 1961.

Hunter, I. M. L. Acquiring complex abilities. *Educational Analysis*, 1982, *4*, 17–25.

Irvine, S. H. Factor analysis of African abilities and attainments: Constructs across cultures. *Psychological Bulletin*, 1969, *71*, 20–32.

Kelley, T. L. *The interpretation of educational measurements.* Yonkers-on-Hudson, N.Y.: World Book, 1927.

Larkin, J., McDermott, J., Simon, D., & Simon, H. Expert and novice performance in solving physics problems. *Science*, 1980, *208*, 1335–1342. (a)

Larkin, J. H., McDermott, J., Simon, D. P., & Simon, H. A. Models of competence in solving physics problems. *Cognitive Science*, 1980, *4*, 317–345. (b)

Lesser, G. S., Fifer, G., & Clark, D. H. Mental abilities of children from different social-class and cultural groups. *Monographs of the Society for Research in Child Development*, 1965, *30*, 4 (Serial No. 102).

MacArthur, R. Some differential abilities of Northern Canadian native youth. *International Journal of Psychology*, 1968, *3*, 43–51.

Messick, S. Beyond structure: In search of functional models of psychological process. *Psychometrika*, 1972, *37*, 357–375.

Messick, S. Multivariate models of cognition and personality: The need for both process and structure in psychological theory and measurement. In J. R. Royce (Ed.), *Multivariate analysis and psychological theory*. New York: Academic Press, 1973.

Messick, S. Personality consistencies in cognition and creativity. In S. Messick (Ed.), *Individuality in learning: Implications of cognitive styles and creativity for human development*. San Francisco: Jossey-Bass, 1976.

Messick, S. *The effectiveness of coaching for the SAT: Review and reanalysis of research from the fifties to the FTC* (ETS RR-80-8). Princeton, N.J.: Educational Testing Service, 1980.

Messick, S. Developing abilities and knowledge: Style in the interplay of structure and process. *Educational Analysis*, 1982, *4*, 105–121. (a)

Messick, S. Issues of effectiveness and equity in the coaching controversy: Implications for educational and testing practice. *Educational Psychologist*, 1982, *17*, 67–91. (b)

Messick, S. Assessment of children. In P. Mussen (Ed.), *Manual of child psychology* (4th ed., 4 vols.), Vol. 1, W. Kessen (Ed.), *History, theories, and methods*. New York: Wiley, 1983.

Messick, S. Cognitive styles in educational practice. *Educational Psychologist*, in press.

Rigney, J. W. Cognitive learning strategies and dualities in information processing. In R. E. Snow, P-A. Federico, & W. E. Montague (Eds.), *Aptitude, learning, and instruction* (Vol. 1). Hillsdale, N.J.: Lawrence Erlbaum Associates, 1980.

Rumelhart, D. E., & Norman, D. A. *Accretion, tuning, and restructuring: Three modes of learning* (Report No. 7602). San Diego: University of California, Center for Human Information Processing, August 1976.

Schwarz, P. A. Prediction instruments for educational outcomes. In R. L. Thorndike (Ed.), *Educational measurement* (2nd ed.). Washington, D.C.: American Council on Education, 1971.

Scriven, M. J. Comments on Ebel's paper: The logic of the aptitude–achievement distinction. In D. R. Green (Ed.), *The aptitude–achievement distinction*. Monterey, Calif.: CTB/McGraw-Hill, 1974.

Simon, H. A. Identifying basic abilities underlying performance of complex tasks. In L. B. Resnick (Ed.), *The nature of human intelligence*. Hillsdale, N.J.: Lawrence Erlbaum Associates, 1976.

Snow, R. E. Aptitude and achievement. In W. B. Schrader (Ed.), *New directions for testing and measurement: Measuring achievement: Progress over a decade—Proceedings of the 1979 ETS Invitational Conference*. San Francisco: Jossey-Bass, 1980. (a)

Snow, R. E. Aptitude processes. In R. E. Snow, P-A. Federico, & W. E. Montague (Eds.), *Aptitude, learning, and instruction* (Vol. 1). Hillsdale, N.J.: Lawrence Erlbaum Associates, 1980. (b)

Sternberg, R. J. *Intelligence, information processing, and analogical reasoning: The componential analysis of human abilities*. Hillsdale, N.J.: Lawrence Erlbaum Associates, 1977.

Stodolsky, S. S., & Lesser, G. S. Learning patterns in the disadvantaged. *Harvard Educational Review*, 1967, *37*, 546–593.

Tomkins, S. S. Affect and the psychology of knowledge. In S. S. Tomkins & C. E. Izard (Eds.), *Affect, cognition, and personality*. New York: Springer, 1965.

Vernon, P. E. *Intelligence and cultural environment*. London: Methuen, 1969.

Viennot, L. Spontaneous reasoning in elementary dynamics. *European Journal of Science Education, 1979, 1,* 205.

Wallmark, M. *Graduate record examinations rescaling study of 1967–68* (SR-69-4). Princeton, N.J.: Educational Testing Service, 1969.

Author Index

Numbers in *italics* indicate pages with complete bibliographic information.

A

Acker, S. R., 65, *86*
Ackoff, R. L., 21, *35*
Adair, F. L., 122, *125*
Adkins, D. C., 148, *153*
Aisner, D. J., 32, *35*
Alderman, D. L., 148, *153*
Anastasi, A., 91, 99, *107,* 129, 130, 132, 134, *139,* 164, 168, *169*
Anderson, G. E., Jr., 21, *35*
Anderson, J. R., 46, *57*
Anderson, R. C., 142, *153, 157, 169*
Arnoff, S. L., 21, *35*
Ausubel, D. P., 165, *169*

B

Baker, F. B., 67, *84,* 112, *126*
Banghart, F., 21, *35*
Baron, J., 52, *57*
Bechtoldt, H. P., 66, *82*
Beck, M., 123, *126*
Beers, F. S., 150, *154*
Behrman, J. R., 18, *35*
Belmont, J. M., 44, 49, *57*
Berdie, R. F., 72, *84*
Bereiter, C., 17, *35*
Bergmann, J., 148, *153*
Berk, R. A., 152, *153*
Bernal, E., 105, *107*
Bernstein, M., 52, 56, *60*
Bersoff, D. N., 15, *35,* 94, 96, 101, 106, *107*
Bingham, W. V., 63, *82*
Blalock, H. M., Jr., 32, *35*
Bloom, B. S., 137, *139,* 143, *153*
Bond, L., 115, *126*
Borkowski, J. G., 44, *57*

Borman, W. C., 72, *83*
Boulding, K. E., 142, *153*
Breen, T. F., III, 29, *37*
Brimm, O., 88, *108*
Brogden, H. E., 79, *82*
Brown, A. L., 44, 49, *57*
Bruner, J. S., 158, *169*
Brush, D. H., 76, *82*
Buros, O. K., 65, *82,* 113, 117, 118, 121, *126*
Burt, C., 162, *169*
Butterfield, E. C., 44, 49, *57*

C

Cahn, E., 97, *107*
Campbell, D. T., 66, 67, *83*
Campbell, J. P., 69, 71, 75, *83*
Campione, J. C., 44, 49, *57*
Cancro, R., 17, *35*
Canfield, J., 21, *37*
Caplan, J. R., 78, *85*
Carroll, J. B., 15, 16, *35,* 48, 49, *58,* 68, *83,* 136, *139,* 162, 167, 168, *169*
Cattell, R. B., 49, *58,* 158, 159, 161, 162, *169, 170*
Chapman, J., 97, *107*
Chapman, L., 97, *107*
Chase, W. G., 45, 47, *58*
Chi, M. T. H., 166, *170,* 45, 46, 53, *58*
Chiesi, H. L., 45, *58, 60,* 166, *170*
Churchman, C. W., 21, 31, *35*
Clark, D. H., 54, *59,* 160, *171*
Clark, H. H., 47, *58*
Clark, K., 97, *107*
Cleary, A., 91, 105, *107*

173

Subject Index